THE ARDEN SHAKESPEARE

GENERAL EDITORS:
RICHARD PROUDFOOT, ANN THOMPSON
and DAVID SCOTT KASTAN

THE TWO GENTLEMEN OF VERONA

THE ARDEN SHAKESPEARE

* Third Series

THE ARDEN EDITION OF THE
WORKS OF WILLIAM SHAKESPEARE

THE TWO GENTLEMEN
OF VERONA

Edited by
CLIFFORD LEECH

The general editors of the Arden Shakespeare have been
W. J. Craig and R. H. Case (first series 1899-1944),
Una Ellis-Fermor, Harold F. Brooks, Harold Jenkins
and Brian Morris (second series 1946-1982)

Present general editors (third series)
Richard Proudfoot, Ann Thompson and David Scott Kastan

This edition of *The Two Gentlemen of Verona*, by Clifford Leech,
first published in 1969 by Methuen & Co. Ltd
Reprinted nine times

Reprinted 1997 by Thomas Nelson & Sons Ltd

Thomas Nelson & Sons Ltd
Nelson House Mayfield Road
Walton-on-Thames Surrey
KT12 5PL UK

I(T)P® Thomas Nelson is an International
Thomson Publishing Company
I(T)P® is used under licence

Editorial matter © 1969 Methuen & Co. Ltd

Printed in Croatia

ISBN 0-416-47490-X (hardback)
ISBN 0-17-443581-9 (paperback)
NPN 9 8 7 6 5 4 3 2

CONTENTS

PREFACE

THE appearance of this volume has been long delayed, for reasons that university teachers and administrators will understand. That it has at last been brought to a conclusion is due to the help I have received from many quarters, notably from the Folger Shakespeare Library, where the holding of a Visiting Fellowship gave me the opportunity to devote three months of uninterrupted work to the play, to the University of Durham for a term's leave of absence, and to the University Grants Committee of New Zealand, whose invitation to visit the universities of that country in 1967 made me free of administration for two months. Most of all, however, I am grateful to the General Editors of the New Arden Shakespeare for the thoroughness of their counsel. Particularly to Dr Harold Brooks I must acknowledge a debt for his advice and his tolerance. It will be apparent in the Introduction that, although he and I hold different views of the likely history of the text and of many points in the play's interpretation, he has generously put his ideas at my disposal: it is my hope that his views are properly represented here and that a sufficient indication is given of his contribution to my own thinking on the play. In the annotations his share is very considerably more substantial than the frequent acknowledgments indicate: it may, indeed, be said that this part of the volume is as much his work as mine, although he certainly does not go along with some of the comments that are included.

CLIFFORD LEECH

Toronto
5 October 1967

ABBREVIATIONS AND USAGES

Quotations from other Shakespeare plays, except where otherwise indicated, are from the Globe edition, edited by W. G. Clark and W. A. Wright (1865). In collation and notes Shakespeare's plays and poems are referred to by the abbreviations listed in C. T. Onions' *A Shakespeare Glossary* (1911, revised edition 1946).

The following abbreviations are used for editions of Shakespeare, and for other sources of readings, referred to in introduction, collation, and notes:

F	The First Folio (1623).
F2	The Second Folio (1632).
F3	The Third Folio (1663–4).
F4	The Fourth Folio (1685).
Rowe	*Works,* ed. Nicholas Rowe (1709).
Pope	*Works,* ed. Alexander Pope (1725).
Theobald	*Works,* ed. Lewis Theobald (1733).
Hanmer	*Works,* ed. Sir Thomas Hanmer (1743–4).
Warburton	*Works,* ed. Alexander Pope and Thomas Warburton (1747).
Victor	*The Two Gentlemen of Verona . . . With Alterations and Additions,* by Benjamin Victor (1763).
Johnson	*Plays,* ed. Samuel Johnson (1765).
Capell	*Comedies, Histories, and Tragedies,* ed. Edward Capell (1767–8).
Steevens	*Plays,* ed. Samuel Johnson and George Steevens (1773).
Steevens ii	2nd edition of preceding (1778).
Rann	*Works,* ed. J. Rann (1787).
Malone	*Plays and Poems,* ed. Edmund Malone (1790).
Malone ii	*Plays and Poems,* ed. Edmund Malone (1821) ['Third Variorum'].
Singer	*Dramatic Works,* ed. S. W. Singer (1826).
Knight	*Pictorial Edition,* ed. Charles Knight (1838–43).
Collier	*Works,* ed. J. Payne Collier (1842–4).
Sargent	*The Two Gentlemen of Verona,* in *Modern Standard Drama,* ed. E. Sargent (New York, 1846).
Halliwell	*Works,* ed. J. O. Halliwell[-Phillipps] (1853–65).
Halliwell MS.	Readings quoted by Halliwell in the above edition from 'a Manuscript Common-place-book of the seventeenth century': Halliwell saw these readings as 'unauthorized alterations'.
Collier (MS.)	Readings allegedly found in a manuscript-corrected copy of F2, published in Collier's *Notes and Emendations to the Text of Shakespeare's Plays* (1853).

Delius	*Shakespeares Werke*, ed. N. Delius (Elberfeld, 1854–65).
Dyce	*Works*, ed. Alexander Dyce (1857).
Grant White	*Works*, ed. R. Grant White (Boston, 1857).
Collier ii	*Comedies, Histories, Tragedies, and Poems*, ed. J. Payne Collier (1858).
Staunton	*Plays*, ed. Howard Staunton (1858–64).
Camb	*Works*, ed. W. G. Clark and J. Glover (1863–6) ['Old Cambridge'].
Keightley	*Plays, ed.* Thomas Keightley (1864).
Chambers	*The Two Gentlemen of Verona*, in *Plays* (Falcon edition, 1886–91).
Marshall	*Works*, ed. Henry Irving and F. A. Marshall (1888–90).
Craig	*Complete Works*, ed. W. J. Craig (1904) ['Oxford edition'].
Bond	*The Two Gentlemen of Verona*, ed. R. Warwick Bond (1906) ['Old Arden'].
N.C.S., *NCS*	*The Two Gentlemen of Verona*, ed. Sir Arthur Quiller-Couch and J. Dover Wilson (1921) ['New Cambridge'].
Alexander	*Complete Works*, ed. Peter Alexander (1951) ['Tudor Shakespeare'].
Sisson	*Complete Works*, ed. C. J. Sisson (1954).
Munro	*The London Shakespeare*, ed. John Munro (1958).

Other references to readings and annotations are quoted from the notes to editions listed above.

Other abbreviations:

Abbott	E. A. Abbott, *A Shakespearian Grammar* (1879).
Bullough	*Narrative and Dramatic Sources of Shakespeare*, ed. Geoffrey Bullough, Vol. 1 (1957).
Chambers, *E.S.*	E. K. Chambers, *The Elizabethan Stage*, 4 vols. (1923).
Franz	W. Franz, *Die Sprache Shakespeares* (Halle, 1939).
J.E.G.P.	*Journal of English and Germanic Philology*.
Kennedy	*A Critical Edition of Yong's Translation of George of Montemayor's Diana and Gil Polo's Enamoured Diana*, ed. Judith M. Kennedy (Oxford, 1968).
Kökeritz	Helge Kökeritz, *Shakespeare's Pronunciation* (1953).
Long	John H. Long, *Shakespeare's Use of Music* (Gainesville, Florida, 1955).
Marlowe	*Works* (general editor R. H. Case), 6 vols. (1930–3).
M.L.N.	*Modern Language Notes*.
M.S.R.	Malone Society Reprints.
O.E.D.	*Oxford English Dictionary*.
Onions	C. T. Onions, *A Shakespeare Glossary* (1911, revised edition 1946).
Partridge	Eric Partridge, *Shakespeare's Bawdy* (1955).
P.M.L.A.	*Publications of the Modern Languages Association of America*.
P.Q.	*Philological Quarterly*.

Romeus	*The Tragicall Historye of Romeus and Juliet* (in Bullough, pp. 284–363).
Sisson	C. J. Sisson, *New Readings in Shakespeare*, 2 vols. (1956).
Schmidt	Alexander Schmidt, *Shakespeare-Lexicon*, 2 vols. (1874–5).
S.P.	*Studies in Philology.*
Tannenbaum	S. A. Tannenbaum, *The New Cambridge Shakespeare and The Two Gentlemen of Verona* (New York, 1939).
Tilley	M. P. Tilley, *A Dictionary of the Proverbs in England in the Sixteenth and Seventeenth Centuries* (1950).

INTRODUCTION

I. THE TEXT

The Two Gentlemen of Verona was first printed in the Shakespeare Folio of 1623, appearing as the second play in the volume, immediately after *The Tempest*. Those who decided on the order in which the plays should be presented to the public must have known that *The Tempest* came at or near the end of Shakespeare's career: it would be reasonable enough to follow it with a play of his earliest years.

Charlton Hinman's analysis of the Folio printing leads to the conclusion that the text of *The Two Gentlemen* was set alternately by Compositor A and Compositor C: we are thus free from the problem posed by Compositor B's employment of 'substitutions involving words without any graphic similarity'.[1] On the other hand, that Compositor A was in general more faithful in following copy than the other compositors who worked on the volume[2] is not of great help to us here, for we are very much in the dark concerning the kind of copy that was available for *The Two Gentlemen*.

The play is divided regularly into acts and scenes, and the stage-directions are given in a form that associates this play with *The Merry Wives of Windsor* and *The Winter's Tale*. All three of these plays in the Folio list in the heading of each scene the characters that are going to appear throughout the scene, without regard for their moment of entry. Exits are occasionally indicated. This feature of the printing led Crompton Rhodes[3] and J. Dover Wilson,[4] following a suggestion of Malone's, to put forward the

1. *The Printing and Proof-Reading of the First Folio of Shakespeare*, Oxford, 1963, ii. 353–71.
2. *Ibid.*, i. 10.   3. *Shakespeare's First Folio*, Oxford, 1923, pp. 96 ff.
4. 'The Task of Heminge and Condell' in *Studies in the First Folio written for the Shakespeare Association*, 1924, pp. 72 ff.; the 'New Cambridge' editions of *The Two Gentlemen of Verona* (1921, reprinted 1955, pp. 77–8), *The Merry Wives of Windsor* (1921, reprinted 1954, pp. 93–4), *The Winter's Tale* (1931, reprinted 1959, pp. 121–7). In his 1955 edition of *The Two Gentlemen* Dover Wilson has recognized that the 'theory of assembled texts . . . is now generally discredited' (p. 82).

theory of 'assembled texts'. Where no author's manuscript or prompt-book or transcript of either was available, the Folio editors could, it was suggested, have put together a text by conflating the 'plot' of the play (i.e., the outline of entries in each scene which was pasted to a board and hung in the tiring-house for the benefit of the book-holder and the actors) and the separate parts which had been prepared for the individual actors. The scene-heading would thus be taken from the 'plot' and the text for each scene would be made up by running the separate parts together. E. K. Chambers was sceptical about the theory, pointing out the difficulty of the assembler's task (in particular because the surviving part of Orlando from Greene's play *Orlando Furioso* does not show characters' names attached to cues, which often consist only of a word or two), and noting that in such an assembled text we should expect an occasional false sequence of speeches and an occasional inclusion of cues in the following lines.[1] W. W. Greg, taking the same view, added that we should also expect the use of the phrase 'to them' in stage-directions, for it occurs frequently in the surviving 'plots'.[2] We may recognize, too, a special difficulty in the case of *The Two Gentlemen*. *The Winter's Tale* and *The Merry Wives of Windsor* were doubtless in the repertory of 1622-3, when the Folio was being printed. It is highly unlikely that *The Two Gentlemen* was acted much later, say, than the reference to it in Francis Meres' *Palladis Tamia* (1598). Experience of the theatre tells us that parts are the most vulnerable of all theatrical documents, and it is difficult to believe that those for an out-dated play would have survived for a quarter of a century beyond the time of its being performed. Moreover, the practice of 'massed entries' is by no means confined to the three Shakespeare plays mentioned. Greg refers to the 1623 quarto of Webster's *The Duchess of Malfi* and to one of the manuscripts of Middleton's *A Game at Chess* in the hand of Ralph Crane.[3] It should be added that in the earlier years of the Elizabethan drama we can find the practice—not employed throughout a play but in some instances freely though inconsistently—in Lyly's *Sapho and Phao*, *Campaspe*, *Mother Bombie*, *Endimion*, *Love's Metamorphosis*, and *Midas*, in Gascoigne's *Supposes*, and in *The Buggbears*, attributed to John Jeffere. What we have in the massed entries in these instances and in the three Shakespeare plays is a kind of compromise between the normal mode of indicating entries and the 'continental-classical' mode used in Renascence printing of Latin drama and taken over into English in, for example,

1. *William Shakespeare: A Study of Facts and Problems*, Oxford, 1930, i. 155.
2. *The Shakespeare First Folio*, Oxford, 1955, p. 157.   3. *Ibid.*, pp. 157-8.

Udall's *Ralph Roister Doister* and regularly in Jonson's plays. While the former procedure marks each entry at the place within the scene where it is specifically required, the latter begins a new scene, with a new scene-number, at every entry, and in the heading to the scene lists the characters who are going to appear. This 'continental' procedure results in numerous and usually brief 'scenes'. The procedure we are confronted with in *The Two Gentlemen* employs the same number of scenes as in the normal English procedure but has a suggestion of classical method and dignity in its massed entries. It is the kind of compromise which we should expect in Italianate comedy, as in Lyly's and the other early plays we have noted, and which might well be taken up by a professional scribe who wished to make his transcripts have an air of authority. Certainly there was no need for Crane's manuscript of *A Game at Chess* to have been put together by 'assembling', for two other manuscripts of the play (in Crane's and Middleton's hands respectively) exist. Crane is believed to have prepared transcripts of some of the Shakespeare plays for the Folio, so the easiest explanation of the special features of *The Two Gentlemen*, *The Merry Wives*, and *The Winter's Tale* is that in each of these instances Crane prepared a transcript and used the 'massed entries' that on occasion he certainly used elsewhere.[1] Some slight confirmatory evidence is provided by the free use of parentheses and hyphens, a Crane characteristic.[2]

The Folio text of *The Two Gentlemen* is in many ways a good one. It rarely needs emendation of a substantive character, and it has little mislineation. When, however, we look at the text's plain statements, we are forced to consider what may have been the play's history before Crane or another made a tidy manuscript of what lay before him. Of course there is hardly a Shakespeare play which does not contain contradictions of detail, and Shakespeare notoriously played freely with place and time. Yet *The Two Gentlemen* takes these things to extremes. It may be best to note first the statements, or absence of statements, concerning place:

(1) Apart from the title of the play, there is no indication that the opening scenes take place in Verona or that Valentine, Proteus, and Julia come from there.

(2) In I. i Valentine is evidently going to Milan (ll. 57, 61, 71).

(3) In I. iii we are told by Panthino that 'youthful Valentine' 'Attends the Emperor in his royal court' (ll. 26–7), and

1. *Ibid.*, p. 158.
2. *Ibid.*, p. 217. See, further, F. P. Wilson, 'Ralph Crane, Scrivener to the King's Players', *The Library*, September 1926, vii. 194–215.

Antonio decides to despatch Proteus also 'to the Emperor's court' (l. 38). Other gentlemen of the town are travelling 'to salute the Emperor' (l. 41), and Proteus can accompany them. Proteus says he has heard that Valentine is 'daily graced by the Emperor' (l. 58), and Antonio says his son shall 'spend some time / With Valentinus, in the Emperor's court' (ll. 66–7). Bond suggested that Shakespeare's Duke was actually the Emperor, the dramatist being royally free concerning royal titles, and thought that these references to the Emperor may have been due to the influence of Lyly's *Euphues*, where the Emperor holds court at Naples.[1] Nevertheless, we must be struck by the fact that the Duke is a Duke in certain scenes and, apparently, an Emperor sometimes when he is off-stage.

(4) In II. iii Launce, an untrustworthy witness but here exactly echoing Antonio and Panthino in I. iii, says he is 'going with Sir Proteus to the Imperial's court' (l. 4).

(5) In II. iv, though the Duke is always a Duke, he says that Proteus, if Valentine has described him truly, is 'as worthy for an empress' love / As meet to be an emperor's counsellor' (ll. 71–2).

(6) In the same scene there is a notable vagueness about the place where Valentine and Proteus have come from: the Duke refers to a letter from Valentine's 'friends' (l. 46), and to 'Don Antonio, your countryman' (l. 49); Silvia says she will leave the two friends to talk of 'home affairs' (l. 114); and Valentine asks Proteus 'how do all from whence you came' (l. 117).

(7) Also in this scene we may note that the Duke, always a Duke in speech-headings and stage-directions, is referred to vaguely and informally. 'Here comes my father', says Silvia (l. 43). A servant addressing Silvia speaks of 'my lord your father' (l. 111). And Valentine can mention simply 'her father' when speaking of Silvia (l. 170). This vagueness is continued in II. vi, where Proteus, soliloquizing on his planned betrayal of his friend's planned elopement with Silvia, refers also merely to 'her father' (l. 36).

(8) In II. v Speed welcomes Launce to Padua (l. 1).

(9) In II. vii Julia tells Lucetta of her plan to follow Proteus, but does not name the place she is to go to.

(10) In III. i vagueness continues: the Duke refers to his having

1. Bond, p. 18. For Harold Brooks' explanation, see below, p. xxxi.

thought to banish Valentine from 'my court' (l. 27), and Valentine says he is happy 'at your court' (l. 57). When the young man is actually banished, it is simply from 'my territories' (l. 163) and 'our royal court' (l. 165). Similarly Valentine is vague about where his letters to his friends are going: they are simply 'letters to my friends' (l. 53).

(11) Yet in this same scene Verona is mentioned for the first time, and in such a way as to suggest that it is the locality of this scene. The Duke, tricking Valentine into a revelation of his love for Silvia and their planned elopement, says he himself is in love with 'a lady in Verona here' (l. 81).

(12) In IV. i Valentine tells the outlaws he is on his way from Milan to Verona (ll. 16–19), though of course here he need not be believed.

(13) In this same scene the Third Outlaw says he was banished from Verona for an offence remarkably similar to Valentine's: 'For practising to steal away a lady, / An heir, and near allied unto the Duke' (ll. 48–9). Historically there was no Duke in Verona, but that would not have seemed of moment to Shakespeare, and we need not regard the point as suspicious in itself.

(14) In IV. ii Proteus and Thurio plan to meet at Saint Gregory's Well (l. 81), which was in Milan.

(15) In IV. iii. Silvia says she will travel to Mantua, where she hears Valentine is (l. 23).

(16) In IV. iv Launce, who in II. iii was going to 'the Imperial's court', refers to 'the Duke' (ll. 18, 22).

(17) In V. ii the Duke says that Silvia and Eglamour have fled to Mantua (l. 46).

(18) In V. iv Verona is mentioned as if Thurio came from there: Valentine says that, if Thurio once again refers to Silvia as his, 'Verona shall not hold thee' (l. 127).

(19) In this final scene the Duke says he will 'repeal' Valentine 'home again' (l. 141). It is of course to the Duke's home that Valentine will return, yet the phrase is still odd.

(20) And, still in V. iv, we have a sudden return to imperial affairs when the Duke asserts that he now sees Valentine as 'worthy of an empress' love', a curious echoing of II. iv. 71–2 noted above.

From all this it appears that the main action of the play (II. i, iv–vi, III, IV. ii–iv, V. i–ii) takes place either in Milan (2, 12, 14), or in

Verona (11, perhaps 13, 18), or in Padua (8). In addition we find vagueness where precision might on occasion have seemed probable (1, 6, 7, 9, 10).

We find, moreover, another sequence of puzzling references and incidents. Many of these are such as can easily be paralleled in other Shakespeare plays: it is well known how he could, as in *Othello*, combine 'long time' with 'short time', and how what Schücking called 'episodic intensification' could lead to inconsistency between scene and scene. Nevertheless, the length at least of the following list makes it deserving of consideration and comment:

(1) In I. i Proteus uses Valentine's servant Speed to take his letter to Julia, though later in the play we find he has a servant of his own, Launce.

(2) In the same scene Speed says he gave the letter to Julia (l. 95), but in I. ii it appears he gave it to Lucetta (ll. 34–40).[1] Proteus speaks of finding 'some better messenger' (l. 145), as if Launce were not the obvious candidate.

(3) In I. ii Sir Eglamour is one of Julia's suitors: later, in IV. iii and v. i, ii, the same name is used for the man who helps Silvia to escape from her father's court. (This, of course, may be merely the result of Shakespeare's forgetting, but the example is fairly extreme.)

(4) In the same scene, Julia has a father who 'stays' for her coming to dinner (l. 131).

(5) In I. iii Proteus wishes that 'our fathers' (his and Julia's) 'would applaud our loves' (l. 48).

(6) In II. i, where we first learn of Valentine's love for Silvia, there is no mention of her having a ducal father who may be unsympathetic to Valentine's love. (This could be due to the playwright's still being new to his craft.)

(7) In II. iv the Duke says Proteus has come to court 'With commendation from great potentates' (l. 74), although it appeared in I. iii that Proteus was going directly to join Valentine.

(8) In this scene Valentine jibes at Thurio's poverty and niggardliness (ll. 40–2), yet refers to his 'possessions' as 'so huge' (l. 171), a passage echoed in v. ii. 26–9. In III. i. 65–6, when speaking to the Duke and therefore doubtless not speaking his mind, Valentine refers to Thurio as 'full of . . .

1. Harold Brooks has suggested in a private note that Speed thought Lucetta was Julia.

bounty, worth and qualities / Beseeming such a wife as your fair daughter'.[1]

(9) Also here Valentine asks Proteus to go with him to his chamber (l. 180), although he had previously said he must follow Silvia at once (ll. 172–3). (Harold Brooks has shrewdly suggested that the change of mind is to be explained by Valentine's at first not intending to tell Proteus of the planned elopement and then being provoked to it by Proteus' 'But she loves you?' (l. 174). But for this to emerge excavation work has to be done on the text.)

(10) II. vi is a soliloquy by Proteus, who had ended II. iv with a similar soliloquy on love–friendship strife: the oddity is reinforced by the use of '*solus*' in the opening stage-direction. (It can be argued, as Harold Brooks has suggested to me, that the two soliloquies are needed to show Proteus gradually coming to the point of betrayal.)

(11) In II. vii Julia, planning to join Proteus, makes no mention of her father and leaves her possessions in Lucetta's hands (ll. 86–7). Like Valentine in II. iv. 180, she asks Lucetta to 'go with me to my chamber' (l. 83), a repetition possible for an author but suggestive either of piecemeal composition or of the intervention of someone else's memory.

(12) In III. i. 222–36 Proteus describes Silvia's petitioning of her father for Valentine's repeal: there was no time for this to happen between the Duke's exit (l. 169) and Proteus' entry (l. 188), but this by itself should arouse no suspicion, being a telescoping of time familiar to readers of Shakespeare.

(13) In III. i. 262 Launce tells us he thinks his master 'a kind of a knave', yet there is no way for him to have learned of Proteus' villainy: again, however, this by itself should not arouse our suspicion of the text.

(14) In III. ii. 3–4 Thurio complains of Silvia's increased hostility since Valentine's exile, but at ll. 11–13 we learn that Valentine has only just gone: another insignificant telescoping of time.

(15) In IV. ii. 74 Julia asks after Launce, with whom she has had no previous association in the play, Speed having been concerned with the business of the letter in I. i, ii, and Launce

---

1. I agree with the view, expressed to me by Harold Brooks, that the apparent complication can be explained by Valentine's first jibe being taken as a deliberately false deduction of poverty from niggardliness. But if this is the true explanation, Shakespeare has written very lamely at the beginning of II. iv.

not having been present when she took her farewell of Proteus in II. ii. Again, a minor point by itself.

(16) In IV. ii. 75–7 the Host tells Julia that Launce has 'Gone to seek his dog, which to-morrow, by his master's command, he must carry for a present to his lady'. This is, of course, palpably absurd, and is inexplicable without reference to what follows.

(17) In IV. iii Sir Eglamour is presented as a valiant and trustworthy knight, but in V. iii we learn that, when the outlaws attacked, he proved 'nimble-footed' and abandoned Silvia to them. We may say the character has been sacrificed to the plotting, but surely quite egregiously so.

(18) In IV. iv. 6–7 Launce says he was 'sent to deliver' Crab 'as a present to Mistress Silvia', which again is palpably absurd and is contradicted by what we hear later about his being instructed to take a pet-dog and his having presented Crab to Silvia because the other dog was stolen (ll. 47–57).

(19) In IV. iv. 132–3 Silvia says she has heard Proteus 'say a thousand times' that Julia gave him at his departure from her the ring he is now offering to Silvia. As in our text Proteus falls in love with Silvia at first sight, it is odd that he should so frequently refer in her presence to his old love and Julia's gift.

(20) In IV. iv. 119–22 Julia, as Proteus' ambassador, gives a letter to Silvia which she takes back because it is the wrong letter: the nature of this letter is never explained. We may assume it was one from Proteus to Julia, but we have to deduce this, and it would have been easy for Shakespeare to give Julia an aside to explain it. (Harold Brooks has conjectured it was the torn letter of I. ii, obviously pieced together so that the audience could recognize it: in that case, I think it would get a laugh.)

(21) In V. iv. 87–94 there is a similar device when Julia first gives Proteus the ring that he gave to her when they separated, and then says she has given him the wrong ring and produces the one he had charged her to give to Silvia (the one presumably that Silvia refused at IV. iv. 130–5). Julia's statement that the delivery of the ring to Silvia '(out of my neglect) was never done' may be explained as a fabrication meant to lead up to her revealing her identity immediately afterwards. But, while the confusion about the rings makes sense in its way, the confusion about the letters in the earlier scene is merely distracting: it may be meant to indicate

both Julia's inclination to tangle things and a certain
poverty of device in her. If so, it is not as skilfully done as
one might expect from the dramatist. We could indeed be
led to wonder whether the incident in IV. iv does not derive
from someone else's remembering of the incident in V. iv.

Thus in this play Julia has a father who disappears (4, 5, 11); the
name Eglamour is used for two very different persons (3); Proteus
seems to forget he has a servant of his own (1); Speed's evidence
about the letter in I. i, ii conflicts with Lucetta's (2); Silvia does not
appear to have a ducal father on her first appearance (6); Proteus'
journey to the court is presented as both direct and circuitous (7);
Thurio's wealth (perhaps) comes and goes (8); Valentine can
change his mind within a few lines (9); the two soliloquies of
Proteus in II. iv and II. vi present a strange repetition, the mystery
being increased by the Folio's unique use of '*solus*' in II. vi (10);
time may be telescoped (12, 14) and a character may acquire information without our being told how (13, 15) or behave in a way
apparently contrary to our justified expectation (17, 19); the
attempt to give Crab to Silvia is first presented as if Proteus had
ordered it (16, 18); a clumsy plot-device is almost exactly repeated
(20, 21).

As we have seen, not all of these oddities are of equal weight. No
suspicion need have been aroused by (9) and (12)–(15), and not
much by (3)–(5), (8), (11). When, however, we consider the number of such minor oddities in the play, and particularly when we
find them along with (2) and (16)–(19), we are bound to grow
suspicious of the text. It seems difficult to believe that the manuscript in front of Compositor A and Compositor C was a copy of a
play that Shakespeare wrote at one time. In the next section of this
Introduction we shall have to consider some now generally discredited suggestions that have been made concerning the possibilities of (i) revision and (ii) the presence of another hand than
Shakespeare's: little as we may be convinced by many of the
theories put forward, a brief survey of them will be useful in indicating the need that so many commentators have felt to explain the
state of the Folio text.

II. DATE AND POSSIBLE STRATIFICATION

The only piece of external evidence that helps us with the dating
of *The Two Gentlemen* is the reference to the play in Francis Meres'
Palladis Tamia (1598), as already noted. Meres mentions 'his
Gentlemen of Verona' first among six comedies named, the others

being *The Comedy of Errors, Love's Labour's Lost, 'Love's Labour's Won'*, *A Midsummer Night's Dream*, and *The Merchant of Venice*.[1] The fact that *The Two Gentlemen* comes first need not mean that Meres thought it Shakespeare's earliest comedy, but it may be significant that it is put so closely with *The Comedy of Errors*.

E. K. Chambers, seeing it as an example of 'hasty composition' soon after the establishment of the Lord Chamberlain's Men, found no case for revision or for double authorship, and placed it in the season 1594–5.[2] This makes it two years later than, in his scheme, *The Comedy of Errors*, one year later than *The Taming of the Shrew*. It also puts it in the same season as *Love's Labour's Lost* and *Romeo and Juliet* and only one year before *Richard II* and *A Midsummer Night's Dream*. James G. McManaway, noting T. W. Baldwin's argument that Shakespeare took over from Brooke's poem *Romeus and Juliet* the adage that a nail drives out a nail and used it in *The Two Gentlemen, Romeo and Juliet*, and *Lucrece* (in that order),[3] observes that this would put back the date of *The Two Gentlemen* 'more than one year'. 'It is safe', he nevertheless concludes, 'to date *The Two Gentlemen* about 1594.'[4]

We are faced with the fact that a good deal of the verse in this play is ungainly, with a laborious filling out of the line, as in:

> *Duke.* Sir Thurio, fear not but that she will love you
> Now Valentine is banish'd from her sight.
> *Thu.* Since his exile she hath despis'd me most,
> Forsworn my company, and rail'd at me,
> That I am desperate of obtaining her.
> *Duke.* This weak impress of love is as a figure
> Trenched in ice, which with an hour's heat
> Dissolves to water, and doth lose his form.
> A little time will melt her frozen thoughts,
> And worthless Valentine shall be forgot.
>
> (III. ii. 1–10)

Here the simple image of ll. 6–8 is uneconomically handled (especially in l. 7 with its unhelpful balancing on the caesura and its six monosyllables), and is then laboriously applied to Silvia's love for Valentine. Dramatically much more effective is the kind of verse which depends on rhetorical repetition, as in:

> To leave my Julia, shall I be forsworn;
> To love fair Silvia, shall I be forsworn;

1. Chambers, *William Shakespeare*, ii. 194.   2. *Ibid.*, i. 270, 330–1.
3. *William Shakspere's Small Latine & Lesse Greeke*, Urbana, Illinois, 1944, ii. 345.
4. 'Recent Studies in Shakespeare's Chronology', *Shakespeare Survey*, 3 (1949), 22–33; p. 25.

> To wrong my friend, I shall be much forsworn.
> And ev'n that power which gave me first my oath
> Provokes me to this three-fold perjury.
> Love bade me swear, and Love bids me forswear.
>
> (II. vi. 1–6)

The third consecutive line ending in 'forsworn' continues the basic structure of the first two, but gets variety and simple climax by incorporating 'much', and there is effective summation in the 'three-fold' of l. 5. The balancing of l. 6 is of an effectively different pattern from that of the first three lines. Yet even this is rather thin, and 'gave me first my oath' is inadequate, for Proteus thinks of himself as sworn both to Valentine and to Julia. Moreover, Proteus can only be regarded as committing three offences if we distinguish (as indeed he does) his desertion of Julia from his preferring another woman to her: a straining for a rhetorical structure seems to take command of the thought. This is the kind of verse that we can find easily in *The Comedy of Errors*:

> The time was once when thou unurg'd wouldst vow
> That never words were music to thine ear,
> That never object pleasing in thine eye,
> That never touch well welcome to thy hand,
> That never meat sweet-savour'd in thy taste,
> Unless I spake, or look'd, or touch'd, or carv'd to thee.
>
> (II. ii. 113–18)[1]

Here the desperate attempt to get in a fourth of the senses leads to the over-particularized l. 117, but the mode of summation in l. 118 is what we can find in Kyd:

> Here lay my hope, and here my hope hath end:
> Here lay my heart, and here my heart was slain:
> Here lay my treasure, here my treasure lost:
> Here lay my bliss, and here my bliss bereft:
> But hope, heart, treasure, joy and bliss,
> All fled, fail'd, died, yea, all decay'd with this.
>
> (*The Spanish Tragedy*, IV. iv. 90–5)[2]

The piling up of the nouns in l. 94 and of the verbs in l. 95 is echoed by Shakespeare in the *Errors* passage. Proteus' words move a little more easily, and, though lacking Richard of Gloucester's vigour and humour, are basically of the type we find in:

> Was ever woman in this humour woo'd?
> Was ever woman in this humour won?
>
> (*Richard III*, I. ii. 228–9)

1. Text from Arden edition, ed. R. A. Foakes, 1962.
2. Text from Revels edition, ed. P. Edwards, 1959.

Yet not all the verse of *The Two Gentlemen* is either ungainly or too obviously patterned. These lines of Valentine, though end-stopped like the rest of the play's verse, are economical and relatively complex in imagery:

> O thou that dost inhabit in my breast,
> Leave not the mansion so long tenantless,
> Lest growing ruinous, the building fall,
> And leave no memory of what it was. (v. iv. 7–10)

The contradiction of 'inhabit' and 'so long tenantless' is effective, for some absentees, however desperate the condition of neglect induced by their absence, can be felt as permanent presences. There is, too, a useful antithesis between 'growing' and 'fall' in l. 9, implying respectively a slow process of decay and a sudden catastrophe. The monosyllables of l. 10 suggest a long recession of time and can be contrasted with the limping monosyllables of III. ii. 7 already noted.

This glance at the matter suggests that we are dealing with a play basically of a very early date, and, possibly from the evidence of the verse alone, one not written all at the same time. F. G. Fleay in a paper given to the New Shakspere Society took the view that the first two acts belong to 1593–4, and that the last three followed about 1595. When he read the paper to the Society, he suggested a non-Shakespearian authorship for the later part but withdrew this before publication, insisting only on a difference in date.[1] Then, in his *Chronicle History of the Life and Work of William Shakespeare*, he argued that 'the play was produced in 1591, with work by a second hand in it, which was cut out and replaced by Shakespeare's own in 1595'.[2] Among other such views may be noted Hugo Norpoth's (dependent on metrical tests) that Shakespeare began by writing Acts I and III, then wrote Act II, and rather later Acts IV and V.[3] His explanation of the procedure was that Shakespeare needed at once to come to grips with his two source-stories (Felix and Felismena, and Julio and Hippolita),[4] which were linked by the character of Proteus. So he started off with the love for Julia and the friendship with Valentine, and then proceeded to Proteus' double treachery. It is, however, difficult to believe that a dramatist would postpone the movement towards treachery which

1. 'On Certain Plays of Shakespeare of which Portions were written at different Periods of his Life', *New Shakspere Society Transactions*, 1874, pp. 285–317.
2. *A Chronicle History of the Life and Work of William Shakespeare*, 1886, pp. 188–91.
3. *Metrisch-chronologische Untersuchung von Shakespeares Two Gentlemen of Verona*, Dülmen, 1916.
4. See Section III of this Introduction.

we see in Act II. That will be his major problem in the play, and his method of dealing with it is bound to affect his treatment of the treachery itself: it therefore cannot be put off, though of course a dramatist might go back and revise his handling of it. Norpoth interestingly illustrates the strong impulse to see the play in strata written at different times, but his theory is too mechanically tied to act-division.[1] More thorough-going was J. M. Robertson, who saw Shakespeare as responsible merely for a re-writing of the first section of the play, making some insertions and doing some occasional re-touching. As Robertson points out, Hanmer in 1743 doubted whether Shakespeare had done more than 'the enlivening of it with some speeches and lines thrown in here and there', and John Upton in 1746 saw the 'manner and style' of both this play and *Love's Labour's Lost* as non-Shakespearian. Robertson thought the basic text was Greene's, with some insertions possibly by Peele and (for Launce and his dog) Nashe.[2] But deservedly the best-known essay in disintegration is that of Dover Wilson in his edition of the play. Not only the inconsistencies already noted, but the frequent occurrence of short verse-lines and the extreme brevity of the forest-scenes (for it is indeed remarkable that Proteus' rescue of Silvia, his attempt to rape her, Valentine's denunciation of him, Proteus' repentance, Valentine's magnanimous offer of Silvia, Julia's revelation of her identity, the Duke's capture, and his acceptance of Valentine as a son-in-law, are all fitted into a scene of 171 lines) led him to conjecture a Shakespeare text which had been severely and negligently handled by a reviser.[3] It is worth noting that S. A. Tannenbaum, though strongly combating the theory of a reviser and often inaccurately representing Dover Wilson's arguments, believed that the play had been re-written by Shakespeare as late as 1598, when Yong's translation of Montemayor's *Diana* was published.[4] Meanwhile George B. Parks had sketched a more drastic theory: at first Shakespeare planned a faithless-friend story, set in Verona, to which the girl-page story (from the *Diana*) was added. He suggested that Launce was the original bearer of the letter to Julia in I. i, ii,[5] though that would leave

1. See Section VI of the Introduction, pp. lxxii–lxxiii.

2. *The Shakespeare Canon: Part II*, 1923, pp. 1–44.

3. N.C.S., pp. 77–82. It should be noted that in the 1955 edition of the play Dover Wilson implies a withdrawal of much at least of his textual theory (cf. above, p. xiii).

4. *The New Cambridge Shakspere and The Two Gentlemen of Verona* (Shakspere Studies No. 4), New York, 1939. On the *Diana* and the doubtful relevance of the publication date of Yong's translation, see Section III of this Intro., pp. xli–xlii.

5. 'The Development of *The Two Gentlemen of Verona*', *Huntington Library Bulletin*, No. 11 (April 1937), pp. 1–11.

unexplained the apparent contradiction concerning whether Julia or Lucetta received it from Proteus' messenger.[1] T. M. Parrott found the play's events all too hastily presented, and conjectured that a reviser had cut down an original that he found burdened with conceits.[2] Chambers, as we have seen,[3] felt no need to postulate either revision or anything more drastic than a limited amount of abbreviation.

In what follows in this section we must move towards conjecture, and it will be best to begin with the difference in kind between Speed and Launce. This difference is disguised in the Folio in the list of 'Names of all the Actors' which is printed at the end of the play: there Speed is '*a clownish seruant to Valentine*' and Launce is '*the like to Proteus*'. Capell saw the inaccuracy of this, and his reading is followed in the list of dramatis personae in the present edition. As T. M. Parrott put it,

> to group Speed and Launce together as Clowns is to ignore Shakespeare's plain intention. There is nothing of the Clown in Speed, unless the term is stretched to cover every type of merry-maker. We hear of Speed early in the play as 'Sir Valentine's page', and a sensitive reader will recognize him on his appearance in the first scene of the play as a typical Lylian page, saucy, critical both of his master and of his master's friend, and very wide-awake to what is going on about him. It is he who picks up the glove Silvia has dropped for a love-token, unnoticed by her dreamy lover, and it is he who interprets to his master the significance of the letter that Silvia first bade him write and then returned to him. That a modern editor should call Speed 'a poor stick without character' betrays a strange misapprehension of the role he plays.

Launce, on the other hand, is a true clown, along with Costard and Bottom and Dogberry. He gets the better of Speed in the two scenes they share. The part was doubtless Kempe's.[4] Then we should notice that Launce makes only four appearances in the play, and that all but one of them are easily detachable from the text:

> (1) In II. iii he appears with his dog and talks to the audience about his imminent departure with Proteus. At the end of the scene he is sent on his way by Panthino, as Proteus had been in the previous scene. The parallel may not have been in the first draft of the play.

1. See p. xviii, above, for the view that the contradiction is not a real one.
2. *Shakespearean Comedy*, New York, 1949, pp. 108–18.
3. See above, p. xxii.   4. Parrott, *loc. cit.*

(2) In II. v he meets Speed in Padua.

(3) At III. i. 188 he enters with Proteus and they find the banished and grief-stricken Valentine. This is the only time we see him without his dog, and the first time we have seen him with Proteus, whom he serves. He retires from the conversation at l. 216 and is briefly addressed by both Valentine and Proteus as they leave the stage.

There follows a soliloquy (l. 261) in which he shows his suspicion of Proteus and his love for the maid whose 'cate-log' of qualities he gets Speed to read when he has entered at l. 277.

(4) In IV. iv he is back with his dog, and talks to the audience on the dog's offences. When Proteus and Julia enter at l. 40, we have the belated explanation of Launce's offering his own dog to Silvia and then Launce's rapid dismissal.

Thus in these four appearances we have three soliloquies and two duologues with Speed. The first, second, and fourth appearances could all be additions (with which we should in that case have to associate Julia's odd exchange with the Host at IV. ii. 72–7); so could the later section of his third appearance (i.e., III. i. 261 ff.). When, moreover, we look at III. i. 188–260, we find him here oddly like Speed. He is called 'boy' (l. 188), as Speed is at III. i. 257 and 374. (We may note that Speed is also 'Sir Valentine's page' at I. ii. 38 and is called 'sweet youth' by Launce at II. v. 2.) And Launce's speeches in this scene have a brevity, a simple playing with the word or a mistaking of the word that we can find in Speed, especially in II. i. Thus we may compare:

Spe. Sir, your glove.
Val. Not mine: my gloves are on.
Spe. Why, then this may be yours; for this is but one.

Val. . . . Ah, Silvia, Silvia!
Spe. Madam Silvia! Madam Silvia!
Val. How now, sirrah?
Spe. She is not within hearing, sir.
Val. Why, sir, who bade you call her?
Spe. Your worship, sir, or else I mistook.

Spe. Is she not hard-favoured, sir?
Val. Not so fair, boy, as well-favoured.
Spe. Sir, I know that well enough.
Val. What dost thou know?
Spe. That she is not so fair as, of you, well-favoured.

(II. i. 1–3, 6–11, 47–51)

with:

> *Pro.* What seest thou?
> *Lau.* Him we go to find. There's not a hair on 's head but 'tis a Valentine.
> *Pro.* Valentine?
> *Val.* No.
> *Pro.* Who then? His spirit?
> *Val.* Neither.
> *Pro.* What then?
> *Val.* Nothing.
> *Lau.* Can nothing speak? Master, shall I strike?
> *Pro.* Who wouldst thou strike?
> *Lau.* Nothing.
> *Pro.* Villain, forbear.
> *Lau.* Why, sir, I'll strike nothing. I pray you—
>
> (III. i. 190–203)

If we join this evidence with the facts that Launce does not take the letter to Julia referred to in I. i. ii, that he does not accompany Proteus to the court in II. iv (though Speed is in attendance on Valentine there), and that he makes no appearance with his master in the forest,—that, indeed, he takes no part at all in the plot[1] (while Speed does)—the case for seeing the Launce-section of the play as a result of second thoughts seems considerable. Speed the Lylyan page acquires as a companion a new type of comic figure, one that Shakespeare was to develop in Bottom, Launcelot Gobbo, Dogberry. Not, of course, that Launce is identical with these other figures, or that they are identical with one another. But all four enjoy their own naïveté, which indeed goes along with some shrewdness. When Shakespeare had determined on the insertion of Launce, it was understandable that he should build up the part by giving him Speed's lines in III. i. 188–260, and should join them to a Launce soliloquy and a Launce–Speed duologue which were, of course, new. I have noted that there would be a consequential alteration in IV. ii. 72–7: similarly III. i. 257–9 would be new, the original scene ending at l. 260 following l. 256.

The Launce-element in the play has been seen as separate. Apart from that, *The Two Gentlemen* brings together two basic plots: the Valentine–Proteus–Silvia story (the faithless friend) and the Proteus–Julia–Silvia story (the faithless lover). G. B. Parks wondered if the play originally concerned itself only with the first of

---

1. Unless we except his truancy and his mistake about the dog as providing the occasion for Proteus' employment of 'Sebastian'. However, it would have been easy enough to contrive this without Launce being involved.

But of course there were other faithless friends in sixteenth-century English literature, the most famous being Lyly's Euphues in *Euphues, The Anatomy of Wit* (1578). Euphues falls in love with Lucilla, the mistress of his friend Philautus, only to be abandoned by her in his turn, and then being reconciled to Philautus. Conceivably Shakespeare echoes a scrap or two of Lyly's language. Euphues, having been taken by Philautus to see Lucilla, says to himself: 'As Philautus brought me for his shadow the last supper, so will I use him for my shadow till I have gained his saint.'[1] Silvia is a 'saint' for Valentine at II. iv. 140, and there is talk of her, of Proteus, and her picture as 'shadows' in IV. ii. 121–7 and IV. iv. 195 (in both places the idea of worshipping a shadow being employed). Harold Brooks has suggested to me that Thurio's name comes from Curio in *Euphues* and Lucetta's from Lucilla there.

More importantly we have the German play *Julio und Hyppolita*, which exists in a collection called *Englische Comedien vnd Tragedien*, published in Germany in 1620. Albert Cohn, reprinting the play in his *Shakespeare in Germany* (1865), suggested that we have here a bad text derivative from a performance by English players about 1600. Clearly we cannot determine the priority between this play and Shakespeare's, but that a connection exists seems likely. Romulus and Julius are two friends, both Romans on a visit to a prince's court. Romulus is betrothed to Hyppolita, the prince's daughter, and leaves to announce to his parents his forthcoming marriage. He commends Hyppolita to Julius' care, but Julius loves her and begins to wonder what he should do about it. He proceeds to withhold Romulus' letters, and gets his clownish servant Grobiano to deliver forged letters in their place—letters rejecting Hyppolita and mocking the prince. The girl is advised by her father and Julius to forget Romulus. The wedding festivities of Hyppolita and Julius are interrupted by the return of Romulus as a masquer: he stabs Julius, and Hyppolita, still thinking Romulus faithless, stabs herself. Romulus follows her example, and the prince announces his intention to turn hermit. There are a number of incidental resemblances to *The Two Gentlemen*. When Romulus is leaving his friend, he says: 'so bald ich zu Rom angelange, wil euch mit Schrifften visitiren' ('as soon as I have arrived in Rome I will visit you with letters'), thus coming close to the stiff phrasing of Valentine's words in I. i. 57–60.[2] The servant Grobiano, as has been noted,[3] talks of a dog, though hardly in Launce's way. When Hyppolita receives what she thinks is Romulus' letter, she kisses it;

1. *Euphues: The Anatomy of Wit; Euphues and his England*, ed. M. W. Croll and H. Clemons, 1916, p. 45.
2. See Bond, p. 113.   3. See Bond, p. 114; Bullough, p. 209.

new identity to the place of the main part of the action: he calls it
'Milan', but at times he still thinks in terms of the emperor and
empress mentioned in II. iv. 71–2, v. iv. 139. This prefixing of the
new 'Verona' scenes, however, must have been anterior to the
introduction of Launce, or surely he and not Speed would have
carried the letter referred to in I. i, ii.

We may thus conjecture four stages in the play's composition,
remembering that during any one of these stages minor changes
may have been made with consequent inconsistency:

(1) The play begins with Valentine at Verona, in love with
Silvia, a nobleman's daughter. Proteus comes on a visit
during his travels, and plans to take Silvia from Valentine.
During the course of composition Shakespeare makes Silvia's
father into a sovereign prince, but does not decide firmly on
his particular rank. Julia enters Proteus' service, having followed him to Verona. The play ends, as now, in the forest.

(2) The first three scenes and II. ii, vii of the extant play are
added, involving a change in the place of the main part of the
action, a change not consistently carried through.

(3) A new character, Launce, is introduced: scenes are devised
specially for him, and Speed's part in III. i. 188–260 is transferred to him. A few small consequential changes are made.
The references to Launce's taking of his dog to Silvia are
never properly managed, because all this stage of composition is carried out by hurried insertion without sufficient
regard for the order in which items of information are given
to us.

(4) A new soliloquy for Proteus (II. vi) is inserted after a new
(Launce) scene and, ironically, immediately before II. vii,
where we see Julia planning to follow Proteus. The insertion
is now possible because the new Launce-scene will separate
this soliloquy from the one at the end of II. iv.

This does not explain the conflict of evidence between Speed (I. i)
and Lucetta (I. ii) as to whether he gave the letter to Julia or to
Lucetta. But there can, as Chambers noted, be no doubt of hasty
composition in some stages: in writing I. ii Shakespeare certainly
found it convenient to make Lucetta the initial recipient, and he
did not go back to adjust Speed's statement in I. i.

It should be emphasized that this is not a 'revision-theory' in the
customary sense of the term. If the above conjectural reconstruction of the stages of composition is correct (and no one is more conscious than the present editor that any such reconstruction is most

unlikely to be correct in all its particulars), we have Shakespeare working on a play and modifying his original conception as the work grew under his hands. Something similar seems to have occurred much later in his career, when in III. i of *Measure for Measure* he found his way out of a difficulty by inventing Mariana and taking over the bed-trick he had already used in *All's Well that Ends Well*. He did not there go back and reconcile his new invention with the Duke's appointment of Angelo as deputy in I. i. In the case of *The Two Gentlemen*, as in this later instance, I do not think two or more complete versions successively existed: the play was not regarded as 'finished' until it reached the form in which we now have it.

As will be suggested below, the manuscript that Crane or another transcribed was in all probability Shakespeare's 'foul papers'. When a prompt-book was made for performance, there may have been some ironing out of the discrepancies in our text. On that point, however, even conjecture is a profitless exercise.

In listing the play's puzzles above, I have indicated how frequently and generously Dr Harold Brooks has made suggestions which, in his view, can make it easier to accept the text as written in one piece, with no 'stratification' theory needed. Although he does agree there is a case for believing that Shakespeare had not thought of Launce when he wrote I. i, he finds no other evidence for the dramatist's having 'second thoughts' during the course of composition. His argument takes account of the discrepant references to locality. For him the opening is securely in Verona, and the central part of the action equally securely in Milan. The references to the Emperor's court came from Montemayor's *Diana*[1] where the father of Don Felix (the prototype of Proteus) 'sent him to the great Princesse *Augusta Caesarinas*[2] court, telling him, it was not meete that [he] . . . should spende his youth idly at home'. Certainly Shakespeare echoes this sentence at I. iii. 14 ('let him spend his time no more at home'). The repeated phrase about 'an empress' love' may be due to an association in Shakespeare's mind of Silvia, the chief lady of the court to which Valentine and Proteus go, with the Empress who was chief lady where Felix went (though his love was Celia, not the Empress). Verona gets confused with Milan because at the point where the rope-ladder comes in (III. i) Shakespeare's source was Brooke's *Romeus and Juliet*,[3] where of course that town was the place of action. This will also explain why

1. See Section III of this Introduction.
2. The name, obviously, has the strongest 'Imperial' suggestion.
3. See again Section III.

Mantua is spoken of as Valentine's place of refuge, and Shake-speare reverts momentarily to Brooke's poem when Valentine is addressing Thurio at v. iv. 127. As for Padua in II. v, Dr Brooks suggests that here Shakespeare inadvertently slipped back to *The Taming of the Shrew* (which may have preceded *The Two Gentlemen*, may for all we know have been in his mind at the same time): in that play Petruchio, like Valentine and Proteus, was travelling for educational purposes and had come from Verona to Padua. More-over, there are two servants there as in *The Two Gentlemen*—Petruchio's own Grumio and Lucentio's Tranio.

It should be noted that on one point Dr Brooks and I are at one: the manuscript transcribed for the Folio was Shakespeare's 'foul papers'. Whereas, however, he sees Shakespeare as fluctuating between three major possibilities for the locality of the central action (Milan, the Emperor's court, Verona) according to whether he was (i) following his original plan (Milan) or (ii) remembering Montemayor (the Emperor's court) or (iii) remem-bering *Romeus and Juliet* (Verona), I find it more probable that the fluctuations are due to interruptions in the play's composition, as will be suggested below,[1] and to later insertions of material within parts of the text already written. What I would not contest is that Shakespeare's memories of *Diana* and *Romeus* were instrumental in causing the confusion, and I am most grateful for Dr Brooks' sug-gestion here. What I find more difficult to credit is that he could work straight on from I. i to the end and, just because he had this or that source immediately in front of him, could switch from Milan to the Emperor's court to Verona. It suggests a degree of absent-mindedness remarkable even for Shakespeare.

We must return, however, to dating. There is a passage in Lyly's *Midas* (to be dated fairly confidently 1588–9)[2] where the pages Licio and Petulus discuss a woman's qualities:

Licio. ... But sirrha, for thy better instructions I wil vnfold euery wrinkle of my mistres disposition.
Pet. I pray thee doe.
Licio. But for this time I wil only handle the head and purte-nance.
Pet. Nothing els?
Licio. Why, wil not that be a long houres work to describe, that is almost a whole daies work to dresse?
Pet. Proceed.
Licio. First, she hath a head as round as a tennis ball.

1. Cf. pp. xxxiv–xxxv.
2. G. K. Hunter, *John Lyly: The Humanist as Courtier*, 1962, p. 76.

Pet. I would my bed were a hazard.

Licio. Why?

Pet. Nothing, but that I would haue her head there among other balles.

Licio. Video, pro Intelligo. Then hath she an haukes eye.

Pet. O that I were a partridge head.

Licio. To what end?

Pet. That she might tire with her eyes on my countenance.

Licio. Wouldst thou be hanged?

Pet. Scilicet.

Licio. Well, she hath the tongue of a Parrat.

Pet. Thats a leaden dagger in a veluette sheath, to haue a black tongue in a faire mouth.

Licio. Tush, it is not for the blacknesse, but for the babling, for euerie houre she wil crie 'walk knaue, walke.'

Pet. Then will I mutter, 'a rope for Parrat, a rope.'

Licio. So maist thou be hanged, not by the lippes, but by the neck. Then, sir, hath she a calues tooth.

Pet. O monstrous mouth! I would then it had been a sheepes eye, and a neates tongue.

Licio. It is not for the bignes, but the sweetnes: all her teeth are as sweet as the sweet tooth of a calfe.

Pet. Sweetly meant.

Licio. She hath the eares of a Want.

Pet. Doth she want eares?

Licio. I say the eares of a Want, a Mole, thou dost want wit to vnderstand me. She wil heare though she be neuer so low on the grounde.

Pet. Why then if one aske her a question, it is likely she wil hearken to it.

Licio. Hearken thou after that. Shee hath the nose of a sowe.

Pet. Then belike there she weares her wedding ring.

Licio. No, she can smel a knaue a mile off.

Pet. Let vs go farther *Licio*, she hath both vs in the wind.

Licio She hath a bettle brow.

Pet. What is she beetle browed?

Licio. Thou hast a beetle head! I say the brow of a beetle, a little flie, whose brow is as black as veluet.   (I. ii. 19–67)[1]

Shakespeare seems to have used this on two occasions, in *The Two Gentlemen* and in *The Comedy of Errors*, and his two versions are fairly close together. In *The Comedy of Errors* Dromio of Syracuse is telling his master Antipholus how Luce the kitchen-maid, wife to Dromio of Ephesus, has claimed him as her husband, and a catalogue of her qualities then follows. The Dromio–Antipholus dialogue has more

1. Text from *The Complete Works of John Lyly*, ed. R. W. Bond, 1902. The resemblance between this passage and the Launce-Speed scene was apparently first noted by F. W. Fairholt in his edition of Lyly's plays (1858).

of witty fancy than the Launce–Speed dialogue of *The Two Gentle-men*, III. i: in particular it makes use of a series of geographical analogues which R. A. Foakes has suggested may come from Friar John's geographical account of the head and body of Panurge (*Gargantua and Pantagruel*, Book III, Chap. 28).[1] But the two Shake-speare passages are close in general ideas, thus:

> *Spe.* 'Item, she is not to be kissed fasting in respect of her breath.'
> > (*Two Gentlemen*, III. i. 317–18)
>
> *Syr. Ant.* Where Spain?
> *Syr. Dro.* Faith, I saw it not; but I felt it hot in her breath.
> > (*Errors*, III. ii. 128–30)
>
> *Spe.* 'Item, she hath no teeth.'
> *Lau.* I care not for that neither; because I love crusts.
> *Spe.* 'Item, she is curst.'
> *Lau.* Well; the best is, she hath no teeth to bite.
> > (*Two Gentlemen*, III. i. 332–5)
>
> *Syr. Ant.* Where England?
> *Syr. Dro.* I looked for the chalky cliffs, but I could find no white-ness in them. But I guess it stood in her chin, by the salt rheum that ran between France and it.
> > (*Errors*, III. ii. 123–7)[2]

Of course, a dramatist in a hurry may do over again and more imperfectly something he has done before: nevertheless, the Launce–Speed duologue is manifestly less thoroughly contrived than the Antipholus–Dromio duologue and is therefore more likely to have come first. If I am right in suggesting that the Launce-part was the latest (except for II. vi) stratum in *The Two Gentlemen*, this means that the play a as whole probably preceded *The Comedy of Errors*. The difficulty is that we are by no means sure of the date of that play. R. A. Foakes suggests it 'was written not long before or immediately after the long spell of plague which caused all acting to be prohibited in London throughout most of the year 1593'.[3] This does not controvert the possibility that the internal contra-dictions of *The Two Gentlemen* may in part derive from its first stratum being written before the plague closed the theatres and its later strata, or some of them, when the theatres were open again and there was at last a renewed demand for fresh plays. Chambers' suggestion that the outset of the career of the Lord Chamberlain's Men (after the re-opening of the theatres) was 'a not unlikely time for hasty composition' would be given additional significance if Shakespeare were not writing an entirely new play but getting into shape one that had initially caused him trouble. Later we shall see

---

1. *The Comedy of Errors*, new Arden edition, 1962, p. 55.
2. *Errors* text from Arden edition, 1962.   3. *Ibid.*, p. xxiii.

that *The Two Gentlemen* was, for him, a new type of comedy, one
that he may well have found difficulty in fashioning: perhaps, indeed, it was his first comedy of all. That, of course, may explain its
unevenness of quality, which is evident apart from its inconsistencies of statement. But in any event 1594–5 seems too late. We
may guess (and it is only a guess) at 1592 for the first phase (*not*
version), and late 1593 for the putting of the play into its present
shape. *The Two Gentlemen* continued to be known till at least 1598,
when Meres included it in his list. But for a long time we may
assume only a manuscript survived, this being Shakespeare's com-
posite draft (consisting of fragments from each phase of composition), and then about 1622 Ralph Crane or another of similar
habits made a transcript for the printer.[1]

There seems thus no sufficient reason to assume that the extant
play is only partly Shakespeare's, even though there are moments
when one is at first inclined to think in terms of a report. Indeed the
reconstruction of the play's composition here put forward suggests
that the additions made during the course of composition include
some of the best things in the text (most especially Launce's contribution). It does, however, seem beyond doubt that the play was
finally put together in some haste.

The play remained active in Shakespeare's mind. In *Romeo and
Juliet, The Merchant of Venice, Twelfth Night,* he used over again
elements that first appeared in *The Two Gentlemen.*[2]

III. SOURCES

The Two Gentlemen of Verona derives from, and makes its contribution to, the great mass of friendship-literature that extends
through the Middle Ages to the seventeenth century. We shall be
later concerned with the special character of the play in its relation
to this literature,[3] but here we must consider the evidence of direct
indebtedness. And we may note, too, that even in the fourteenth
century friendship is not always victorious in its conflict with love.
Normally it is: the romance *Amis and Amiloun,*[4] for example, shows
Amis ready to kill his own children in order that his friend Amiloun

---

1. W. W. Greg, *The Shakespeare First Folio*, pp. 216–17, argues against Crane's
copy being foul papers only on the grounds that 'the directions in their fashion'
'provide for the presence of all necessary characters' and 'there is no irregularity
in their description'. But Crane, we assume, re-arranged entries, and this is a
play with a small and easily manageable cast-list. It is harder to believe that all
the play's confusions survived in a prompt-copy. Cf. above, p. xxxi.

2. See Section VI of the Introduction, p. lxxi.   3. *Ibid.*, pp. liv–lvi.

4. Edited by MacEdward Leach (Early English Text Society, no. 203, 1937).

may be cured of leprosy, and the climax of the story tells how the two men punish Amiloun's wife for her desertion, imprisoning her and restricting her diet to bread and water till she dies. But in *The Knight's Tale* Palamon and Arcite come to open conflict through their joint love of Emily, and Arcite has to die so that a wryly happy ending for Palamon may be secured. When, in all probability, Shakespeare at the end of his career worked with Fletcher on a dramatization of Chaucer's story, the title of their play *The Two Noble Kinsmen* surely echoed that of *The Two Gentlemen of Verona*. Moreover, *The Two Noble Kinsmen* is linked with *A Midsummer Night's Dream* in their common use of Theseus' wedding as a framework-action. Just as *Pericles* looks back to the early *Comedy of Errors*, so *The Two Noble Kinsmen*—using Chaucer as a source-book as *Pericles* used Gower—was a reversion to the beginning of Shakespeare's career. The point is worth making at this moment, for if the *Two Gentlemen* story was in any way linked in Shakespeare's mind with *The Knight's Tale*, we must not let resemblances between the early play and more conventional examples of friendship-literature—and resemblances there certainly are—make us equate the respective dominant attitudes.

That Shakespeare knew Chaucer we need not doubt, but there are two friendship-stories told in the sixteenth century, those of Titus and Gisippus and of Damon and Pithias, that may well have made a direct contribution to the play. In Sir Thomas Elyot's *The Boke named the Gouernour* (1531) we find in Book II, chapter xii, '*The wonderful history of Titus and Gisippus, and whereby is fully declared the figure of perfet amitie*'. The scene of the story is Athens, Titus having come there from Rome. He and Gisippus are identical in appearance. Gisippus is prevailed on to marry by his friends and relations, but likes well enough the lady Sophronia who is suggested to him. Before the marriage Titus is taken by his friend to see Sophronia, loves her, consequently falls ill, and confesses his love to Gisippus. So Gisippus suggests that after the public wedding ceremony Titus shall take his place in bed, the essential part of the marriage-contract being the giving of a ring in bed, and the loosening of the bride's girdle. This plan is carried out, and Titus takes Sophronia, now his legal wife, back to Rome with him. The later part of the story tells how the Athenians reproached Gisippus for his management of the affair, confiscated his property and exiled him. He goes to Rome and is at first not recognized by Titus. But when he is accused of a murder, Titus does recognize his friend and claims that he himself is the murderer. They are both saved when the real murderer, touched by their magnanimity, confesses.

Titus takes an army to Athens, punishes Gisippus' enemies and reinstates him in his possessions.

The differences from *The Two Gentlemen* are many: Titus tells his friend of his love immediately, while Shakespeare's Proteus hides his; in Elyot Gisippus is the contriver always, in Shakespeare Proteus (corresponding to Titus); Sophronia is the passive party in an arranged marriage, while Silvia confesses her love for Valentine and shows enterprise in her flight from court; Gisippus is not much in love ('more estemynge true frendship than the loue of a woman, where unto he was induced by his frendes, and nat by violence of Cupide constrained'[1]), in contrast to Valentine; Titus has no previous attachment, in contrast to Proteus. On the other hand, Gisippus' lamenting in Rome when Titus has not recognized him, so that he thinks his friend is ungrateful, could be compared with Valentine's lament in v. iv. 62–72 over Proteus' actual treachery. A closer kinship may exist between Valentine's words in renouncing Silvia to Proteus (v. iv. 82–3) and those of Gisippus in renouncing Sophronia to Titus: 'Here I renounce to you clerely all my title and interest that I nowe haue or mought haue in that faire mayden.'[2]

Elyot had the story from the *Decameron*, Day x, Novel viii, and in Boccaccio there are some notable differences from Elyot's version. Titus and Gisippus are not identical in appearance. Sophronia, when she discovers the cheat, is sorrowful and indignant (cf. Silvia's rebuke to Proteus just before he attempts a rape on her, v. iv. 33 ff.). Boccaccio says nothing of the friends going to Athens to take revenge on Gisippus' enemies: instead, Titus bestows his sister Fulvia on Gisippus, and 'they all lived together in one house, he with his Fulvia, and Titus with his fair Sophronia, to their mutual satisfaction, every day adding something, if possible, to their felicity'.[3] We may be reminded of the last line of Shakespeare's play: 'One feast, one house, one mutual happiness' (v. iv. 171). Moreover, when Titus in Boccaccio finds himself in love, he argues with himself concerning the claims of love and friendship in a way similar to that of Proteus in ii. vi, reaching at one point the heretical notion that 'The laws of love are of greater force than any other; they disannul those of friendship'.[4]

The Titus and Gisippus story is also found in two verse-redactions of the sixteenth century: by William Walter (*c.* 1530), apparently based on Beroaldo's Latin version of Boccaccio (1491),

---

1. *The Gouernour* (Everyman's Library), reprinted 1937, p. 177.
2. *Ibid.*, p. 172.   3. *The Decameron*, London, 1911, iv. 281.
4. *Ibid.*, iv. 256–8.

and by Edward Lewicke (1562), based on Elyot. No evidence of Shakespeare's indebtedness to either of these has been observed. There were also a Latin play for schoolboys, *De Titi et Gisippi firmissima amicitia*, acted at Hitchin in 1538, and a lost English play, *The History of Titus and Gisippus*, acted by Paul's Boys at Whitehall on 19 February 1577.[1] It is more than probable that Shakespeare knew *The Gouernour*, and the story of Titus and Gisippus is likely enough to have been in his mind when he told his own friendship-story of Valentine and Proteus. Yet he may have had another channel of access to Boccaccio, whose version he is, we have seen, closer to than he is to Elyot's. Titus and Gisippus were certainly famous friends: both Elyot and Spenser (*The Faerie Queene*, Book IV, Canto x, st. 26–7) list them with Damon and Pithias.

In 1571 was published Richard Edwards' play *The excellent Comedy of two the moste faithfullest Friendes, Damon and Pithias*, which had been acted in 1565.[2] Here there is no love–friendship conflict, the friends being always devoted and ready to die for each other: Pithias does indeed make the simple assertion that he will 'doo more for a man' than Gronno the hangman 'woulde for a woman'.[3] Yet there are some remarkable connections between Edwards' play and Shakespeare's. In the list of '*Speakers names*' we find Damon and Pithias described as '*two gentlemen of Greece*', and we may note that the friends share one servant (as there may originally have been only one in *The Two Gentlemen of Verona*[4]). Stephano the servant complains that he is hungry, while his masters have other things in mind (ll. 436–62), as Speed complains that, unlike Valentine and 'the chameleon Love', he needs food (II. i. 162–5). The word 'noddy', which grows tiresome in *The Two Gentlemen*, I. i. 109–12, is used in *Damon and Pithias* at ll. 40, 43, 1568, 1583, and the word 'lubber' is in *The Two Gentlemen* at II. v. 40 and in *Damon and Pithias* at l. 1226. At ll. 123–4 Aristippus says of the parasite Carisophus: 'A Villaine for his life, a Varlet died in Graine, / You lose Money by him if you sel him for one knaue, for he serues for twaine'—which may help to explain Launce's comment on Proteus: 'my master is a kind of a knave; but that's all one, if he be but one knave' (III. i. 262–3). There is an irony in the situation if, as appears to be the case, Shakespeare had this story of woman-free friendship in his mind as he wrote of his changing Proteus.

1. Ralph M. Sargent, 'Sir Thomas Elyot and the Integrity of *The Two Gentlemen of Verona*', *P.M.L.A.*, lxv (December 1950), 1166–80. Cf. Chambers, *E.S.*, iv. 93, 152.

2. Chambers, *E.S.*, iii. 310.

3. M.S.R., 1957, ll. 1079–80. All line-references are to this edition.

4. See above, pp. xxvi–xxviii.

these,[1] but if so Shakespeare's first planning or first version cannot even in outline be reconstructed: the two stories are inextricably intertwined in the play as we have it. Many of the play's inconsistencies, however, would disappear if we assumed an original outline (involving both stories) on the following plan.

The scene is Verona, where Valentine, recently arrived from elsewhere, has fallen in love with Silvia. She is the daughter of a noble, not a sovereign prince, and hence the informality of his presentation in II. iv and of his fabricated wooing-story in III. i. As the play proceeds, Shakespeare finds it convenient to make him a prince, so that his sentence of banishment (with an echo from Brooke's *Romeus and Juliet*)[2] can be introduced. Proteus, Valentine's friend in the place they both come from, appears 'With commendation from great potentates' (II. iv. 74), and at this stage Shakespeare is not sure whether to turn Silvia's father into an emperor (II. iv. 72). In scenes now lost, Valentine may have shown Proteus Silvia's 'picture' (II. iv. 205) and Proteus may have referred to Julia in conversation with Silvia (IV. iv. 132–3). The first of these conjectures is unnecessary, for in the play as extant Proteus can mean only that he has had a mere glimpse of Silvia (her 'picture' or mere external appearance) as yet: for this reason the passage referred to here has not been mentioned above in our list of the play's puzzles. But Julia, already arrived in Verona, disguises herself and enters Proteus' service. The play would then proceed more or less as we have it, except that—after the insertion of Launce—Shakespeare added II. vi to make it clear that Proteus was hesitant in his treachery, which would explain the introductory stage-direction with its '*solus*', a form easily used by a dramatist inserting a scene wholly made up of soliloquy.[3]

But perhaps the play was proving too short. Perhaps Shakespeare, who already had a journeying element in the play (from Verona to the forest), decided to profit from the example of his main source, Montemayor's *Diana*, and to trace the movement of the action from the place where the two young men and Julia came from. But they had been 'the two gentlemen of Verona' because that is where they were when the love–friendship conflict began to operate. Now, with a beginning in their own town, that is the obvious place for them to be primarily associated with. But Shakespeare is not sure about this and does not name Verona in the added first act. He does, however, decide to give a

1. See above, p. xxv.   2. See Section III of this Introduction, p. xliii.
3. The '*solus*' could of course be Crane's addition, but he did not use it for Valentine's soliloquy at the beginning of V. iv.

when she has read it, she tears it and throws it on the ground—thus performing Julia's actions in I. ii. 100–17. Grobiano tells Hyppolita: 'Mein Herr Julius lest Jhr Gn. zu 1000 malen grüssen' ('My master Julius sends you a thousand greetings'), and Hyppolita responds: 'O das tausendt mal grüssen thönet noch stets von meinen Ohren' ('O how the thousand greetings still resound in mine ears') —an exchange that might be mocked in Valentine's and Silvia's offering of 'a thousand good-morrows' and 'two thousand', with Speed's amusement at the extravagance (II. i. 91–4). Grobiano has to labour to extract a ducat from Hyppolita for bringing her the forged letter, as Speed laboured for a fee in connection with his carrying Proteus' letter, again a ducat being mentioned (I. i. 130–9).[1] Doubtless it is a coincidence that, when Romulus comes in disguise at the end of the play, he is described by a servant as coming from Padua (cf. *The Two Gentlemen*, II. v. 1).[2] On the other hand, the friends in the German play are from the same city and visiting a prince's court where all the action takes place (as perhaps originally was almost the case in Shakespeare's play). The name Julius (at times Julio in the German text) may be linked with Shakespeare's name Julia, though that may have come from Brooke's *Romeus and Juliet*, as we shall see.[3] As already noted, there seems to be no substantial evidence whether or not the English original of *Julio and Hyppolita* preceded *The Two Gentlemen*.[4] There is no sufficient reason to identify the play with the *Phillipo and Hewpolyta* recorded by Henslowe as acted several times between 9 July 1594 (when it is marked 'ne') and the following October.[5]

All the possible sources glanced at so far have been concerned with a main action in a single place: only the Titus and Gisippus story has a continuation of the Athens-story in Rome; *Damon and Pithias* and *Julio and Hyppolita*, though involving journeys in their stories, are wholly located for their action in Syracuse and the court of an unknown prince respectively. None of these writings gives a hint of a character corresponding to Julia, even if her name is a link with the German play. Yet in Shakespeare there is a marked stress on the girl that Proteus loved and abandoned and found again, and moreover the action of his play, as we have it, involves notable changes of locality, from one town to another, back and forth between town and town, and then back and forth between town and forest. This links *The Two Gentlemen* with those

1. See Bond, p. 114; Bullough, *loc. cit.*   2. See Bond, p. 115.

3. Some other possible resemblances are noted by Bond, pp. 113–15.

4. Cf. Bond, p. xxiv; Bullough, p. 209.

5. *Henslowe's Diary*, ed. R. A. Foakes and R. T. Rickert, Cambridge, 1961, pp. 22–4.

romantic plays which we know from Sidney's evidence in *An Apology for Poetry* were popular in the theatres of 1570–80: of the few examples extant, *Sir Clyomon and Clamydes* (which includes our earliest English girl character in boy's disguise) and *Common Conditions* may well be typical enough. When the stage grew more sophisticated, with the writings of the University Wits, it was Greene who in the conduct of his actions kept closest to this established formula. His *James IV* tells of royal faithlessness in love, of a queen's wanderings in male disguise, of her final reunion with her repentant husband. Despite its title (and its title-page reference to the Battle of Flodden) this is sheer romance of the journeying kind, with a powerful stress on the disguised and suffering Dorothea, a slighter but effective degree of stress on the equally virtuous but less threatened Ida. It has a villain, a mocking servant (more acid in his comments than anyone in Shakespeare's play), a fairy-land induction and framework, and a vague background of national events. There is no question of *James IV* being a source for *The Two Gentlemen*, but they do belong basically to the same genre, despite the much wider scope of Greene's play. *James IV* is difficult to date: it was entered in the Stationers' Register in 1594, Greene having died in 1592. Chambers suggests 1591 for its composition[1]: most probably, then, it preceded *The Two Gentlemen*.

If Shakespeare had a dramatic source for the Julia-story, it would surely have been in a play of this type. In her disguise, her wanderings, her feminine appeal to our sympathy, Julia belongs in the *James IV* kind of drama.[2] And it is possible that there was such a play for Shakespeare to make direct use of. The Elizabethan Revels Accounts record a performance of '*The history of felix & philiomena*' given by 'her maiesties servauntes on the Sondaie next after newe years daye' in 1585.[3] Though the play is lost, there can be no doubt that it was a dramatization of the story of Don Felix and his love Felismena which is included in the *Diana* of the Portuguese writer Jorge de Montemayor, probably published in 1559, in French translation in 1578 and 1587, and in an English translation by Bartholomew Yong in 1598.[4] Shakespeare's source for the Julia-story may have been the lost play[5] or the French translation of

1. Chambers, *E.S.*, iii. 330.

2. Shakespeare's use of a Greene story for *The Winter's Tale* is another indication of his readiness in his final plays to return to certain features of his beginnings.

3. Chambers, *E.S.*, iv. 160.   4. Bullough, pp. 205–6.

5. T. P. Harrison, Jr, 'Concerning *Two Gentlemen of Verona* and Montemayor's *Diana*', *M.L.N.*, xli (April 1926), 251–2, suggests Shakespeare would not be likely to have access to *Felix and Philiomena* because the Queen's Men were in the provinces in 1593–4. But this assumes the date of *The Two Gentlemen* is certain.

Montemayor or Yong's English version, for in his preface Yong stated that he had begun his translation 'About nineteene yeeres past' and that it 'hath lyen by me finished *Horaces* ten and six yeeres more'. Certainly, as Kittredge pointed out, Yong went on to say that he had sent to the printer the only copy he had, which was 'verie darke and enterlined',[1] but this is not proof that another copy did not exist or that Shakespeare could not have seen in advance the one that was printed. There were also unpublished partial translations by Edward Paston and Thomas Wilson. The many verbal echoes of Yong's version noted in the commentary to this edition make it almost certain that this was Shakespeare's immediate source.

The main story of the *Diana* concerns Diana and Syrenus: they love, he has to leave the kingdom 'about certaine affaires', she marries another, he grieves on his return. This is contrasted with the story of Don Felix and Felismena. In the main story there is an elaborate leave-taking when the lovers part, which is described in a nymph's song of 516 lines. The farewell includes Diana's giving Syrenus a ring and a final embrace. Conceivably Shakespeare, with a touch of irony, had this incident in mind when making the farewell of Proteus and Julia so brief in II. ii. Felismena, we may note, is an orphan, as Julia appears to be in II. vii though not earlier. In her story, the maid Rosina is like Lucetta in the incident of the first letter sent by Don Felix; the father of Felix opposes their love, as hinted by Shakespeare in I. iii. 48–9; this father argues that his son should not 'spende his youth idly at home' (cf. I. iii. 4–24), and Felix is sent to 'the great Princesse *Augusta Caesarinas* court'; there is a serenade of Felix's second love (cf. IV. ii); Celia, corresponding to Silvia, is concerned about Felix's behaviour to his first love (cf. IV. ii. 92–6, IV. iv. 131–75, V. iv. 45–52); Felismena enters Felix's service as his page and goes on love-embassies to Celia (cf. IV. iv); on these occasions Celia and Felismena talk of Felix's first love. Celia, we should note, falls in love with Felismena in her disguise, as Olivia falls in love with the disguised Viola in *Twelfth Night*, and then dies. At this Felix disappears, distraught.

This part of the story has been told in Book II of the *Diana*. The continuation is to be found in Book VII. There Felismena disguised as a shepherdess rescues Felix by killing two or three knights who are attacking him. She is momentarily 'in such a traunce' when she recognizes him, but then reveals herself and her long sufferings. He swoons, as Julia does in *The Two Gentlemen* (V. iv. 84). On recovery he compares her beauty to Celia's: 'I knowe not wherein to

1. *The Complete Works of Shakespeare*, ed. G. L. Kittredge, 1936, p. 34.

put this fault, that may be so justly attributed to me; ... If to *Celias* beautie, it is cleere, that thine did farre excell hers and all the worlds besides.' Shakespeare suggests equality rather than superiority (v. iv. 113–14).

Thus we have an origin for Julia, the first love of the faithless friend, and we have a story with a changing locality. But Felix is only a faithless lover: there is no question of his being also a faithless friend. Shakespeare has united the story from the *Diana* with the friendship-literature we have already considered. Nevertheless, if he set out with the intention of writing a play with a 'happy ending' (and everything in our text of *The Two Gentlemen* suggests that), it was obviously convenient for him to have a first love for Proteus to be reunited with. The change of plan which I have suggested[1] does not necessarily entail the later use of the *Diana* after Shakespeare had originally planned a faithless friend story. But that at some time he used the *Diana* or a very close derivative from it (the lost play) seems indubitable.

Yet he used more than the *Diana* and the friendship-literature. There can be no doubt that when he was writing *The Two Gentlemen of Verona* he had already read Arthur Brooke's poem *Romeus and Juliet* (1562), which was to be the major source of the tragedy he was to write a few years later. In his edition of the poem J. J. Munro adduced a number of parallels, the most compelling of which are the matter of the rope-ladder (II. iv. 178, II. vi. 33–4, III. i. 117–52), the banishment of both Romeus and Valentine, who go, the one actually, the other presumptively (IV. iii. 23, v. ii. 46), to Mantua, the declaration of Valentine to the outlaws that he has killed a man, as Romeus indeed had (IV. i. 26–9), the reaction of Valentine and Romeus to the sentence of banishment and the advice given to them respectively by the Friar and Proteus (III. i. 241–56), the use of a visit to a friar by Silvia and Juliet under the pretence of confession (IV. iii. 43–4, v. ii. 40–2), the mention of Friar Laurence in *The Two Gentlemen* (v. ii. 36).[2] Also we find that Brooke gives Shakespeare the cue for *The Two Gentlemen*, II. iv. 188–91: 'And as out of a planke a nayle a nayle doth drive, / So novell love out of the minde the auncient love doth rive' (ll. 207–8). We may note too that Juliet is the first to speak of love in *Romeus and Juliet* (ll. 277–9) as Silvia was the first in *The Two Gentlemen*, II. i, and that Brooke's Juliet pleads with Romeus to let her accompany him in his flight (ll. 1605–30), as Silvia decided to follow Valentine when he was sent into exile. So, too, Silvia's father's determination to marry his

1. See above, pp. xxix–xxx.
2. *Brooke's 'Romeus and Juliet'*, ed. J. J. Munro, 1908, p. lvi

daughter to Thurio seems related to Juliet's father's predilection for Paris.[1]

We can thus be reasonably sure of certain things as sources for *The Two Gentlemen*: the friendship-literature (especially 'Titus and Gisippus' in one form or another, *Damon and Pithias*), the *Diana* (directly or, less probably, indirectly), and Brooke's *Romeus*. In addition, Shakespeare certainly drew on the dialogue between Licio and Petulus in Lyly's *Midas*, I. ii,[2] and Speed is evidently a Lyly page throughout. Attempts have been made, without the effect of total conviction, to link *The Two Gentlemen* to particular Italian comedies,[3] and the scenes involving the outlaws, with their reference to Robin Hood (IV. i. 36), have been linked to Robin Hood legend and the literature of the greenwood generally.[4] Miss Dorothy F. Atkinson has argued that the main source of the play is the fifth story in *A Courtlie Controversie of Cupids Cautels*, translated by H. Wotton (1578) from the French of Jacques d'Yver (Paris, 1572).[5] On the whole Bullough seems justified in seeing this as an 'analogue' rather than a source,[6] and we may merely note in passing that Miss Atkinson draws our attention to the early mention of Padua in this story as explaining the odd reference to that town in *The Two Gentlemen*, II. v. i.

From the name of the play, with its echo of the '*two Gentlemen of Greece*' in *Damon and Pithias*, we can assume that the friendship-literature was the starting-point of *The Two Gentlemen*, that the *Diana* (immediately or via the lost play) and Brooke's poem *Romeus and Juliet* came in at some stage, and that behind the total concept of the play were the romantic drama of preceding years, brought to a point of some maturity by Greene, and the patterned love-arrangements of Lyly (with his use of song). Many incidental echoings of Lyly are observed in the commentary notes to the present edition. Certainly we have here, at the beginning of Shakespeare's career, an example of the use of multiple sources for a play, for it is unlikely that the lost *Felix and Philiomena* brought so much together as this early Shakespeare comedy contrived to do. In that

1. These resemblances have been noted by Mozelle Scaff Allen, 'Broke's *Romeus and Juliet* as a Source for the Valentine–Silvia Plot in *The Two Gentlemen of Verona*' (University of Texas Publication No. 3826: Studies in English, 1938, pp. 25–46).

2. See above, pp. xxxii–xxxiii.

3. Cf., e.g., O. J. Campbell, '*The Two Gentlemen of Verona* and Italian Comedy', *Studies in Shakespeare, Milton and Donne by Members of the English Department of the University of Michigan*, 1925, pp. 49–63.

4. Cf. Bullough, p. 207.

5. 'The Source of *Two Gentlemen of Verona*', *S.P.*, xli (April 1944), 223–34.

6. Bullough, p. 208.

respect it stands in sharp contrast to the almost exactly contemporary *Comedy of Errors*, with its nearly total reliance on two comedies of Plautus.

In the first volume (1957) of *Narrative and Dramatic Sources of Shakespeare*, edited by Geoffrey Bullough, extracts from the following are given in relation to *The Two Gentlemen of Verona*: the Titus and Gisippus story from *The Gouernour*, *Euphues*, Yong's translation of the *Diana*, the *Arcadia*, Flaminio Scala's *Flavio Tradito* (one of a series of scenarii published as Scala's in Venice in 1611 and illustrating the commedia dell' arte elements which Shakespeare may have drawn on in the present play and elsewhere), and *Julio und Hyppolita*. This group of extracts is freely drawn upon in the commentary notes to the present edition, as is Bullough's printing of *Romeus and Juliet*, which is given in full, in the same volume, in the section devoted to *Romeo*. Quotations from the *Diana* are, however, given from the edition of Judith M. Kennedy (Oxford, 1968).

IV. STAGE HISTORY

The earliest known performance of *The Two Gentlemen* was given at Drury Lane on 22 December 1762.[1] That is, we have no firm evidence that the play was acted in Shakespeare's life-time (though from Meres' reference to it in 1598 we can assume that it was), or from his death to the Civil War, or in the Restoration,[2] or through the first half of the eighteenth century.[3] The long neglect after 1660 is understandable enough: of the other early comedies, *The Comedy of Errors* and *Love's Labour's Lost* were equally or almost equally neglected, the former achieving only twelve performances (seven of them in an adapted form) before 1750 and the latter having as blank a story as *The Two Gentlemen*.[4] Even *As You Like It* and *Twelfth Night*, close to *The Two Gentlemen* in tone though of course of far greater maturity, made a poor showing until the eighteenth century was well advanced: *As You Like It* did not get on the stage (except for a few performances of an adaptation in 1723) until the 1740s, and *Twelfth Night*, seen a few times in the Restoration playhouse and then unsuccessfully adapted by William

1. The duodecimo edition published in 1734 is preceded by a note from W. Chetwood, prompter at Drury Lane, but the text shows no evidence of theatrical use: it derives from Pope, even to the 'continental' division of scenes and the relegation of certain passages to the foot of the page.

2. Allardyce Nicoll, *A History of English Drama 1660–1900*, Cambridge, i (1952), 172.

3. Charles Beecher Hogan, *Shakespeare in the Theatre 1701–1800*, Oxford, i (1957), 461.

4. *Ibid.*

Burnaby, had to wait for the same decade to take its place on the London stage. Until the shifting of critical standards that marked the middle years of the eighteenth century, there was indeed little interest in Shakespeare's early comic experiments or in the plays of love and fantastic journeying that he wrote shortly before turning to his tragedy of *Hamlet*. Only *Much Ado*, robust in its wit and plotting, had a noticeably better record. *A Midsummer Night's Dream* was material for opera and other modes of adaptation.

What of course, we shall wish to know is the degree to which *The Two Gentlemen of Verona* held the stage in the years immediately after its composition. That the play was known at all in that time we have firm evidence only from Meres, and it is well to remember that before 1623 a knowledge of it could come only from performance or from the reading of a manuscript. We have already noted the possibility that the English original of *Julio und Hyppolita* may be later than *The Two Gentlemen* and may derive from it. There is one other play which may owe a similar debt. This is Heywood's *The Four Prentices of London*, published in 1615 but described in its preface as '*written many yeares since*': the author adds that '*as* Playes were then some fifteene or sixteene yeares agoe it was in the Fashion'. Fleay grandly put the date of composition back to 1594, identifying Heywood's play with the *Godfrey of Bulloigne* acted by the Admiral's Men in that year, but Chambers noted that *Godfrey* was a Second Part and suggested therefore that *The Four Prentices* was the *Jerusalem* acted by Strange's Men in 1592.[1] If Chambers is right, *The Two Gentlemen* could be later than *The Four Prentices* and indebted to it, but the line of argument is highly conjectural and it seems more likely that *The Four Prentices* was written *c.* 1600, possibly as a conflation of an old two-part play with a new citizen-theme worked in. Nevertheless, in noting the resemblances with *The Two Gentlemen*, one must recognize the possibility that Shakespeare was the debtor.

Charles, one of the four noble apprentices, encounters a group of outlaws on his way to Jerusalem. When he kills their captain, they offer him the leadership, which he accepts. In the Presenter's speech which gives an account of this, the outlaws are described as 'such as keepe in Caues' and as 'This crue' (cf. *The Two Gentlemen*, IV. i. 74, v. iii. 11). A little later we see Charles instructing the outlaws in the ways of 'ciuility' and 'ciuil nurture' (cf. *The Two Gentlemen*, v. iii. 12, iv. 154); they are again referred to as a 'crew' and as living in a 'Caue'; he warns them not to rob 'pilgrims, or poore Trauellers' or to commit rape (cf. *The Two Gentlemen*, IV. i. 6, 71–2,

1. Chambers, *E.S.*, iii. 340–1.

v. iii. 12–13, iv. 15); and one outlaw, a Clown, refers to the offences for which they were banished: 'wee haue beene all Gentlemen and House-holders; But I was banisht for nothing but getting of Bastards; but this fellow fled from *Venice*, for killing a man cowardly on the *Rialto*; some for one villany, and some for another' (cf. *The Two Gentlemen*, IV. i. 44–52). Then we have a stage-direction and a snatch of dialogue as follows:

> Enter the Clowne *and the Villaine, dragging the old Earle violently, and rifling him. . . .*
>
> *Vill.* . . . Sirra, stand.
> *Eust.* Yes, I will stand, base wretch, when thou shalt fall, . . .

We can find the use of 'rifle' in relation to an outlaw's attack, and a 'stand'–'sit' pun resembling the 'stand'–'fall' pun here, in *The Two Gentlemen*, IV. i. 3–4. Later the disguised Bella Franca, being pursued by an outlaw, begs aid from Charles and Eustace "'gainst him,/ That in the Forest would haue rauisht me' (cf. *The Two Gentlemen*, v. iv. 21–2). And then we have a '*French* Lady' who follows Guy in the disguise of a page and takes service with him. When at the end she appears in woman's clothes, the dialogue's use of 'wagtail', 'wag', 'boy', 'Page' is notable:

> *Guy.* She is no boy, you do mistake her quite.
> *Eust.* A boy, a Page, a wagtaile by this light:
> What say you sister?
> *Bel.* Sure he told me so,
> For if he be a maide, I made him one.
> *Eust.* Do not mistake the sex, man, for he's none.
> It is a rogue, a wag, his name is *Iacke*,
> A notable dissembling lad, a Cracke.

(Cf. *The Two Gentlemen*, v. iv. 85–6, 162–4). Of the resemblances noted between the two plays, some are indeed slight and perhaps inevitable in situations involving outlaws. But they are numerous, and an indebtedness of one dramatist to the other seems likely. If that is true, the probability is that Heywood had seen *The Two Gentlemen* on the stage and remembered the outlaws' scenes.[1]

We move on to firmer ground in the late eighteenth century. The performance at Drury Lane on 22 December 1762, under Garrick's management, was of the alteration by Benjamin Victor

[1]. It has been suggested by Paul Becker, *Das Verhältnis von John Marston's 'What You Will' zu Plautus' 'Amphitruo' und Sforza D'Oddi's 'I Morti Vivi'*, Halle, 1904, p. 28, that the discussion of suitors in *What You Will*, IV. i, is indebted to *The Two Gentlemen*, I. ii. But (as remarked by Anthony Caputi, *John Marston, Satirist*, Ithaca, 1961, p. 167 and n.) the situation is commonplace. The debt, if any, could equally be to *The Merchant of Venice*, I. ii.

published in the following year. In his 'Advertisement' Victor said he had tried to remove the 'weeds' without cutting the threads of the 'several poetical flowers' with which the play was adorned. He also aimed at giving 'a greater uniformity to the scenery, and a connection and consistency to the fable', and added two scenes for Launce and Speed in Act v. So in I. i Valentine's journey is to be by horse, not boat, Speed says he gave the letter to Lucetta, and Proteus explains he used Speed as his messenger in order to keep his love secret from Julia's family. We proceed to I. iii, with the reference firmly to Milan, not the Emperor's court, and with Launce making a brief entry with Proteus. The following scene is an ingenious conflation of I. ii, II. ii, and II. vii, but with Victor slipping momentarily when Lucetta refers to having just received the letter from 'Sir Valentine's page', who left for Milan in I. i. Thus all the 'Verona' scenes are now in the first act. Victor's II. i is a conflation of Shakespeare's II. i and II. iv, omitting Thurio's near-bankruptcy and the reference to Proteus' sea-journey. II. ii conflates Shakespeare's II. iii (Launce already being in Milan) and II. v, with references to Milan instead of 'the Imperial's court' and Padua, and with the omission of Panthino's entry. II. iii is Shakespeare's II. vi; III. i and ii are as in Shakespeare, but with the Duke's imaginary lady in Milan, not Verona, and with Valentine's poem to Silvia omitted. The original's Act IV is largely preserved, but v. i is added to it in order that virtually the whole of Act v may be in the forest. Valentine says he will 'counterfeit some story' if he meets outlaws; the Host says Launce has gone 'to seek his master's dog'; Silvia makes the appointment for flight 'This evening coming on at nine'; Launce explains in his soliloquy that Proteus' 'dog Squirrel' was lost; Silvia explains giving the picture to Proteus by saying it 'may divert him from my intended flight'. In the fifth act, v. i is Shakespeare's v. ii; v. ii consists of the first eighteen lines of v. iv; v. iii shows Launce and Speed captured by outlaws; v. iv brings together v. iii and v. iv from the end of Valentine's speech now in v. ii. In this last scene, Valentine's offer of Silvia to Proteus is omitted, Silvia joins the hands of Proteus and Valentine, Valentine says to Thurio 'Milan shall not behold thee', and Launce and Speed come in almost at the end, Launce through Speed's contrivance believing he is in danger of death. Victor's additions are largely in prose, occasionally in halting verse. He has done a neat job on the play, showing where he found it faulty (over-frequent changes of scene, contradictions, Valentine's renunciation, insufficient use of Launce and Speed towards the end, and apparently an old-fashionedness in Valentine's poem). If he had written better, his version might have held the stage longer. In fact it had only six performances in 1762 and 1763, and the original play returned for a single performance in 1784 (Covent Garden) and for three performances in 1790 (Drury Lane) under Kemble's management.[1] The playbills announced the play in 1790 as 'not acted twenty years'.[2] In 1808 Kemble put on his own alteration of Victor's adaptation: it omitted Proteus' attempt at rape and included 'a good deal of stilted stuff about Valentine's sending off Proteus to await sentence'.[3] The production was given only three times.[4] In 1821 came the operatic version by Frederic Reynolds, with music by Bishop, under Charles Kemble's management at Covent Garden. Scattered through the play were songs from other Shakespeare plays, and Shakespeare sonnets.[5] The words of the songs were published without date (though clearly near to the time of the performances), and from this we can see that Kemble's version gave Reynolds the basis for his. For all its shortcomings, this production was certainly the most popular presentation of the play so far recorded: there were twenty-nine performances in the first season. The playbills announced a 'Carnival in the Great Square of Milan' with a grand 'Emblematical Procession of the Seasons and the Elements', and the preface to Oxberry's edition of 1823 remarked that without the new musical and scenic devices the play 'would at once relapse into its former obscurity'.[6] However, Shakespeare's version came back at Bath in 1822, at Drury Lane (unsuccessfully) under Macready in 1841, and at the Park Theatre, New York, in 1846 under Charles Kean (who gave it also at the Haymarket in 1848). Macready's scenery was praised in *The Times* and in *John Bull*, for it did not 'overlay the drama' and 'quite enough was done and yet not too much'.[7] Kean, whose version was published in New York in 1846 prior to performance, omitted III. ii and V. i and abbreviated and expurgated throughout. Phelps tried the play at Sadler's Wells in the 1850s, and Osmund Tearle at Stratford-upon-Avon in 1890.[8] Augustin Daly's version then appeared at Daly's, New York, in February 1895, and at Daly's, London, the following July. In London it had the honour of a review from Bernard Shaw,

1. Hogan, *op. cit.*, ii. 672–4. The duodecimo edition of 1776, with a text derived from Capell, makes a number of critical observations 'by the Authors of the Dramatic Censor', all suggesting that the play would do well if it were put on the stage. Victor is disregarded, and the return of the original play was still eight years distant. This edition was reprinted in Volume VIII of *Bell's English Theatre* (1792).

2. G. C. D. Odell, *Shakespeare from Betterton to Irving* (1921), ii. 50.

3. *Ibid.*, ii. 61–2.   4. N.C.S., p. 105.

5. Odell, ii. 138–40; N.C.S., p. 106.   6. Odell, ii. 160–1.

7. *Ibid.*, ii. 205, 228, 277; N.C.S., p. 106.   8. N.C.S., p. 106.

who commented on the cuts (some indeed going back to Victor), the musical embellishments, the follies of the scenery, and the general inadequacy of the acting. Ada Rehan and Maxine Elliot played Julia and Silvia respectively, and Shaw gave them honourable mention.[1] The published New York text shows that the *Henry VIII* epilogue was used, with 'pair' substituted for 'one' in line 11.

The Two Gentlemen of Verona was one of the plays that particularly engaged the attention of William Poel. In 1892 he directed a recital-performance at the St James's Hall, which was repeated in costume, in the open air, before the members of the Albany Club at Kingston. A new production was given in the Merchant Taylors' Hall in November 1896 and in the Great Hall of the Charterhouse in January 1897. Then, most remarkably, Sir Herbert Tree invited Poel to direct *The Two Gentlemen* at His Majesty's Theatre during the Shakespeare Festival there, an apron being built out over the orchestra pit for the first time in that theatre. The production was given at His Majesty's on 20 April 1910 and at the Gaiety Theatre, Manchester, on the following 25, 26, and 30 April.[2]

Other twentieth-century productions, which have not been very frequent, include one at the Royal Court Theatre, London, in 1904.[3] The play has also been done at Stratford-upon-Avon, at the London Old Vic, and at the Theatre Royal, Bristol. The Bristol production (later transferred to London) took a cue from Reynolds and incorporated several songs from other plays. There was a French version by Maurice Olivaint done at the Odéon, Paris, in 1902, which omitted Launce, changed the location only twice (at some considerable cost to coherence), and translated Valentine's famous couplet as: 'J'y mets tout mon pardon, et te rends l'amitié / De Sylvie, si j'en puis disposer.'[4] It is evident, indeed, that some of the things that worry the play's critics have worried the directors too.

V. THIS EDITION

Using modern spelling, the text of this edition remains otherwise as faithful to the Folio as convenience will allow.

No localities are inserted in scene-headings: they are always

1. *Our Theatres in the Nineties*, 1931, i. 178–85.

2. Robert Speaight, *William Poel and the Elizabethan Revival*, 1954, pp. 73, 119–22, 280, 281, 283. This book includes a photograph from the 1896 performance in the Merchant Taylors' Hall, which was briefly referred to in a Shaw review (*Our Theatres in the Nineties*, ii. 298–9).

3. N.C.S., p. 106.   4. Published in Paris, 1902.

likely to give a wrong impression of Elizabethan stage-practice, and in the present instance (where we do not know from the text where we are in Act I, and where the locality of the Duke's court is given variously as Milan, Verona, and Padua) they would seriously distort the character of the Folio text. The major harm that Rowe and his successors did to the plays and their readers (though in his text of *The Two Gentlemen* Rowe himself was content with merely inserting 'A Forest' in IV. i) can at least here be disregarded.

As noted above, each scene in the Folio has a list at its head, giving the names of all the characters who will make an entry in that scene. In this edition the usual 'English' mode is adopted. The characters who come on stage at the beginning of the scene are named in an entry at the head; the other characters listed are given their entries in square brackets at appropriate places within the scene. The original forms of the entries are recorded in the collation.

Editorial stage-directions are inserted in square brackets, and the collation refers to the earliest edition which has totally or substantially (*'subst.'*) introduced the direction. In the case of a few stage-directions which are easily deducible from the text, but which it has seemed convenient to insert here, no collation is given: it can be assumed that such stage-directions are original with this edition, although something approaching them may be found elsewhere.

The Folio text of *The Two Gentlemen*, like the Folio texts in general, is heavily punctuated. However, for this play it would seem wrong to make the pointing too light. We are dealing with dramatic writing contemporary with Marlowe's and Kyd's, and the language of the 'romantic' characters at least has something of the deliberateness generally characteristic of the stage around 1590. So, although colons are avoided where they are used in the Folio simply to mark a substantial pause (being replaced here by, most often, a semi-colon or a full stop), the punctuation is closer to the Folio's than is usually the case in modernized editions. Question-marks in the Folio with the sense of exclamation-marks are silently changed. The collation indeed records punctuation only when a change affects interpretation.

The Folio's elisions within a word are preserved when the verse-line seems unquestionably to run better if they are used, but when the Folio has an elision (in a verse passage) which the present text disregards, the original form is given in the collation. The Folio's use of '-'d' in preterites and past participles is silently disregarded in prose passages. The Folio is followed in all cases where elision involves more than one word: for example, the Folio's 'it is' is not contracted even when metrical considerations would suggest 'it's'.

The brackets of the Folio are frequently retained when they do not seem likely to disturb a modern reader. Their use can make the general shape of a sentence more immediately clear than a double use of commas or dashes.

The collation in general is concerned to indicate those cases where an editorial choice has to be made. It records all substantive departures from the Folio (except, as noted, in the case of some editorial stage-directions enclosed in square brackets, and except for some obvious misprints which are silently corrected), and any noteworthy substantive emendations of the play's text made in the history of the play's editing. Only the first editor to introduce a change is named, although, where a conjecture has been offered by one and then incorporated into the text by another, both names are given.

The act- and scene-divisions are those of the Folio.

VI. THE COMEDY

The Two Gentlemen of Verona has been the recipient of indulgence rather than praise. Rowe, noting that it immediately follows *The Tempest* in the Folio, was sure that it was written long before that play: 'if his Fire may be suppos'd to abate in his Age, yet certainly his Judgment increas'd, but most of the Faults of this Play are Faults of Judgment more than Fancy.'[1] He added that '*Silvia* and the rest' do not behave themselves 'like Princes, Noblemen or the Sons and Daughters of such'.[2] Pope praised the style as '*less figurative, and more natural and unaffected, than the greater Part of this Author's, though suppos'd to be one of the first he wrote*', yet took exception to '*the lowest and most trifling conceits*' in it, which he attributed to '*the gross taste of the age he liv'd in*'.[3] For Theobald, it was simply 'One of the very worst' of Shakespeare's.[4] Hanmer thought '*It may well be doubted whether* Shakespear *had any other hand in this play than the enlivening it with some speeches and lines thrown in here and there.*'[5] Johnson conjectured that the text had escaped corruption 'only because being seldom played, it was less exposed to the hazards of transcription'.[6] Malone was kinder, thinking that, as perhaps the earliest of Shakespeare's plays, it 'may surely be pronounced a very elegant and extraordinary performance'.[7]

On the whole, as we should expect, the nineteenth century was more sympathetic. Coleridge thought the play only doubtfully

1. Rowe, vii (1710), 274.   2. *Ibid.*, p. 275.
3. Pope, i. 155, 157.   4. Theobald, i. 153, n. 1.   5. Hanmer, i. 145.
6. Johnson, i. 180.   7. Malone, iv. 7.

Shakespeare's,[1] and in Dowden's view the play's worst feature, its carelessness in the last act, was due to Shakespeare's handing over his manuscript to the actors 'while a portion of it still remained a hasty sketch',[2] but at least he admired the symmetry in the arrangement of the characters—Proteus balancing Valentine, Silvia Julia, and Launce Speed.[3] R. G. Moulton looked further than this and noted how each of the three journeys (Valentine's, Proteus', and Julia's) added to the complication of the action, and how the outlaws' encounters with a series of the play's characters (Valentine, Silvia, Proteus, and Julia) constituted the 'Resolving Accident'. Moreover, he saw the sub-plot (Launce and Speed) and the lighter exchanges of the dialogue as constituting a contrasting pattern to that of the romantic main plot.[4] Critics more concerned with characters praised Launce and Julia and Silvia: Ulrici wrote of 'the inimitable Launce, one of those delightfully amusing characters which we meet nowhere else but in Shakespeare',[5] and Brandes drew attention to 'the beauty and clearness with which the two young women are outlined' and to 'the true English humour' that Launce brings to the play.[6] Yet Ulrici also found in *The Two Gentlemen* a strong satiric element, presenting love as 'the foundation and ruling spring of life' but a foundation marred by 'instability and rottenness': 'love is presented under the most diversified forms, but in all equally weak, foolish, perverse, and self-indulgent.'[7] We may think this a rather heavy-handed presentation of the play, but the emphasis on satire is notable. Warwick Bond in his Arden edition (1906) and Quiller-Couch in his introduction to the New Cambridge edition (1921) represent a commoner and less bold approach. For Bond the play is worthy of praise for its key position in the development of romantic comedy, as constituting the 'earliest positive achievement surviving' in this form in English —only Greene's *Friar Bacon and Friar Bungay* and *James IV* having comparable status.[8] For 'Q' it is 'a light and jocund Italianate comedy', with 'notable promise, too, in the characters'.[9] Both Bond and 'Q' were worried about Valentine's renunciation of Silvia, but Bond convinced himself that Valentine only meant that his love was as much Proteus' as Silvia's (Julia unfortunately misunder-

1. T. M. Raysor (ed.), *Coleridge's Shakespearean Criticism*, 1930, ii. 308, n. 2.

2. *Shakspere: A Critical Study of his Mind and Art*, 3rd edition [1881], p. 51.

3. *Ibid.*, pp. 52–3.

4. *Shakespeare as a Dramatic Thinker*, New York, 1907 (2nd edition), pp. 222–8, 341.

5. Hermann Ulrici, *Shakespeare's Dramatic Art: and his Relation to Calderon and Goethe*, 1846, p. 286.

6. George Brandes, *William Shakespeare: A Critical Study*, 1898, i. 62–4.

7. *Op. cit.*, pp. 285–7.   8. Bond, p. xxxv.   9. N.C.S., pp. vii, xi.

standing his words and therefore swooning)[1] and 'Q' fell back on a belief that the text had been tampered with by another hand.[2]

Commentators of the last forty years have come nearer to a recognition that the play—sketch as it is for fuller development in the years that lay ahead for Shakespeare—has its own degree of complexity. They are not so inclined to take refuge in the state of the text or to explain away Valentine's renunciation by a disregard of its palpable sense. And they are not so ready to praise Launce and Julia without considering the significance of their co-existence within the play. Miss M. C. Bradbrook has insisted that we must recognize the force of the Friendship Cult, must see Valentine as 'displaying in transcendent form the courtly virtue of Magnanimity, the first and greatest virtue of a gentleman'.[3] The stress, she argues, is on the young men, with the young women merely materials for demonstration of the great virtue:

> At this point the two young men may be well down on the forestage, but with Valentine's forgiveness and proffer, Silvia and Julia are brought into the action again. It has been asked how Silvia should be expected to react to this summary disposal of her favour. Clearly she should not react at all. She is the prize, for the purpose of argument, and must not call attention to herself, but stand like the 'mistress' in *Cynthia's Revels* before whom the courtiers conduct their amorous verbal duels, a lay figure. Leading ladies may not relish this, but leading boys would have been more tractable.[4]

It is wrong, she thinks, to imagine that Julia swoons with calculation, such an idea being 'part of the modern vulgar search for "personality" at all costs': we must think of that incident as merely the dramatist's device for precipitating the dénouement.[5] She argues, consistently if dubiously, that the parodic elements—as when 'Launce's "parting" from his family completely kills Proteus' parting with Julia'—are used merely as contrasts with the romantic elements: 'the high style and the low were used in contrast, as black and white, and not allowed to blend.'[6] This view of things is not quite received doctrine, but certainly it has been influential on the general view of the play. 'We would not see, or present, things in that way', is frequently the reader's sentiment, 'but of course Shakespeare with the Friendship Cult working powerfully on him could do it.' Stanley Wells, while accepting the theoretical basis of it all, suggests that Shakespeare fails here in an attempt at synthesis: he did not manage to fit his characters convincingly into the

1. Bond, p. xxxviii.   2. N.C.S., pp. xvii–xviii.
3. *Shakespeare and Elizabethan Poetry*, 1951, p. 151.   4. *Ibid.*, p. 152.
5. *Ibid.*, p. 153.   6. *Loc. cit.*

pattern that his friendship-plot demanded.[1] Wells sees more
danger in juxtaposition than Miss Bradbrook suspected: Speed's
mockery of Valentine in II. i makes 'the tenderness . . . in great
danger of being lost in the absurdity'; but the comic commentary
can sometimes be wholly successful in providing 'a perfectly legitimate comic counterpoint'.[2] It is not clear why Wells makes this
distinction, but his discussion of the play seems rightly to refuse the
escape dependent on suggesting a simple dichotomy between the
Elizabethan and the twentieth-century consciousness. Moreover,
he has most usefully indicated the play's general reliance on soliloquies and duologues, a reliance which indeed makes the juxtapositions too starkly apparent—so starkly that their relationship
has been looked at with incredulity, or merely disregarded, by
most of the play's critics. The fullest, and I think most perceptive,
account of these juxtapositions is given in an article by Harold F.
Brooks.[3] Taking up H. B. Charlton's round assertion, 'Launce . . .
has no real right within the play except that gentlemen must have
servants, and Elizabethan audiences must have clowns',[4] he insists
on the way that many small details in the play have their echoes in
other details. Even the famous song's praise of Silvia ('Love doth to
her eyes repair / To help him of his blindness') links with Speed's
insistence to Valentine in II. i that he cannot properly see Silvia
because he loves her. In the same way, Launce's refusal to tell
Speed the name of his love contrasts with Valentine's readiness to
tell all to Proteus, and Brooks goes so far as to 'hint' a comparison
between Proteus and Crab:

> I am hinting a comparison of Proteus with Crab; and I do not
> think it extravagant, provided one is not too serious about it, to
> see reflected in Crab, comically and a little pathetically, the
> transgressor in Proteus. The want of sensibility to old ties and to
> his friend Launce's feelings which Crab is alleged to show at
> parting from home, is ominous as a parallel to Proteus' parting
> from Julia and impending reunion with Valentine. As a present
> for Silvia, Crab resembles the love that Proteus proffers her. He
> is a sorry changeling for the true love gift Proteus meant to
> bestow. He is unfit for Silvia (persecuting her with most ob-
> jectionable attentions!), and offensive where true courtliness
> should rule. Like Proteus, he gets his friend into trouble. And

1. 'The Failure of *The Two Gentlemen of Verona*', *Shakespeare-Jahrbuch*, xcix
(1963), 161–73; p. 170.
2. *Ibid.*, pp. 167, 171.
3. 'Two Clowns in a Comedy (to say nothing of the Dog): Speed, Launce (and
Crab) in "The Two Gentlemen of Verona"', *Essays and Studies 1963*, 1963,
pp. 91–100.
4. *Shakespearian Comedy*, 1938, p. 41.

as Crab is only saved by Launce's quixotic, self-sacrificial affection, so Proteus is only saved by the extremes to which Valentine
is ready to carry his friendship and Julia her love.[1]

Though Brooks is evidently aware of the danger, the tone of this
comment may suggest that the effect is more ponderous than it is.
Nevertheless, we are at least taken in a direction which is in general
true to the play. Less thorough-going, but thoroughly useful, is
Bertrand Evans' introduction to his Signet edition of the play[2]: he
shows that the romantic-comedy line that Shakespeare followed
after writing *The Two Gentlemen* was one in which the comic aspect
of a sympathetically drawn hero (Valentine) was rarely overlooked
for long, and that the moral imperfections of Proteus firmly anticipate traits of which we are all conscious in Claudio and Bertram.
He is able to exhibit, too, the vivid existence of Julia in her own
right and not merely as a preliminary sketch for Rosalind and
Viola. Evans' account is too heavily weighted on the side of character to let the complications of this play's writing emerge fully, but
he does excellently bring out the adult nature of Shakespeare's
attitude towards the figures he uses. Much as we owe to Miss Bradbrook's demonstration of the play's link with the Friendship Cult,
Evans makes it plain that this is no simple cult-play but a play in
which human beings are thought about as such.

In an attempt to look at *The Two Gentlemen* afresh, it seems worth
while to begin by noting one of its strongest peculiarities. Shakespeare's seventeen comedies (the fourteen in the Comedies section
of the Folio, together with *Cymbeline* in the Tragedies section,
Troilus and Cressida originally there too but transferred to a no-
man's-land between Histories and Tragedies, and *Pericles* omitted
from the Folio) show three main ways in which locality is employed.
Eight of them (*The Comedy of Errors, The Taming of the Shrew, Love's
Labour's Lost, Much Ado about Nothing, Twelfth Night, The Merry
Wives of Windsor, Measure for Measure, The Tempest*) have the whole
of the action presented in or near a single place. To this place, in
every instance but *Measure for Measure*, strangers come, and the
action depends primarily on the impact of the strangers (who
generally bring with them a sense of another locality, which is not
presented on the stage) on the normal inhabitants of the locality.
Shakespeare thus in these plays adheres, sometimes in a strict and
sometimes in a fairly free way, to the notion of Unity of Place. On
occasion (*The Comedy of Errors, Love's Labour's Lost, The Merry
Wives of Windsor, The Tempest*) there is adherence also, again to a

1. *Op. cit.*, p. 99.   2. New York and London, 1964.

greater or lesser extent, to the notion of Unity of Time. This, for all the romantic admixture that is frequently present, is comedy in a direct line of development from the classics, most obviously in *The Comedy of Errors* but evident enough too even in *The Tempest*. It is a comic mode that lends itself to elaborate incident, to a contrasting of events and of characters, and to a pattern of action that depends on the Terentian formula—an encounter leading to a plot, the working out of that plot to a point of *epitasis* where complication co-exists with impasse, and then a new movement that leads to resolution.[1] Its English predecessors are to be found in, for example, *Ralph Roister Doister*, *Gammer Gurton's Needle*, *Damon and Pithias*, *Campaspe*, *Mother Bombie*. But we have noticed that in using this kind of action Shakespeare generally implies a second locality, and he gives to it a much greater place in the play's economy than Plautus, for example, gave in *The Menaechmi* to the Syracuse from which one of his twins came to find the other in the play's Epidamnum. The royal court of France in *Love's Labour's Lost*, the war from which Don Pedro and the rest came to Messina in *Much Ado*, the world of Prince Hal which Falstaff had abandoned for love-making in Windsor, the Italy which was home for almost all the characters that met on the island in *The Tempest*—these unseen localities contribute something important to the plays, and to some extent we find the unseen locality being played off against the locality presented. Not surprisingly, therefore, in five comedies Shakespeare alternated his scene between two localities, whose interrelations are of major importance to their plays' economies: *A Midsummer Night's Dream*, *The Merchant of Venice*, *As You Like It*, *Troilus and Cressida*, *The Winter's Tale*. In *A Midsummer Night's Dream* and *The Winter's Tale* we begin in one place, move to another, and then return to the first. In *The Merchant of Venice* and *Troilus and Cressida* there is repeated alternation between the two localities. In *As You Like It* Act I belongs to the court, Acts II–V almost wholly to the Forest (with three short moments of return to the court); yet here we may note that there is to be at the end of the play a general return to the court, bringing this play nearer to the pattern of *A Midsummer Night's Dream* and *The Winter's Tale*. Court and forest, Sicilia and Bohemia, Venice and Belmont, Troy and the Greek camp: in each pair of localities, there is reciprocal comment, both overt and implied. It was a comic mode that may have developed out of Shakespeare's interest in locality-contrast already seen in the plays of the first group, but it nevertheless seems to be a kind of writing of

1. Cf. T. W. Baldwin, *Shakspere's Five-Act Structure*, Urbana, Illinois, 1947, especially pp. 112, 231–2.

his own invention. Certainly it is non-classical, but may take its rise ultimately from the court–country antithesis that underlies pastoral writing. It is noticeable that a forest is of major importance in two of the plays, that in *The Winter's Tale* a pastoral element is strong, and that the Belmont of *The Merchant of Venice* is felt as non-urban. Particularly suitable for satire, this pattern of comedy is much less naturally fitted for comedy of incident than the first type, and its characters are likely to be presented in the light of a contrast with corresponding figures in the juxtaposed locality. Plays written in this way may well embody thought of the more serious kind.

Four Shakespeare comedies belong to neither of these types. *The Two Gentlemen of Verona*, *All's Well that Ends Well*, *Pericles* and *Cymbeline* are wandering plays, changing their locality more than once, not usually for the sake of a special significance in the fresh locality (the forest in *The Two Gentlemen* being a place of convenient meeting rather than the place where magic is done in *A Midsummer Night's Dream* or the place where the wind blows and people mature in *As You Like It*, and even the Welsh hills in *Cymbeline* being only incidentally contrasted with the royal court), but in order that the characters may ultimately find their way to a sorting out of their tangled patterns of life. We may note that, if my conjectures are justified concerning the stages of composition that *The Two Gentlemen of Verona* went through, this play may have originally been a two-setting play, with a gradual move from town to forest as there was to be later in *As You Like It*. Without question, however, the re-writing, if such it was, was an improvement, for this play is stronger as a play of wandering than it would have been as a play where localities are in an important way contrasted. We should note, too, that *The Two Gentlemen* is the only early play of this type, and that its mode was not one that Shakespeare was ever to make frequent use of. Doubtless *Cymbeline* grew out of the example of *Pericles*, its close predecessor; doubtless the reversion to other modes apparent in the later romances, *The Winter's Tale* and *The Tempest*, indicate that the dramatist felt a need for tighter organization than the wandering play gave him. Nevertheless, we have the four experiments with it, and one of them, the play we are immediately concerned with, came at or near the beginning of his career.

Ancestry in this case presents no problem. We are dealing here with a derivative from romantic narrative, remotely from Hellenistic and medieval exemplars, and finding its place in the drama at an understandably early date. Sidney in *An Apology for Poetry* mocked at plays that were liberal both with place and time, 'where you shall have *Asia* of the one side, and *Affricke* of the other, and so manie other under-Kingdomes, that the Player when he comes in, must ever begin with telling where he is, or else the tale will not be conceived',[1] thus clearly indicating the prevalence of the wandering play in the 1570s. As we have seen, surviving examples from these years and the following decade are not numerous, but *Sir Clyomon and Clamydes* (*c.* 1570) and *Common Conditions* (before 1576) give us a notion of what this type of dramatic romance was like before the University Wits improved it.[2] Greene's *Friar Bacon and Friar Bungay* and *James IV* and Lyly's *Endimion* are obviously more sophisticated, but equally depend on a series of journeys to bring things into order. And all the time, of course, prose romance was being written, where a writer most frequently took his characters from place to place as they worked out their patterns of adventure and misadventure. Here the *Arcadia* was of course the great exemplar in England: its progeny was numerous, but its influence was strengthened by the availability of Italian and French prose stories of wandering, Shakespeare going to Montemayor for *The Two Gentlemen of Verona* and to Boccaccio for *All's Well that Ends Well*.[3]

Part of the attraction is in the wandering itself, for the continuing novelty of setting emphasizes a separateness from everyday life. The reader of a romance and the spectator of a 'wandering' romantic comedy are taken on holiday into far places which, even if they existed in the form that the writing gives them, would be normally inaccessible. It was therefore appropriate that such writing should present a code of conduct aspired after but not realized in the course of everyday life. The popular romance of the twentieth century still adheres to this, making its characters behave either according to a notion of correct behaviour that is no longer current or directly contrary to this. The writers of prose romance in the late sixteenth century could exalt the friendship idea which they had inherited from antiquity and the Middle Ages just as they could pay homage to courtly love: both had become a little out of key, but no one would be uneasy about this if the setting were remote—even less if the narrative took one with easy mobility from place to place. Not that the prose romance always presented the

1. *The Prose Works of Sir Philip Sidney*, ed. Albert Feuillerat, reprinted 1963, iii. 38.

2. See above, p. xli.

3. I have discussed Shakespeare's varying use of locality, in similar terms, in 'Ephesus, Troy, Athens: Shakespeare's Use of Locality', *Stratford Papers on Shakespeare 1963*, Toronto, 1964, pp. 151–69, and in *Twelfth Night and Shakespearian Comedy*, Toronto, 1965, pp. 5–7.

traditional attachments without mockery. Nashe's *The Unfortunate
Traveller* (1594) had great fun with the Earl of Surrey's alleged
devotion to 'Geraldine', and the sexual relations of this piece of
writing were generally rooted in a commoner kind of satisfaction.
And the wandering drama too could burlesque itself. Peele's
The Old Wives' Tale (?1591–4) gives us the supreme example of a
thorough-going burlesque, not only of the wandering play as such,
but of its high-minded assertion of the debt of friend to friend.
Eumenides, the romantic hero whose quest is the freeing of his love
Delia from the power of the magician Sacrapant, has entered into
a bargain with the cheerful ghost Jack: they are to share equally
whatever each gains in his adventures. Finally Delia is released
from enchantment, Eumenides has her love, and Jack makes his
demand:

> *Jack.* So, master, now ye think you have done; but I must have
> a saying to you: you know you and I were partners, I to
> have half in all you got.
> *Eum.* Why, so thou shalt, Jack.
> *Jack.* Why, then, master, draw your sword, part your lady, let
> me have half of her presently.
> *Eum.* Why, I hope, Jack, thou dost but jest: I promised thee half
> I got, but not half my lady.
> *Jack.* But what else, master? have you not gotten her? therefore
> divide her straight, for I will have half—there is no remedy.
> *Eum.* Well, ere I will falsify my word unto my friend, take her
> all: here, Jack, I'll give her thee.
> *Jack.* Nay, neither more nor less, master, but even just half.
> *Eum.* Before I will falsify my faith unto my friend, I will divide
> her: Jack thou shalt have half.
> *1st Bro.* Be not so cruel unto our sister, gentle knight.
> *2nd Bro.* O, spare fair Delia! she deserves no death.
> *Eum.* Content yourselves; my word is passed to him.
> Therefore prepare thyself, Delia, for thou must die.
> *Del.* Then farewell, world! adieu, Eumenides!
>
> *He offers to strike, and* Jack *stays him.*[1]

The burlesque here goes quite far, for the angel's intervention at the
sacrifice of Isaac seems remembered. But so too is the belief that in
the interest of friendship one must do anything, even the slicing of
one's love. Though we do not know whether or not *The Old Wives'
Tale* preceded *The Two Gentlemen*, it is manifest that there is some
relationship between them. Is Peele burlesquing a convention that
Shakespeare accepted, or is Peele doing more obviously what

1. Text from *Five Elizabethan Comedies*, ed. A. K. McIlwraith (World's Classics),
1934.

Shakespeare did more discreetly? An examination of the general conduct of Shakespeare's play, with help from the observations of Harold F. Brooks, will suggest that the dramatist, accepting the data of the wandering play and responding to them with some sympathy, nevertheless made fun of the normal asseverations of romance.[1]

It quickly becomes evident that Shakespeare uses parody again and again in the juxtaposition of scenes. We begin in I. i with Proteus and Valentine, Proteus being presented as the lover and Valentine as the man immune to love, but immediately after we see Proteus and Speed together, with Speed's comic comments making Proteus' devotion seem a little less than important. The next scene shows Julia both as genuinely in love and as comic in her behaviour, anxious to hide her love from Lucetta yet thoroughly human in her anxiety to read the message from the suitor she favours. In the last scene of the first act Proteus contrives to conceal from his father that he is reading a letter from Julia, thus paralleling his love's behaviour immediately before: this does not suggest insincerity in either lover, but does underline the comedy of their relationship. Valentine's dullness of wit in II. i, as he fails to see Silvia's signs of love for him, has already been commented on.[2] This is quickly followed by Proteus' farewell to Julia and the immediate burlesque offered by Launce on his first appearance: the parallelism of these scenes is emphasized by their both ending in the entry of Panthino, Antonio's servant, who comes to tell Proteus and Launce they must hurry to embark. Julia has hardly a word to say as Proteus leaves her, and is totally silent after their kiss ('What, gone without a word?'). The dog Crab is reproached for his silence when Launce has been taking leave of his noisily affected family. That Julia is staying while Crab is going is a fitting antithesis, for after all Julia is human and charming while Crab is what he is; that there is a similarity in their behaviour is a linking that goes along with the antithesis and retrospectively brings Julia within the orbit of mockery that Crab, because of his animal immunity, escapes. II. iv opens with some indifferent exchanges between Valentine, now Silvia's accepted lover, and Thurio, her father's choice, but soon the Duke announces Proteus' arrival and Valentine pours forth his praise of his friend. Proteus sees Silvia and is entangled at once, but he is able to make Valentine's hyperboles look silly when they are alone together:

1. A study of the relation between *All's Well* and earlier examples of comedies with a multiplicity of scene would, I think, help to bring out the special character of that play.
2. See above, p. xxvi.

> *Pro.* ... Was this the idol that you worship so?
> *Val.* Even she; and is she not a heavenly saint?
> *Pro.* No; but she is an earthly paragon.
> *Val.* Call her divine.
> *Pro.*   I will not flatter her.
> *Val.* O flatter me; for love delights in praises.
>
>   (II. iv. 139–43)

For the moment Valentine is ready to accept the idea that the praise he demands is flattery, and Proteus reminds him that once their positions were reversed and Valentine then gave him 'bitter pills' in his talk of love. The transposition may suggest that neither young man may be entirely discreet in his devotion, or at least that words as used by Valentine go beyond their proper scope. And in a moment he loses again his sense of decorum.

> *Val.* Then speak the truth by her: if not divine,
>   Yet let her be a principality,
>   Sovereign to all the creatures on the earth.
> *Pro.* Except my mistress.
> *Val.*   Sweet, except not any,
>   Except thou wilt except against my love.
> *Pro.* Have I not reason to prefer mine own?
> *Val.* And I will help thee to prefer her too:
>   She shall be dignified with this high honour,
>   To bear my lady's train, lest the base earth
>   Should from her vesture chance to steal a kiss,
>   And of so great a favour growing proud,
>   Disdain to root the summer-swelling flower,
>   And make rough winter everlastingly.
> *Pro.* Why, Valentine, what braggardism is this?
> *Val.* Pardon me, Proteus, all I can is nothing
>   To her whose worth makes other worthies nothing:
>   She is alone.   (II. iv. 146–62)

There is something almost touching in this last admission, as the lover's sense of his lady's rareness makes him feel the inadequacy of his soaring speech. But Proteus' response is sharp ('Then let her alone'), and Valentine escapes from the implication that the paragon is of its nature not for human enjoyment by at once confessing, and delighting in, his plan to win possession. Proteus, left alone, reveals his new love to us and his determination to reject the claims of friendship. Again the effect is retroactive, and we are conscious of Valentine's rashness in telling all. The Friendship Cult is manifestly a dangerous game to play at when friends, as necessarily, are the flesh and blood that Valentine does not credit his mistress with being.[1] And then Launce and Speed appear, Launce refusing to make a plain statement about the future of the Proteus–Julia love-affair. These two friends exchange abuse and make jests at each other's expense, but they go off to drink ale together. Proteus then returns to speak another soliloquy, reaffirming his decision to betray Valentine and announcing his plans in detail. The second act ends ironically with Julia planning to set out in disguise, to find the Proteus whose fidelity she makes no question of:

> *Jul.* ... A thousand oaths, an ocean of his tears,
>   And instances of infinite of love,
>   Warrant me welcome to my Proteus.
> *Luc.* All these are servants to deceitful men.
> *Jul.* Base men, that use them to so base effect;
>   But truer stars did govern Proteus' birth,
>   His words are bonds, his oaths are oracles,
>   His love sincere, his thoughts immaculate,
>   His tears, pure messengers sent from his heart,
>   His heart, as far from fraud as heaven from earth.
> *Luc.* Pray heav'n he prove so when you come to him.
> *Jul.* Now, as thou lov'st me, do him not that wrong,
>   To bear a hard opinion of his truth.   (II. vii. 69–81)

The girl's situation is of course one that she herself recognizes as comic:

> *Luc.* What fashion, madam, shall I make your breeches?
> *Jul.* That fits as well as 'Tell me, good my lord,
>   What compass will you wear your farthingale?'
>   (II. vii. 49–51)

Our knowledge of Proteus' loss of love makes her situation poignant, but her over-confidence in the man simultaneously makes her comically vulnerable. She joins Valentine and the Proteus of the early scenes in believing that liking is necessarily for ever and that oaths carry weight. In *The Two Gentlemen* we have no oaths that the swearer meant to break when swearing them, but the play's oaths are still fragile.

Act III begins with Proteus' disclosure of Valentine's plans to the Duke. He extracts a promise of secrecy, so when Valentine opportunely appears the Duke sets up as amateur detective. He pretends he wants advice on how to pursue a love affair, and Valentine falls

---

1. In Jean de Meun's section of *The Romance of the Rose*, both Reason and The Friend insist on the propriety of revealing one's love to a 'faithful friend' (cf. the translation by Harry W. Robbins, New York, 1962, pp. 103–4, 199).

into the trap by recommending the use of a rope-ladder concealed beneath a cloak. The Duke insists on removing Valentine's own cloak, and discovers not only the rope-ladder that was to be used for the elopement but also a verse-letter addressed to Silvia. Throughout the Duke has behaved with scant dignity in talking of his alleged love-predicament, and Valentine's worldly-wise advice shows the younger man at his most callow. Moreover, the pose Valentine here adopts reflects on the 'braggardism' of his claims for Silvia in II. iv: this young man can talk any language, it seems, that he believes appropriate to the moment. When the Duke denounces him as a Phaëton, the image is manifestly disproportionate, as is Valentine's burst of lamentation at his sentence of banishment. Launce, coming with Proteus, increases the difficulty of our taking this with full seriousness, and then we see Valentine's quick acceptance of Proteus' assurance of help. When the gentlemen have left the stage, Launce tells us of his own love and deliberates with Speed on whether or not he should proceed with his wooing. If his final determination is caused by the girl's money, we are at least ready to see this as a kind of rough wisdom: if we retain some involvement with Valentine's emotional condition, we nevertheless see it as vulnerable in its irrationality. And Launce's pleasure in Speed's discomfiture at the end of the scene ('an unmannerly slave, that will thrust himself into secrets') again reflects on Valentine's over-easy confiding in his friend. Next we see Proteus deceiving the Duke and Thurio as he has deceived Valentine: he undertakes to conduct Thurio's wooing, and his advocacy of poetry brings the processes of romantic love into further ridicule, just as the Duke's admiring comment ('Ay, much is the force of heaven-bred poesy') brings him within the same sort of absurdity as Marlowe contrived for Mycetes King of Persia ('And 'tis a pretty toy to be a poet', *1 Tamburlaine*, II. ii. 54).

The forest-setting is introduced at the beginning of Act IV. The outlaws who offer Valentine the choice between death and kingship over them are frank in confessing their offences:

> *3 Out.* Know, then, that some of us are gentlemen,
>   Such as the fury of ungovern'd youth
>   Thrust from the company of awful men.
>   Myself was from Verona banished,
>   For practising to steal away a lady,
>   An heir, and near allied unto the Duke.
> *2 Out.* And I from Mantua, for a gentleman,
>   Who, in my mood, I stabb'd unto the heart.
> *1 Out.* And I, for such like petty crimes as these.
>
>   (IV. i. 44–52)

It is odd that the Third Outlaw's reason for banishment is similar to Valentine's, and the Second Outlaw's similar to the offence that Valentine claims was his (ll. 27–9): fighting and eloping, being thus by implication multiplied, seem to become minor and ordinary happenings, and Valentine's love and predicament are the less involving for us. There is, however, an oddity about the whole scene, especially in the outlaws' reasons for choosing Valentine as their king (he is handsome and he is a 'linguist') and in their ready promise, so at odds with their account of past practices, to do 'no outrages / On silly women or poor passengers'. If 'No, we detest such vile base practices' were ironic, it would make Valentine's new position intolerable: we must rather take it as an indication that these outlaws are meant to be figures of fun, despite their threats, are meant indeed to appear as pasteboard figures like the Duke himself.

The rest of Act IV reintroduces us to Julia (her first appearance since II. vii), and the degree of concentration on her distress makes the immediately preceding light treatment of Valentine's story appropriate. We are the readier to feel with Julia because Valentine's story has moved into a world of mock-fantasy. IV. ii is one of the play's most successful scenes, incorporating the song 'Who is Silvia?', which is sung to Silvia apparently by Proteus, accompanied by musicians hired by him, nominally on behalf of Thurio. Julia and the Host of the inn where she lodges are unnoticed watchers and listeners, and it is during this scene that Julia learns of Proteus' falseness to Valentine and Thurio and herself. The quiet exchanges between her and the Host are in prose, thus effectively differentiated from both the song and the blank verse dialogue of the other characters. Julia, who in the earlier scenes was merely excited and enterprising, is here for the first time made deeply acquainted with distress. We can see that it was dramatically sound to have her almost silent at the moment of Proteus' leave-taking in II. ii, for her previous control makes the present strain altogether stronger. And her prose makes her seem genuine and the other figures all tainted with affectation: it was perhaps in line with this that Shakespeare allowed Silvia to agree that Proteus should have her picture, even Silvia thus entering into the love game that Proteus now dominates. Yet Julia's prose is not merely quiet and gentle. In playing upon the Host's meanings, she shows a wit that co-exists with, sets off, grows out of, and deepens her sadness (ll. 54–69).[1] During the talk between Proteus and Silvia

---

1. I cannot agree with Stanley Wells (*op. cit.*, p. 172) in thinking that her replies are 'misunderstandings'.

the Host falls asleep: it is good to have Julia alone here, freed from the need to comment (except sparsely aside) and with her isolation emphasized. It is also appropriate that the good-natured Host, like any plain man, is kept by sleep from any full involvement in the romantic action. Then in IV. iii we see Silvia's plans for her escape, with a highly romanticized portrait of Eglamour which may be a little difficult to credit after the previous scene's deflation of high romance. With IV. iv, however, we have Launce (on his last appearance in the play) complaining about the way his dog has made him suffer for his devotion to it. This suggests a kind of parallel to Julia's suffering through Proteus' behaviour, this Launce–Julia relation being perhaps more cogent than the Crab–Proteus relation that Harold F. Brooks has suggested.[1] The effect is to prevent our taking Julia too seriously, and we are made to respond lightheartedly to Silvia too when we hear of Crab's behaviour with her farthingale and of her indignant rejection of Crab as a gift. When Proteus and Julia are alone together, and when Julia approaches Silvia as Proteus' envoy, Julia's situation is again pathetic—though the situation is presented with more obvious contrivance than her overhearing of the serenade in IV. ii. She is, after all, in a position of advantage in her disguise, and she sees to it that a remembrance of Julia is forced into both of these conversations. She shows some power of invention in the account of the playing of Ariadne in the Pentecostal pageant (ll. 156–70), for the incident, if not totally fictitious, has obviously been ingeniously transposed: she, as a woman, could not have taken part in such a performance; yet the boy playing the part of Julia could have done so: the play-world and the world of the actors playing in it have become subtly intertwined. The scene ends with a soliloquy in which Julia, expressing gratitude for Silvia's kindness, admits that she has an impulse to scratch out the eyes of the picture she is to take to Proteus: it is a reminder of the Julia who tore up Proteus' letter in I. ii, and in thus binding the later Julia with the earlier it brings her again within the compass of light comedy. Moreover, her conduct here shows her gradually winning mastery over the other figures: clearly we do not have to worry about her ultimate success.

Act V begins with Silvia and Eglamour setting out for the forest, and then the Duke's discovery of her absence and his laborious working out of what it signifies (V. ii. 34–47). The baiting of Thurio by Proteus and Julia at the beginning of V. ii relaxes the tension, such as it is, notably. In scene iii the outlaws are on their best behaviour with Silvia, but Eglamour has taken to his heels

with astonishing rapidity—or at least with a rapidity that would
astonish us if the romantic picture of this knight in iv. iii had not
already been brought within the bounds of suspicion. The play's
last scene first presents Valentine remembering his love and commenting on his difficulty in making the outlaws accept his high
code:

> These are my mates, that make their wills their law,
> Have some unhappy passenger in chase.
> They love me well; yet I have much to do
> To keep them from uncivil outrages.   (v. iv. 14–17)

He withdraws to watch Proteus, who has rescued Silvia, renewing
his suit and then deciding on rape. Reprehensible as this is, we
cannot help noticing that Silvia is a little churlish about her
rescue:

> Had I been seized by a hungry lion,
> I would have been a breakfast to the beast,
> Rather than have false Proteus rescue me.   (v. iv. 33–5)

This does switch our sympathy a little in Proteus' direction, and the
girl's choice of image has a touch of the ludicrous. When the
shocked Valentine intervenes, there is something risible in his first
cry:

> Ruffian! Let go that rude uncivil touch,
> Thou friend of an ill fashion.   (v. iv. 60–1)

And he goes on with his speeches to Proteus without a word to his
twice-rescued love. And so we proceed to the famous renunciation.
Surely by now we can be in little doubt as to its intended effect.
We have seen Valentine made fun of as a lover (mocking the god in
i. i and being the god's faithful but unperceptive servant in ii. i), as
a credulous friend (so much less discreet than Launce), as a man
helpless under the sentence of exile, as a sanguine teacher of good
behaviour to outlaws. Now his continued preoccupation with the
demands of friendship makes him ready to hand over his love to the
man who has just been trying to rape her. The absurdity is pointed
by Julia's well-timed swoon: that this is a deliberate one is suggested by the equally well-timed producing of the wrong ring
immediately after.[1] Of course these matters lead to her revealing
her identity and to Proteus' remorse. At first sight it looks odd that
Julia, coming to herself, speaks in prose, and yet this is highly effec-

---

1. It should be emphasized that neither of the General Editors of this series has
been persuaded that the swoon is other than genuine. One doubt expressed is
that a performer cannot make an audience aware that a swoon is deliberate:
surely, however, it is not beyond compassing?

tive: common day breaks, and Julia's plain attachment to it (despite her earlier sentence-capping with Lucetta) is evidenced here as with her prose in IV. ii. It is appropriate too that on recovering from her 'swoon' she should speak in a disordered fashion. The elaborate masquerade in which all here have been playing is momentarily dissolved, paradoxically, in Julia's fresh practice of deceit. Silvia, on the other hand, says no further word in the scene, and Valentine never addresses her from the moment of his entry. This need not be attributed to a faulty state of the text, or to the necessary subordination of women (as Miss Bradbrook suggested) in a play of friendship, but rather can be taken as a further incursion of reality: Valentine is no longer the almost hopelessly aspiring lover but is the dispenser of magnanimity and, before the play is done, the Duke's accepted son-in-law. It is a transformation he hardly notices: friendship is maintained, his love is securely won, and never in the play has he shown any recognition of his own folly or excess. There are, however, touches of final absurdity. Valentine is ready to threaten Thurio if he does not abandon his claim to Silvia, showing a formal violence hardly called for; the Duke is ready to accept Valentine as Silvia's betrothed and goes so far as to think him 'worthy of an empress' love'—a volte-face which only Valentine's position of power in the forest might ironically explain; Valentine asks the Duke to find employment for the outlaws, as men 'full of good, / And fit for great employment'—a description hardly accordant with his account of them in v. iv. 14–17; the Duke at once agrees.[1] Valentine looks forward to a double wedding for himself, Silvia, Proteus, Julia, and apparently also to a shared household: 'our day of marriage shall be yours, / One feast, one house, one mutual happiness.'

The antitheses come thus throughout the play. Shakespeare has used no character directly as a commentator, and has let the comic light play on Valentine, Silvia, Proteus, Julia while at the same time getting us interested in a double romantic story. In this respect, as in so many details, he anticipates his later romantic manner. Readers of *As You Like It*, *Much Ado*, and *Twelfth Night* frequently argue about how this character or that is to be taken, and attempt to impose a simple pattern of assertion on these plays so much more complex than *The Two Gentlemen*. Jaques represents a point of view to be rejected, Claudio is a wholly admirable though mistaken young man, Orsino is a proper enough duke—

1. For a consideration of this Duke along with others of his rank in Shakespeare's comedies, see the editor's article 'Shakespeare's Comic Dukes', *Review of English Literature*, v (April 1964), 101–14.

these are judgements of the kind we have come to expect from readers allegedly qualified to know. There is indeed an insufficient recognition that in his 'romantic' writings Shakespeare could simultaneously induce concernment and a sense of friendly mockery. That he did this as early as *The Two Gentlemen of Verona* should not surprise us when we can see it happening much more obviously in *Love's Labour's Lost*, which cannot have been written much later. It will be well to remember, moreover, the close relationship of *The Two Gentlemen* and *The Comedy of Errors*: in the neo-Plautine affair he wrote with extreme economy, and achieved a sense of distance through the multiplying of farcical event; in the earliest of his romantic comedies he has a similar economy in his composition and a not altogether dissimilar sense of remoteness. We may observe in passing that the appearance of condensation in the last scene of *The Two Gentlemen* may be due, not to abridgement as Dover Wilson suggested,[1] but to Shakespeare's purpose of reducing involvement by the very speed with which incident followed incident. Seen in this way, the play's mockery comes into focus as a more subtle thing than the sharp merriment of Peele when he ridicules the Friendship Cult in *The Old Wives' Tale*.

Yet it is possible to take another view of the play's antitheses. Attention has been drawn to Harold Brooks' discussion of them,[2] but in a private communication he has assured me he does not see them as ironic at the expense of the friends and the lovers. They are in his view chiefly to be seen as 'lightning-conductors, allowing the audience to laugh at the extremes of the convention, so that laughter shall not disturb our response when we are required to accept the convention, extremes and all'. Remembering that in all probability *The Two Gentlemen of Verona* was written about the time when Shakespeare was at work on some at least of the Sonnets, he cannot believe that the dramatist could stand as far outside the experience of either love or friendship in the way that I have suggested.

Certainly one must recognize links between this play and the Sonnets. Valentine's verses at III. i. 140–51 constitute a sonnet minus one quatrain (as do Beatrice's in *Much Ado about Nothing* at III. i. 107–16 and Orlando's in *As You Like It* at III. ii. 1–10). Moreover, the 'sonnet-story' presents two friends, a woman loved by both, and the narrator's renunciation of the woman for the sake of friendship. The friend's infidelity to the narrator is seen as a worse thing than the loss of the woman (Sonnet 42), and the claims of friendship can be carried to a point of quixotry (Sonnet 88). And

1. N.C.S., p. 81.   2. Cf. above, pp. lv–lvi.

in both the play and the poems we get the use of themes common in sixteenth-century sonneteering: sight and blindness (e.g., II. i. 60 ff., II. iv. 87 ff., 192 ff.), shadow and substance (e.g., II. iv. 205, III. i. 177, IV. ii. 117–24, IV. iv. 182 ff., 199), appearance and reality (*passim*, necessarily, in a play where the arch-intriguer is named Proteus). Neo-platonism goes along with a frank recognition of sensual appetite in the Sonnets; in the play the attitudes are simpler, never I think being so strenuously aspired to or so dangerously brought into association with the body's urges. When one is considering the effect of what Shakespeare did in the play, it seems to me important that he was writing in very different circumstances from those that governed the Sonnets. In them he was contributing to that store of semi-private literature that abounded in the last years of the sixteenth century: they did not—apart from the doubtless fortuitous publication of two sonnets in *The Passionate Pilgrim* of 1599—encounter the press until 1609. But, though we know nothing of the play's early staging, we can be sure it was written to be acted, to be made immediately into a public thing. Moreover, the dramatist was experimenting with different types of comedy in these earliest years of his career: Plautus and Lyly and Greene were all being drawn upon in what we may call his search for a comic mode in which he would feel most at home. In that situation he would not be likely to wear his heart upon his sleeve (even if we assume he came nearer to doing that in the Sonnets), and he could be more frankly concerned with the comic side of a situation which at another time he might find painful.

That it was possible for a writer in the early 1590s to mock at love is evident from Nashe's *The Unfortunate Traveller*; that he could find the friendship cult amusing we have seen from Peele's *The Old Wives' Tale*. Moreover, it seems illuminating to compare *The Two Gentlemen* with another play with which we have seen it to have close relations: *Romeo and Juliet*. There too Shakespeare can make Romeo's love-sickness amusing, and not only when he is in love with Rosaline. Moreover, his lamentations at his sentence of banishment are as extreme as Valentine's, and he has to be firmly handled by the Friar. The love of Romeo and Juliet is juxtaposed with the ordinary current of life and with the special dangers in Verona: it is exposed to a kind of testing in our eyes, and we come, as Nicholas Brooke has pointed out, to accept its validity as an important contribution to human experience—but only just.[1] The testing takes place also in *The Two Gentlemen*, and there I believe the

---

1. 'The Tragic Spectacle in *Titus Andronicus* and *Romeo and Juliet*', *Shakespeare: The Tragedies: A Collection of Critical Essays*, ed. C. Leech, Chicago and London, 1965, pp. 243–56; cf. especially pp. 252–5.

effect is different. The relations between Valentine and Silvia, between Proteus and Julia, are too fragile a thing to stand up to the play's ironic implications through parallel and antithesis, or to the frequent absurdity of the romantic characters' own conduct and of the play's total atmosphere (as felt both in the ducal court and in the forest). That Shakespeare intended it in this way seems to me probable, though no one can prove that the play did not get out of hand and away from his first image of it. Still, when he decided to put Launce in, he must have realized that romance was being given a most powerful competitor.

No one is likely to claim that *The Two Gentlemen of Verona* is a masterpiece, or anything like it. But its seminal nature for Shakespeare—anticipating *The Merchant of Venice* in the account of Julia's suitors in I. ii, *Romeo and Juliet* in the planned elopement, the rope-ladder, the banishment of the lover and his extravagant response to it, *Twelfth Night* in Julia's employment as Proteus' messenger to Silvia, *As You Like It* in the use of a forest-setting, and a whole group of Shakespeare's plays in Julia's disguise—indicates that this was a play he did not readily put from his mind. If it were as poor a thing as has been commonly thought, he would have been less likely to take so many hints from it in the eight years or so subsequent to its writing. But there are signs that the play is beginning to be seen in proper perspective. We have noted Harold F. Brooks' sketching of the play's ironic parallels, and Hereward T. Price has commented on the critical presentation of the characters through the giving to them of over-elaborate speech and has expressed himself forcibly on the subject of renunciation:

> Then Valentine gives Sylvia to Proteus. It ought to be clear that by this action Shakespeare is wringing the last drop of silliness out of Valentine's conventions. With the idea of smashing a particularly ridiculous convention, Shakespeare has set out to prove Valentine a fool. Any explanation of this scene that implies that Shakespeare was serious does rather less than justice to Shakespeare's sense of humor. It is like Shakespeare to make Valentine at once noble and silly; indeed the nature of his folly is allied to his nobility and may be said to spring from it. The heroes of these romantic comedies usually have their two sides; they have their follies, of which they are cured, and their fineness which persists.[1]

Valentine is not cured, though Julia's swoon saves him from the effects of his folly. Nevertheless, Price's insistence on a doubleness

---

1. 'Shakespeare as a Critic', *P.Q.*, xx (1941), 390–9.

of impression seems right. Other commentators, of course, have taken some steps in the same direction, as when Franklin M. Dickey wonders whether 'Shakespeare is burlesquing himself' in the last scene, with its 'downright silliness'.[1] Not self-burlesque but a rather too direct kind of comic counterpoint is likely to be a considered verdict.

Such a notion of careful and, within its limits, subtle dramaturgy is consonant with the obvious care that has ultimately been given to the play's general shape. Certainly in its present form *The Two Gentlemen of Verona* suggests that Shakespeare made one or two false starts and that he did not, as far as we know, get rid of inconsistencies resulting from changes of plan;[2] nevertheless, the play as we have it has achieved neatness of outline. There are three journeys (Valentine's, Proteus', Julia's) to the place of the main action, all accomplished in Acts I and II, and three localities nicely correlated with act-division:

Act I. First locality.
    II. Second locality (i, iv, v, vi); first locality (ii, iii, vii).
    III. Second locality.
    IV. Third locality (i); second locality (ii, iii, iv).
    V. Second locality (i, ii); third locality (iii, iv).

The introduction of a fresh locality in the fourth act is in line with Shakespeare's frequent practice (as in *The Taming of the Shrew, Coriolanus, Titus, Timon, Julius Caesar, Macbeth*),[3] and the use of a locality for Act I which will not be the play's main locality is something he returned to in *A Midsummer Night's Dream, As You Like It, All's Well*, and *Othello*. Moreover, T. W. Baldwin seems right in suggesting that the play fits quite well into the typical Terentian pattern as interpreted by Landino in 1482 and Willichius in 1539: the love–friendship theme is introduced in Act I and brought to a point of crisis in Act II (the two acts together constituting the *protasis*); Act III shows the *epitasis* or point of maximum complication, as Proteus' intrigue leads to the exile of Valentine; Act IV introduces two counter-actions when Valentine becomes king of the outlaws and when Julia arrives to oversee Proteus' conduct. The failure of Proteus' wooing of Silvia in Act IV indicates that the plans of both young men have come to nothing: the initiative now passes to the girls. The general movement to the forest in Act V

1. *Not Wisely But Too Well: Shakespeare's Love Tragedies*, San Marino, 1957, p. 70, n. 7.
2. See above, pp. xxx–xxxi.
3. Cf. the editor's article 'Shakespeare's Use of a Five-Act Structure', *Die Neueren Sprachen*, Neue Folge, vi (January 1957), 249–63.

(movement *to* in scenes i and ii, movement *in* in scenes iii and iv) induces the catastrophe or resolution.[1] Moreover, the alternation of locality in Act II increases suspense and shows all the four main characters at their points of maximum initiative. It contrasts with the use of a single locality in Act III and most of Act IV: in this central block of the play we have the collisions prepared for in Act II.

The Two Gentlemen of Verona is not a play where detailed comment on the characters is a worth-while occupation. Valentine and Silvia are graceful, a little impercipient, though Silvia (for all her readiness to give Proteus her picture and her unnecessary sharpness of tongue when he rescues her in the forest) is the more attractive and the more intelligent of the two. The Duke is what we expect of a ducal figure in the early Shakespeare. Speed is the pert boy of Lylyan comedy. Thurio is in line with Lyly's Sir Thopas in *Endimion*. Proteus is the worried victim of plotting, his own and the dramatist's. The rest are lay-figures, except for Launce and Julia. Launce, though he appears only four times in the play, has justifiably acquired fame for his enjoyment of his own appearance of naïveté and for his ability to get the better of any of the people we see him meeting in the play. Even his dog has, in the nature of things, no reply to his master's reproaches. Because he is without the briskness of Speed or of the Dromios in *The Comedy of Errors*, he can slacken the tempo of *The Two Gentlemen of Verona* and make us think with amusement of the romantic way of existence that is totally foreign to him. If we ask why Shakespeare omitted to bring either Launce or Speed into Act V, we may answer that he wanted the high-mindedness of Valentine and the remorse of Proteus to speak for themselves: a glance from Launce to Crab or a pert comment from Speed would have too obviously deflated the romancing of the two gentlemen, too deeply underlined Julia's ability to make herself mistress of the ultimate situation. And Julia, of course, though she is not given many words to speak, is indeed the voice of common day in the last scene. 'Q' quoted Sir George Young's view that Julia is, 'in comparison with Silvia, something of an ordinary wench; that she and Proteus together are portrayed as "lovers of common clay, of less than second-rate refinement", meant to be a foil to chivalrous Valentine and Silvia'. 'Q' would not have it so: it is the abridger's fault if we find Julia a bit 'common'.[2] But a mid-twentieth-century reader or spectator is likely to find Julia in need of no such excuse. She is alive and enterprising and ready to swoon

1. T. W. Baldwin, *op. cit.*, pp. 719–41. Cf. also Leech, 'Shakespeare's Use of a Five-Act Structure', *loc. cit.*, p. 251.
2. N.C.S., pp. xviii–xix.

and reveal her identity if that is the only way of countering Valentine's absurd offer of Silvia to Proteus. Afterwards she may blush
(v. iv. 163), but it is she who has exhibited wit in difficult circumstances in her talk with the Host in iv. ii and has conducted her
embassy to Silvia in iv. iv with a careful contrivance of pathos. We
are on her side if Sir George Young is not, and are glad that Shakespeare gave her successor Rosalind a more obviously active part in
the working out of the resolution in *As You Like It*.

Perhaps more important is a comment on the use of prose and
verse in this play. Prose of course for the servants, but prose more
subtly for Julia and the Host during and after the serenading of
Silvia in iv. ii, and for Julia when she discovers herself in v. iv. On
the whole it is very good prose, though we may weary of the dialogue about Launce's love in iii. ii. The verse varies from the
mechanical to the deliberately high-flown to the pathetic to (on
rare occasions) the truly eloquent. At its best, it is fully assured
though over-sweet, as in Valentine's lines already quoted (v. iv.
7–10) or in these of Proteus:

> O, how this spring of love resembleth
> The uncertain glory of an April day,
> Which now shows all the beauty of the sun,
> And by and by a cloud takes all away.

(i. iii. 84–7)

At its worst the verse, like the prose, is a mechanical capping of
sentence with sentence or of manifest absurdity with obvious
comment.

With *The Two Gentlemen of Verona* we are near the beginning of
Shakespeare's career, and it is one of his first comedies—perhaps,
as already conjectured, even his very first. Nevertheless, it shows
his readiness to see things simultaneously from more than one point
of view. It exhibits his mockery, though also his partially sympathetic understanding, of the Friendship Cult; it presents his robust
deflating, through Launce, of the ideas that men, of the sixteenth
century and later times, like to persuade themselves they live by; it
expresses an admiration for the type of young woman who pursues
the young man who has shown an interest in her. John Masefield
once said of *Twelfth Night* that 'one can see it played night after
night, week after week, without weariness, even in a London
theatre'.[1] That is a large claim for any play, and certainly more
than one can say for *The Two Gentlemen of Verona*: nevertheless,

1. *William Shakespeare*, n.d. (Home University Library), p. 139.

students of Shakespeare have to keep this comedy in mind. Not only does it anticipate in all sorts of ways the 'romantic' plays that followed: it also gives us a clue to the interpretation of Shakespeare's writing as a whole. We have to recognize the double nature of the apparently plain statement, we have to see his characters as coming beneath his gaze and within the orbit of his (here good-humoured) merriment. In some ways *The Two Gentlemen* appears to take its place among his most artificial plays, as a play on the *débat*-theme of love versus friendship, but on a deeper inspection it exhibits the fragility, the minor quality, of both love and friendship. It is not merely that men fall in and out of love, and may betray their friends: the very idea of attachment is in this play presented as a small thing, however large its claim, however high its dignity, for the human beings involved. That does not mean that Julia or Silvia or Valentine or even Proteus is outside the range of our, or the playwright's, sympathy. It does suggest, however, that our involvement is slighter than in some of the later comedies, though even in them there remains always a doubleness of view. Here Julia gets her Proteus, for what he is worth; Valentine gets his Silvia, and all she is worth. The two gentlemen reassume the positions of gentility. Back in the play's second locality, 'One feast, one house, one mutual happiness'. Perhaps Proteus and Julia, taking a long look at each other, might decide to return to the play's first locality. In this instance, with the accumulation of ironies, we are not wrong to speculate about what was to happen when the characters had left the stage. And in that respect too *The Two Gentlemen of Verona* points forward. Julia, though not Silvia, has taken on the kind of life that we rightly associate with the later romantic comedies. We are bound to wonder about the future of Proteus and Julia, though we know that Valentine and Silvia are story-book figures, whose existence stops with the play.

THE TWO GENTLEMEN OF VERONA

DRAMATIS PERSONAE

Duke, *father to Silvia.*

VALENTINE, } *the two gentlemen.*
PROTEUS,

ANTONIO, *father to Proteus.*

THURIO, *a foolish rival to Valentine.*   5

EGLAMOUR, *agent for Silvia in her escape.*

Host, *where Julia lodges.*

Outlaws, *with Valentine.*

SPEED, *page to Valentine.*

LAUNCE, *a clownish servant to Proteus.*   10

PANTHINO, *servant to Antonio.*

JULIA, *beloved of Proteus.*

SILVIA, *beloved of Valentine.*

LUCETTA, *waiting-woman to Julia.*

Servant, *attending the Duke.*   15

Musicians.

DRAMATIS PERSONAE] The names of all the Actors *F* (*at end of play*).   1. Duke]
F; Duke of Milan Pope; Duke, Vice-roy of Milan *Capell.*   3. *Proteus] Malone ii;*
Protheus F (*as throughout play*).   9. *page] Capell; a clownish seruant F.*   10. *a*
clownish servant] this ed.; the like F; Servant Capell.   11. *Panthino] Capell; Panthion*
F.   15. Servant . . . *Duke] Capell* (*subst.*)*; not in F;* Servants *Theobald.*   16.
Musicians] *Theobald; not in F.*

1. *Duke*] T. W. Baldwin, *Organiza-*
tion and Personnel of the Shakespearean
Company (1927), p. 249, suggests that
this part was played by John
Heminges, who in Baldwin's view
specialized in playing 'a more or less
comic, peppery old man of high rank'.

2. *Valentine*] The name suggests
'lover'; cf. III. i. 192 n. and *O.E.D.*,
s.v., 2.

3. *Proteus*] As Steevens pointed out,
it is merely confusing to retain the F
spelling 'Protheus', which in Elizabethan times was interchangeable
with 'Proteus'. The name draws attention to the character's disposition to
change, as the classical Proteus freely
altered his shape when hands were
laid on him. In *Look About You* (publ.
1600), where the Duke of Gloucester

uses a series of disguises, we read:
'Gloster will be a proteus euery houre',
and in *3H6*, III. ii. 191–3, Richard
asserts: 'I can add colours to the
chameleon, / Change shapes with
Proteus for advantages, / And set the
murderous Machiavel to school.'

4. *Antonio*] the form used in the text
at I. iii (opening S.D.) and II. iv. 49.

9. page] See Introduction, p. xxvi.

11. *Panthino*] *NCS* points out that
'Panthino' occurs rather more often in
F than 'Panthion', that it is more
Italianate and therefore more suitable
to this play, and that 'Panthmo' at I.
iii. 76 indicates a MS. reading
'Panthino'. But Bond suggests that the
name may come from Pandion in
Lyly's *Sapho and Phao*.

2

THE TWO GENTLEMEN OF VERONA

ACT I

SCENE I

[Enter] VALENTINE *and* PROTEUS.

Val. Cease to persuade, my loving Proteus;
　　Home-keeping youth have ever homely wits.
　　Were 't not affection chains thy tender days
　　To the sweet glances of thy honour'd love,
　　I rather would entreat thy company　　　　　　　　　5
　　To see the wonders of the world abroad
　　Than (living dully sluggardis'd at home)
　　Wear out thy youth with shapeless idleness.
　　But since thou lov'st, love still, and thrive therein,
　　Even as I would, when I to love begin.　　　　　　10

ACT I

Scene 1

ACT I SCENE 1] *Rowe; Actus primus, Scena prima F;* Act I. Scene 1. Verona *Pope.*
S.D. Enter . . . Proteus] *Valentine : Protheus,* and *Speed F.*

1. i] Harold Brooks has drawn my
attention to the fact that Lyly's *Endimion* (publ. 1591) begins with a duologue between the friends Endimion
and Eumenides. In this opening scene
Eumenides, who later experiences a
conflict between love and friendship,
rebukes Endimion for placing his love
on an impossible object. Shakespeare
may well have been influenced by this,
though the pattern of his relationship
between the friends is of course different.

1. *Proteus*] here trisyllabic, but often
disyllabic in the play.

1–2.] Cf. *Shr.,* 1. ii. 50–2: 'Such wind
as scatters young men through the
world / To seek their fortunes farther
than at home / Where small experience
grows', and Tilley, N 274.

2.] Cf. *Comus,* l. 748: 'It is for homely
features to keep home' (Steevens).

7–8.] Cf. *Diana*: 'spende his youth
idly at home' (Kennedy, p. 87); and
Romeus, l. 106: 'consume away, the
best parte of thine age'.

8. *shapeless idleness*] 'The expression
is fine, as implying that *idleness* pre-
vents the giving any form or character
to the manners' (Warburton).

3

Pro. Wilt thou be gone? Sweet Valentine, adieu;
　　Think on thy Proteus, when thou (haply) seest
　　Some rare noteworthy object in thy travel.
　　Wish me partaker in thy happiness,
　　When thou dost meet good hap; and in thy danger　15
　　(If ever danger do environ thee)
　　Commend thy grievance to my holy prayers,
　　For I will be thy beadsman, Valentine.
Val. And on a love-book pray for my success?
Pro. Upon some book I love, I'll pray for thee.　　20
Val. That's on some shallow story of deep love,
　　How young Leander cross'd the Hellespont.
Pro. That's a deep story, of a deeper love,
　　For he was more than over shoes in love.
Val. 'Tis true; for you are over boots in love,　　25
　　And yet you never swum the Hellespont.
Pro. Over the boots? Nay, give me not the boots.
Val. No, I will not; for it boots thee not.
Pro.　　　　　　　　　　　　　　　　What?
Val. To be in love; where scorn is bought with groans;

---

25. for] *F;* but *Collier ii;* and *or* but *conj. Staunton.*　　26. swum] *Camb;* swom *F;* swam *Collier.*　　28. boots thee] *F;* boots *conj. S. Walker (ap. Camb).*

12. *haply*] perchance.

14. *partaker*] Cf. *Euphues*: 'a friend whom thou maist make . . . partaker of all thy misfortune' (Bullough, p. 218).

17. *Commend*] entrust.

grievance] distress; again in this sense at IV. iii. 37.

18. *beadsman*] one paid to pray on behalf of others.

22.] alluding to Leander's swimming of the Hellespont in order to visit his love Hero. Marlowe's *Hero and Leander* was entered in the Stationers' Register in 1593 but no edition is known before 1598: see III. i. 89–91 n.

25. *for*] The conjectures of Collier and Staunton may be justified.

over boots] Cf. *O.E.D., boot,* sb³, 1b: '*Over shoes, over boots*: expressing reckless continuance in a course already begun'; *Wily Beguiled* (M.S.R., 447–

8): 'I am in loue with her, ouer my high shooes'; and Tilley, S379.

26. *swum*] F's 'swom' represents this form of the verb: cf. Franz, p. 164.

27. *give . . . boots*] Theobald pointed out that Cotgrave interpreted *Bailler foin en corne* as *To give one the boots,* and that Proteus' words therefore mean 'don't make a laughing-stock of me'. In *The Weakest Goeth to the Wall* (M.S.R., 432–3) Bunch, considering himself insulted, exclaims: 'tis not your big belly . . . can carry it away, if ye offer vs the boots.' It may have some connection with the Warwickshire game described by Steevens, in which the 'forfeit' was to be slapped on the breech with a pair of boots, or (less probably) with the torture of the boot. Cf. Tilley, B537.

28. *boots*] profits. Cf. *Romeus,* l. 78: 'What booteth me to love?'

Coy looks, with heart-sore sighs; one fading moment's
    mirth,   30
With twenty watchful, weary, tedious nights;
If haply won, perhaps a hapless gain;
If lost, why then a grievous labour won;
How ever, but a folly bought with wit,
Or else a wit by folly vanquished.   35
Pro. So, by your circumstance, you call me fool.
Val. So, by your circumstance, I fear you'll prove.
Pro. 'Tis Love you cavil at, I am not Love.
Val. Love is your master, for he masters you;
And he that is so yoked by a fool   40
Methinks should not be chronicled for wise.
Pro. Yet writers say: as in the sweetest bud
The eating canker dwells, so eating Love
Inhabits in the finest wits of all.
Val. And writers say: as the most forward bud   45
Is eaten by the canker ere it blow,
Even so by Love the young and tender wit
Is turn'd to folly, blasting in the bud,
Losing his verdure, even in the prime,

---

30. one fading] *F;* one *Hanmer.*   48. blasting] *F;* blasted *Collier (MS.).*

30. *one fading moment's mirth*] Cf.
Romeus, l. 1102: 'Or els such fading
pleasure as by Fortune straight was
reaved'.

33. *a grievous labour won*] As L. Hotson, *Shakespeare's Sonnets Dated and
Other Essays* (1949), points out, Valentine means that, if the object of love is
not gained, all that one has won is a
grievous labour. Hotson used this passage as part of his argument for identifying 'Love's Labour's Won' with *Troil.*

34. *How ever*] in any case.

36, 37. *circumstance*] (1) circuitous
deduction; (2) state of affairs.

39.] Cf. *Romeus*, ll. 94–5: 'love . . .
hath so mastred quite his hart'.

42–4.] Cf. '1576 Pettie *Pet. Pal.*, i.
28: The canker which commonly
breedeth in the fairest rose' (Tilley,
C56), and '1576 Pettie *Pet. Pal.*, ii. 3:
The finer wit he was endued withal,
the sooner was he made thrall and sub-

ject to love' (Tilley, W576). Malone
noted from Sonnet 70: 'For canker
vice the sweetest buds doth love'. Cf.
also Sonnet 35, l. 4.

43–4. *Love . . . all*] Cf. *Euphues*: 'Love
easilye entreth into the sharpe witte
without resistaunce, and is harboured
there without repentaunce' (cited by
Tilley, W576).

44. *Inhabits*] generally, as here, in-
transitive in Shakespeare.

45–6.] Cf. *Ham.*, i. iii. 39–40: 'The
canker galls the infants of the spring, /
Too oft before their buttons be dis-
closed.' And *Rom.*, i. i. 157–9.

46. *blow*] bloom.

48. *blasting*] Abbott gives several
examples of present participles used in
a passive sense. Cf. the frequent 'beholding', found here at iv. iv. 171, and
'soul-confirming', ii. vi. 16.

49. *prime*] spring; cf. Sonnet 97:
'The teeming autumn, big with rich

And all the fair effects of future hopes.   50
But wherefore waste I time to counsel thee
That art a votary to fond desire?
Once more adieu: my father at the road
Expects my coming, there to see me shipp'd.

Pro. And thither will I bring thee, Valentine.   55

Val. Sweet Proteus, no; now let us take our leave.
To Milan let me hear from thee by letters
Of thy success in love; and what news else
Betideth here in absence of thy friend;
And I likewise will visit thee with mine.   60

Pro. All happiness bechance to thee in Milan.

Val. As much to you at home; and so farewell.   *Exit.*

Pro. He after honour hunts, I after love;
He leaves his friends, to dignify them more;
I leave myself, my friends, and all, for love: 65
Thou, Julia, thou hast metamorphos'd me;
Made me neglect my studies, lose my time,
War with good counsel, set the world at nought;
Made wit with musing weak, heart sick with thought.

[*Enter* SPEED.]

Spe. Sir Proteus, 'save you; saw you my master?   70

57. To Milan] *F;* At Millaine *F2;* To Milan— *conj. Malone.*   65. leave] *Pope;*
loue *F.*   all,] *Camb;* all *F.*   69. Made] *F;* Make *conj. Johnson.*   S.D.] *Rowe.*
70. 'save you] *F;* 'save you, sir *Capell.*   saw you] *F;* saw you, Sir, *Hanmer.*

increase, / Bearing the wanton burden
of the prime'.

   50. *future hopes*] hopes for the future.

   53. *road*] roadstead, where ships can
ride at anchor (not necessarily at sea).
Cf. '1617 MORYSON *Itin.* III. 138 The
Towne Gravsend is a knowne Road'
(*O.E.D.*). See Introduction, p. xlviii.

   55. *bring*] accompany.

   57. *To Milan*] Malone interprets:
'Let me hear from thee by letters to
Milan', and compares *Err.*, IV. i. 48–9:
'you use this dalliance to excuse / Your
breach of promise to the Porpentine'
(i.e., to meet me at the Porpentine).

   58. *success*] fortune (good or bad).

   60. *visit*] Cf. *O.E.D.*, *vb* 11: 'To come
to (a person) *with* some accompani-

ment; to supply or enrich with some
benefit', citing this passage and III. ii.
82.

   61. *bechance*] befall.

   64. *dignify*] bring honour to.

   65.] Harold Brooks says: 'No doubt
suggested by *Romeus*, ll. 114, 111–12:
'In that thou lovest such a one, thou
seemst thy selfe to hate' and 'I pray /
That thou . . . become thyne owne.'

   65–7. *for love . . . lose my time*] Cf.
Euphues: 'for loue . . . I haue lost my
time' (ed. Arber, p. 106); and *Romeus*,
l. 693: 'There is no losse . . . to losse of
time'.

   70–141.] Pope described this dialogue as '*compos'd of the lowest and most
trifling conceits*' and explained it by

Pro. But now he parted hence to embark for Milan.

Spe. Twenty to one, then, he is shipp'd already,
And I have play'd the sheep in losing him.

Pro. Indeed a sheep doth very often stray,
And if the shepherd be awhile away.   75

Spe. You conclude that my master is a shepherd, then,
and I a sheep?

Pro. I do.

Spe. Why, then my horns are his horns, whether I wake or
sleep.   80

Pro. A silly answer, and fitting well a sheep.

Spe. This proves me still a sheep.

Pro. True; and thy master a shepherd.

Spe. Nay, that I can deny by a circumstance.

Pro. It shall go hard but I'll prove it by another.   85

Spe. The shepherd seeks the sheep, and not the sheep the
shepherd; but I seek my master, and my master
seeks not me: therefore I am no sheep.

Pro. The sheep for fodder follow the shepherd, the shepherd for food follows not the sheep; thou for wages   90
followest thy master, thy master for wages follows
not thee: therefore thou art a sheep.

Spe. Such another proof will make me cry 'baa'.

Pro. But dost thou hear? Gavest thou my letter to Julia?

---

77. a sheep] *F2*; Sheepe *F*.   89. follow] *F*; follows *Pope*.

---

referring to '*the gross taste*' of Shakespeare's age. He thought that such
scenes were in some instances '*interpolated by the Players*', and was sub-
sequently attacked by Johnson and
Malone for saying that this one was so
interpolated. Malone is more to the
point in suggesting the need to relate
the dialogue here to the work of
Shakespeare's predecessors: see Introduction, p. xxvi.

73. *sheep*] There is plenty of evidence
that 'sheep' and 'ship' were often
homophones. Dyce, *A Few Notes on
Shakespeare* (1853), quotes 'ship-skin
cap' from Dekker's *Satiromastix* (1602).
For the pun, cf. *LLL.*, II. i. 218–19:
'*Boyet.* I was as willing to grapple as he

was to board. *Mar.* Two hot sheeps,
marry. *Boyet.* And wherefore not
ships?' and *Err.*, IV. i. 93–4. The occurrence of Ship Streets in inland towns
is to be explained in the same way.

74–5.] Cf. Tilley, S312.

75. *And if*] if.

79. *my horns are his horns*] i.e., Valentine owns me and therefore my horns:
therefore Valentine is a cuckold (presumably *in posse*).

82 ff.] This mock-academic disputation can be paralleled in *Err.*, II. ii.
62 ff. and in Lyly's *Sapho and Phao*, II.
iii. 45 ff.

84. *circumstance*] as in l. 36.

93. *baa*] Bond suggests a quibble on
'bah!'

Spe. Ay, sir; I (a lost mutton) gave your letter to her (a   95
laced mutton) and she (a laced mutton) gave me (a
lost mutton) nothing for my labour.

Pro. Here's too small a pasture for such store of muttons.

Spe. If the ground be over-charged, you were best stick
her.   100

Pro. Nay, in that you are astray; 'twere best pound you.

Spe. Nay, sir, less than a pound shall serve me for carrying your letter.

Pro. You mistake; I mean the pound, a pinfold.

Spe. From a pound to a pin? Fold it over and over,   105
'Tis threefold too little for carrying a letter to your lover.

Pro. But what said she?

Spe. [*first nodding*] Ay.

Pro. Nod—ay: why, that's 'noddy'.

---

101. Nay, ... astray;] *F* (*subst.*) ; Nay, ... a stray: *Theobald, conj. Thirlby;* Nay: ...
astray, *Camb.*   104. a] *F;* the *Delius, conj. Capell.*   107–8.] *Camb; Pro.* But
what said she? *Sp.* I. *F; Pro.* But what said she? *Speed.* She nodded and said, I.
Pope; Pro. But what said she? Did she nod? [*Speed nods.*] *Speed.* I. *Theobald; Pro.*
But what said she? [*Speed nods.*] Did she nod? *Speed.* I. *Capell.*

---

96. *laced mutton*] Cf. Tilley, M1338.
'Laced mutton' is a frequent term for a
courtesan, either as being tightly
laced or as wearing lace. It is less likely
that the culinary sense of 'lace', to
make a number of incisions in the
breast of a bird), *O.E.D.*, s.v., 8, is
involved. Dyce, *A Few Notes on Shakespeare* (1853), suggested that here we
should interpret, not as 'courtesan',
but as '*a richly-attired piece of woman's
flesh*'. Staunton was convinced that
Speed is describing Lucetta. *NCS*
found it strange that Proteus should
tolerate such a description of Julia.
Bond, however, rightly considered that
the jest is well enough for 'a page of
1590'. In any event, as Dyce conjectured, the term could be used without
reflection on a woman's character; cf.
July and Julian (M.S.R., 297–8): 'on
gentell woman wch wayteth on my
maistris, / a fine pice of laced mutton
dowtlys' (spoken of the play's heroine).
Moreover, in *Gent.* no opportunity for
a pun could be lost, and the talk of
sheep in ll. 73–93 led easily to this.

99. *over-charged*] over-burdened, too
packed; cf. *Mac.*, I. ii. 37: 'cannons
overcharged with double cracks'.

stick] slaughter, with a sexual pun.

101. *Nay, . . . astray*] The Camb.
reading is attractive, but F makes good
sense.

pound] (1) enclose in a pound; (2)
beat. An obvious third meaning
appears in the next line.

104. *pinfold*] enclosure for stray
cattle; cf. *Lr.*, II. ii. 9.

105. *Fold*] This seems to mean 'mul-
tiply', as in, e.g., 'tenfold'; Speed
uses the term in order to echo 'pinfold'.

109. *noddy*] fool, simpleton; cf.
Beaumont and Fletcher, *Knight of the
Burning Pestle*, II: '*Hum.* What do you
think I am? *Jasp.* An arrant noddy.
Hum. A word of obloquy!' 'Noddy'
was also the name of a card-game, and
of the knave in various card-games.
Cf. Tilley, N199. The general sense of
this passage and the stage-business
involved is clear enough, but the reconstruction of its details must be

Spe. You mistook, sir: I say she did nod; and you ask me   110
    if she did nod, and I say 'Ay'.

Pro. And that set together is 'noddy'.

Spe. Now you have taken the pains to set it together,
    take it for your pains.

Pro. No, no, you shall have it for bearing the letter.   115

Spe. Well, I perceive I must be fain to bear with you.

Pro. Why, sir, how do you bear with me?

Spe. Marry, sir, the letter very orderly, having nothing
    but the word 'noddy' for my pains.

Pro. Beshrew me, but you have a quick wit.   120

Spe. And yet it cannot overtake your slow purse.

Pro. Come, come, open the matter in brief: what said
    she?

Spe. Open your purse, that the money and the matter
    may be both at once delivered.   125

Pro. [*giving money*] Well, sir; here is for your pains. What
    said she?

Spe. Truly, sir, I think you'll hardly win her.

Pro. Why, couldst thou perceive so much from her?

Spe. Sir, I could perceive nothing at all from her; no, not   130
    so much as a ducat for delivering your letter; and
    being so hard to me that brought your mind, I fear
    she'll prove as hard to you in telling your mind.

110, 111. say] *F;* said *F2.*   110–11.] *so Capell;* You . . . nod; / And . . . I. *F.*
118. orderly] *F;* motherly (moderly) *conj. Staunton.*   118–19.] *so Capell;*
Marry . . . orderly, / Hauing . . . paines. *F.*   130–5.] *so Capell;* Sir . . . her; / No
. . . letter: / And . . . minde; / I . . . minde. / Giue . . . steele. *F.*   130. her] *F;*
her better *Collier ii.*   132. brought] *F;* brought to her *Collier ii.*   133. your] *F;*
her *F2;* you her *Collier ii.*

speculative: the Camb. S.D. (l. 108)
seems the best suggestion to follow on
the stage.
  116. *bear with*] put up with; but see
following note.
  118. *orderly*] in conformity with
order, duly. Staunton, however, suggested that the right reading may be
'moderly' (i.e., motherly), and that the
theme of child-bearing runs through
the dialogue, in 'bearing', 'bear with
you', 'my pains', 'a quick wit',
'delivered'. But it is unlikely that the
two words would be confused, and the

spelling 'moderly' would be unusual at
the date of the play.
  118–19. *nothing . . . 'noddy'*] 'Note the
quibble' (*NCS*); 'nothing' would probably be pronounced 'noting' (Kökeritz, p. 320).
  130–3. *Sir . . . mind*] Speed's use of
doggerel verse at II. i. 128–33, 155–9,
suggests that F may be right in giving
this too as verse. But Collier's 'corrector' may be right in assuming that
the F lines are imperfect.
  133. *in telling your mind*] i.e., 'When
you address her in person' (Malone).

Give her no token but stones, for she's as hard as
steel.   135
Pro. What said she? Nothing?
Spe. No, not so much as 'Take this for thy pains'. To
testify your bounty, I thank you, you have testerned
me; in requital whereof, henceforth carry your
letters yourself; and so, sir, I'll commend you to my   140
master.   [*Exit.*]
Pro. Go, go, be gone, to save your ship from wrack,
Which cannot perish having thee aboard,
Being destin'd to a drier death on shore.
I must go send some better messenger: 145
I fear my Julia would not deign my lines
Receiving them from such a worthless post.   *Exit.*

SCENE II

Enter JULIA *and* LUCETTA.

Jul. But say, Lucetta, now we are alone,
Wouldst thou then counsel me to fall in love?

136.] *Camb;* What . . . she, nothing? *F;* What . . . she nothing? *F2;* What, . . .
she nothing? *Pope.*   137–9. No . . . me] *so Capell;* No . . . pains: / To . . . me; *F.*
137–8. Take . . . thank you] *F;* I thank you, take . . . pains. To . . . bounty *conj.*
Camb.   138. testerned] *F2 (subst.)* ; cestern'd *F;* tester'd *Hanmer.*   141. S.D.]
Capell.   147. S.D.] *F; Exeunt Rowe; Exeunt severally Warburton.*

Scene II

SCENE II] *Rowe; Scæna Secunda F; Scene III. Changes to Julia's chamber Pope.*

134. *stones*] Bond interprets 'jewels',
but there may be a reference to
Matt., vii. 9, or Luke, xi. 11.

134–5. *hard as steel*] Cf. Tilley, S839.
A link with 'stones' (l. 134) is paralleled in *3H6*, II. i. 201–2: 'as hard as
steel, / As . . . flinty', and in *Ven.*, 198:
'flinty, hard as steel'.

138. *testerned*] The tester was an
Elizabethan sixpence, one-seventh of
the ducat that Speed mentioned in
l. 131. For this comic treatment of a
term applied to the reward in a beg-
ging-routine, cf. Costard on 'guerdon'
and 'remuneration', *LLL.*, III. i. 171–4.

142–4.] Cf. *Tp.*, I. i. 71, where
Gonzalo finds hope in his belief that
the Boatswain will be hanged: 'I
would fain die a dry death.' Cf. Tilley,
B139.

145. *some better messenger*] Cf. Introduction, p. xviii.

146. *deign*] take graciously; the obso-
lete contrary of 'disdain' (Bond).

147. *post*] (1) letter-carrier; (2) type
of stupidity.

Scene II

1–14.] The opening of this scene
anticipates the discussion of Portia's

Luc. Ay, madam, so you stumble not unheedfully.

Jul. Of all the fair resort of gentlemen
 That every day with parle encounter me,   5
 In thy opinion which is worthiest love?

Luc. Please you repeat their names, I'll show my mind,
 According to my shallow simple skill.

Jul. What think'st thou of the fair Sir Eglamour?

Luc. As of a knight well-spoken, neat, and fine;   10
 But were I you, he never should be mine.

Jul. What think'st thou of the rich Mercatio?

Luc. Well of his wealth; but of himself, so so.

Jul. What think'st thou of the gentle Proteus?

Luc. Lord, Lord! to see what folly reigns in us!   15

Jul. How now? What means this passion at his name?

Luc. Pardon, dear madam, 'tis a passing shame
 That I (unworthy body as I am)
 Should censure thus on lovely gentlemen.

Jul. Why not on Proteus, as of all the rest?   20

Luc. Then thus: of many good, I think him best.

Jul. Your reason?

Luc. I have no other but a woman's reason:

---

12. Mercatio] *F; Mercutio Sargent.*   15. reigns] *F; feigns conj. anon (ap. Camb).*
19. censure . . . gentlemen] *F; censure thus a lovely gentleman Pope; censure pass on lovely gentlemen Hanmer; censure thus a loving gentleman Collier ii; censure on this lovely gentleman conj. Camb; censure on a lovely gentleman conj. S. Verges (ap. Camb).*   20. of] *F; on Hanmer.*

---

suitors in her conversation with Nerissa (*Mer.V.*, i. ii. 36–108).

4. *resort*] company of persons resorting; cf. *Euphues* (ed. Bond, i. 192): 'my resorte and company, and companions' (Bond).

5. *parle*] talk.

9. *Sir Eglamour*] On the use of this name both for Julia's suitor and for Silvia's '*agent . . . in her escape*', see Introduction, p. xviii. The name may have acquired a burlesque significance: cf. 'Adieu, Sir Eglamour; adieu lute-string, curtain-rod, goose-quill' (Dekker, *Satiromastix*, quoted by Steevens).

10. *neat*] elegant; cf. *Wint.*, i. ii. 123: 'not neat, but cleanly'.

12. *Mercatio*] As Mercutio is a char-

acter in Brooke's *Romeus and Juliet*, which was used for this play (see Introduction, p. xliii), it is tempting to believe that 'Mercatio' is a misprint ('u' and 'a' being easily confused in Elizabethan handwriting). But 'Mercatio' (presumably from Ital. 'mercáto', market) fits the wealth attributed to this suitor: at the same time Shakespeare may well have had Brooke's Mercutio in mind in choosing the name.

17. *passing*] surpassing.

19. *censure*] pass judgment.

lovely] probably 'loving' (cf. *Shr.*, iii. ii. 125: 'seal the title with a lovely kiss') rather than 'beautiful'.

23. *a woman's reason*] Cf. 'Lyly *Love's*

I think him so, because I think him so.

Lul. And wouldst thou have me cast my love on him? 25

Juc. Ay; if you thought your love not cast away.

Jul. Why, he, of all the rest, hath never mov'd me.

Luc. Yet he, of all the rest, I think best loves ye.

Jul. His little speaking shows his love but small.

Luc. Fire that's closest kept burns most of all. 30

Jul. They do not love that do not show their love.

Luc. O, they love least that let men know their love.

Jul. I would I knew his mind.

Luc. Peruse this paper, madam.

Jul. 'To Julia': say, from whom? 35

Luc. That the contents will show.

Jul. Say, say: who gave it thee?

Luc. Sir Valentine's page; and sent I think from Proteus.

He would have given it you, but I being in the way

Did in your name receive it: pardon the fault, I pray. 40

Jul. Now, by my modesty, a goodly broker!

---

28. loves] *F;* lov'd *Keightley.* ye] *F;* you *Capell.* 30. Fire that's] *F;* The fire that's *Pope;* Fire that is *Capell.* 39. in the way] *F;* by *Pope.* 40. the ...pray] *F;* me *Pope.*

Metam., IV. i. 78: Womens reasons; they would not, because they would not' (Tilley, B179, who notes also *Troil.,* I. i. 109).

27. *mov'd*] wooed; cf. v. iv. 57 (F2 reading).

29.] For repudiation of this idea, cf. Sonnets 85 and 23, and II. ii. 16–18.

30. *Fire*] disyllabic; cf. Kökeritz, pp. 291–2.

30.] Cf. *Ven.,* 331–2: 'An oven that is stopp'd ... Burneth more hotly'; and Tilley, F265, citing a passage in *Euphues* concerned with the protagonist as a traitor to love. Cf. also II. vii. 21–8n.

31.] The line echoes the form, and reverses the sentiment, of Sidney in *Astrophel and Stella,* Sonnet LIV: 'They love indeed who dare not say they love'.

32.] Cf. Tilley, L165.

33–7.] Short lines with three accents reappear at ll. 74–5, 92–4. It would appear that Shakespeare is here freely experimenting with the versification, balancing the trimeters with the alexandrines of ll. 39–40. For a similar example of experimentation, probably close in date, note the octosyllabics for soliloquy in Greene's *James IV,* II. i. 736–9. Bond compared *R3,* I. ii. 193–203. Senecan stichomythia sometimes occurred in half-lines: e.g., *Agamemnon,* 791–9, and *Hippolytus,* 242–5.

39–40.] For the contradiction with scene i, see Introduction, p. xviii.

41, 51, 55. *modesty, shame, modesty*] Cf. *Diana:* 'love ... did put a certaine desire into my minde to see the letter, though modestie and shame forbad me to aske it of my maide, especially for the wordes that had passed betweene us' (Kennedy, p. 84).

41. *broker*] agent, especially in love affairs; cf. *Ham.,* I. iii. 127–30: 'Do not believe his vows; for they are brokers, ... Breathing like sanctified and pious bawds.'

Dare you presume to harbour wanton lines?
To whisper, and conspire against my youth?
Now trust me, 'tis an office of great worth,
And you an officer fit for the place.   45
There: take the paper; see it be return'd,
Or else return no more into my sight.

Luc. To plead for love deserves more fee than hate.

                                    [*She drops the letter.*]

Jul. Will ye be gone?

Luc.   That you may ruminate.   *Exit.*

Jul. And yet I would I had o'erlook'd the letter.   50
It were a shame to call her back again,
And pray her to a fault for which I chid her.
What fool is she, that knows I am a maid,
And would not force the letter to my view!
Since maids, in modesty, say 'no' to that   55
Which they would have the profferer construe 'ay'.
Fie, fie; how wayward is this foolish love,
That (like a testy babe) will scratch the nurse,
And presently all humbled kiss the rod!
How churlishly I chid Lucetta hence,   60
When willingly I would have had her here!
How angerly I taught my brow to frown,
When inward joy enforc'd my heart to smile!
My penance is to call Lucetta back
And ask remission for my folly past.   65
What ho! Lucetta!

                    [*Enter* LUCETTA.]

Luc.   What would your ladyship?

Jul. Is 't near dinner time?

---

49. *Luc.*] *F; Luc.* [*aside*] *Hanmer.*   53. fool] *F4*; 'fool *F*; a fool *Camb.*   58. the]
F; his *Halliwell MS.* (*at first quotation of this passage*).   59. presently] *F*; by and
by *Halliwell MS.* (*at first and second quotations of this passage*).   62. angerly] *F*;
angrily *Malone i.*   66. S.D.] *Rowe.*

50. *o'erlook'd*] examined.

52. *pray . . . fault*] pray her to commit
a fault.

53. *fool*] The F apostrophe indicates
elision of 'a'.

55-6.] Cf. Tilley, W660.

59. *presently*] at once.
kiss the rod] Cf. Tilley, R156.

62. *angerly*] angrily.

65. *remission*] pardon. Cf. *Diana*:
'asking *Rosina* forgivenes of what was
past' (Kennedy, p. 86).

Luc.   I would it were,
        That you might kill your stomach on your meat,
        And not upon your maid.   [*She takes up Proteus' letter.*]
Jul. What is 't that you took up so gingerly?   70
Luc. Nothing.
Jul. Why didst thou stoop then?
Luc. To take a paper up that I let fall.
Jul. And is that paper nothing?
Luc. Nothing concerning me.   75
Jul. Then let it lie, for those that it concerns.
Luc. Madam, it will not lie where it concerns,
        Unless it have a false interpreter.
Jul. Some love of yours hath writ to you in rhyme.
Luc. That I might sing it, madam, to a tune.   80
        Give me a note; your ladyship can set.
Jul. As little by such toys as may be possible:
        Best sing it to the tune of 'Light o' Love'.
Luc. It is too heavy for so light a tune.
Jul. Heavy? Belike it hath some burden then?   85
Luc. Ay; and melodious were it, would you sing it.
Jul. And why not you?
Luc.   I cannot reach so high.

70.] *so Collier;* What . . . you / Tooke . . . gingerly *F.*   80. tune] *F;* time *conj.*
Keightley.   81. note;] *F4;* Note, *F.*

67–9. *I would . . . your maid*] Cf. the
proverb 'A hungry man an angry man'
(Tilley, M187: cf. M846).

68. *stomach*] (1) appetite; (2) anger.

68–9. *meat, maid*] As 'meat' would be
pronounced as 'mate', the quibble
would be obvious (cf. Kökeritz,
p. 198).

70.] Cf. *Diana*: 'What is that that
fell downe?' (Kennedy, p. 85).

70. *gingerly*] cautiously; *O.E.D.* records this adverbial use only from the
seventeenth century.

71, 74, 75. *Nothing . . . nothing?
Nothing*] Cf. *Diana*: 'It is nothing
Mistresse' (Kennedy, p. 85).

73. *I let fall*] Cf. *Diana*: 'she let the
letter closely fall' (Kennedy, p. 85).

77. *lie*] with the obvious quibble.

81. *note*] tune; *NCS* suggests a

quibble on 'note' = short letter (i.e.,
a reply to Proteus).

set] compose music for words. Bond
suggests a quibble on 'show the way',
i.e., show me how to answer the letter.
In l. 82 Julia quibbles by taking 'set'
(with 'by') in the sense 'set store by',
'esteem'.

83. *Light o' Love*] a tune mentioned
in *Ado*, III. iv. 44, and in *Two Noble
Kinsmen*, v. iv. There is dramatic
irony here in the association of the
tune with Proteus.

84. *heavy*] serious.

85. *burden*] undersong or bass, sung
throughout the song.

86. *would you sing it*] possibly with a
sexual reference, quibbling on 'burden': if you would bear the burden.

87. *I . . . high*] (1) The tune is too

Jul. [*taking the letter*] Let's see your song. How now, minion?
Luc. Keep tune there still: so you will sing it out.

[*Julia strikes her.*]

And yet methinks I do not like this tune.   90
Jul. You do not?
Luc. No, madam, 'tis too sharp.
Jul. You, minion, are too saucy.
Luc. Nay, now you are too flat;
And mar the concord with too harsh a descant: 95
There wanteth but a mean to fill your song.
Jul. The mean is drown'd with your unruly bass.
Luc. Indeed I bid the base for Proteus.
Jul. This babble shall not henceforth trouble me.
Here is a coil with protestation. [*She tears the letter.*]   100
Go, get you gone; and let the papers lie.
You would be fing'ring them, to anger me.

88.] *so Hanmer;* Let's . . . Song*: /* How . . . Minion *F.*   88. how] *F;* Why, how *Hanmer.*   89. S.D.] *Hanmer (subst.).*   97. your] *F2;* you *F.*   100. S.D.] *Pope (subst.).*

high for me; (2) Proteus is beyond my reach.

88. *Let's see*] Cf. *Diana*: 'Come, come, let me see it' (Kennedy, p. 85).

88, 93. *minion*] Cf. *Diana*: 'an impudent and bolde minion' (Kennedy, p. 84).

89. *so . . . out*] perhaps 'in that way you will finish singing it'.

94. *flat*] 'downright' (Bond); *NCS* suggests that 'sharp' in l. 92 and 'flat' here denote a pinch and a slap, in addition of course to their musical significance.

95. *descant*] Most often this signifies 'singing a part extempore upon a plain song' (Morley, *Plain and Easy Introduction to Practical Music*, 1597, quoted by Staunton). F. G. Fleay, *New Shakspere Society Transactions*, 1874, p. 295, noted that 'descant' occurs in Shakespeare only here and on two occasions in *R3*.

96. *mean*] (1) mean between the 'sharp' and 'flat' of ll. 92, 94; (2) tenor voice (perhaps referring, *NCS* suggests, to Proteus).

97. *with . . . bass*] Tannenbaum, p. 7, wishes to preserve the F reading, interpreting it as 'by you, unruly bass'. *NCS* suggests that Julia quibbles on Lucetta's 'base' conduct. On the playing on 'mean' and 'base', cf. Lyly's *Love's Metamorphosis* (publ. 1601), III. i. 121–4: 'Why, what strings are in Ladies hearts? Not the base. . . . There is no base string in a woman's heart . . . The meane? . . . There was neuer meane in woman's heart.'

98. *bid the base*] (1) sing the bass part; (2) challenge (from the game of prisoner's base). Cf. Marlowe, *Edward II*, IV. ii. 65–6: 'We will find comfort, money, men and friends / Ere long, to bid the English king a base.' Also *Ven.*, 303–4 (Bond).

99. *babble*] senseless talk; *NCS* suggests 'bauble', which might be spelt 'bable'.

100. *coil*] fuss, disturbance; cf. Marlowe, *2 Tamburlaine*, IV. i. 73–4: 'What a coil they keep! I believe there will be some hurt done anon amongst them.'

102. *fing'ring*] touching or, more

Luc. She makes it strange, but she would be best pleas'd
    To be so anger'd with another letter.   [*Exit.*]
Jul. [*gathering up pieces of the letter*] Nay, would I were so
    anger'd with the same!   105
    O hateful hands, to tear such loving words;
    Injurious wasps, to feed on such sweet honey,
    And kill the bees that yield it, with your stings!
    I'll kiss each several paper, for amends.
    Look, here is writ 'kind Julia': unkind Julia!   110
    As in revenge of thy ingratitude,
    I throw thy name against the bruising stones,
    Trampling contemptuously on thy disdain.
    And here is writ 'love-wounded Proteus'.
    Poor wounded name: my bosom, as a bed,   115
    Shall lodge thee till thy wound be throughly heal'd;
    And thus I search it with a sovereign kiss.
    But twice, or thrice, was 'Proteus' written down:
    Be calm, good wind, blow not a word away,
    Till I have found each letter, in the letter,   120
    Except mine own name: that some whirlwind bear
    Unto a ragged, fearful, hanging rock,

---

103. best pleas'd] *F;* pleas'd better *Collier ii.*   104. S.D.] *F2.*   105. *Jul.*] *F;*
om. conj. *Staunton (inserting at l. 106).*   105. S.D.] *Capell (subst.), at l. 109.*
114. love-wounded] *F2;* Loue wounded *F.*   122. fearful, hanging] *F;* fearful-
hanging *Delius.*

probably, pilfering; cf. *Ham.*, v. ii. 15:
'Finger'd their packet', and *3H6*, v. i.
44.
    103. *makes it strange*] pretends to
be surprised or (here) indifferent; cf.
Tit., II. i. 81. Also *Diana* (just before the letter episode): 'many more
[days did Felismena] spende in making the matter strange' (Kennedy,
p. 83).
    105. Jul.] Staunton objects that
here Julia replies to an aside from Lucetta, and he therefore gives this line
to the maid, with a stress on 'I'. But
there is such a device as the half-
aside, which can be overheard. Julia
means that she wishes the letter still
existed for her to get angry over, or
perhaps that she wishes her true

emotion was the anger she pretended.
    110 ff.] Shakespeare's cue for this
dwelling on particular words from the
letter seems to come from *Diana*: 'I
read the letter once againe, pausing
a little at every worde' (Kennedy,
p. 86).
    112–28.] For love-conceits on
'name', cf. *Rom.*, II. ii. 38–57 (where
Romeo says: 'Had I it [his name]
written, I would tear the word'), and
Sonnet 136.
    115–16. *my . . . thee*] Cf. *Ven.*, 1183:
'Here was thy father's bed, here in my
breast' (Malone).
    117. *search*] probe.
    122–3.] Cf. *3H6*, v. iv. 27, 25: 'a
ragged fatal rock', 'a ruthless sea'.
    122. *ragged*] rugged.

And throw it thence into the raging sea.
Lo, here in one line is his name twice writ:
'Poor forlorn Proteus', 'passionate Proteus'.   125
'To the sweet Julia': that I'll tear away.
And yet I will not, sith so prettily
He couples it to his complaining names.
Thus will I fold them, one upon another:
Now kiss, embrace, contend, do what you will.   130

[*Enter* LUCETTA.]

Luc. Madam, dinner is ready; and your father stays.
Jul. Well, let us go.
Luc. What, shall these papers lie, like tell-tales here?
Jul. If you respect them, best to take them up.
Luc. Nay, I was taken up, for laying them down.   135
Yet here they shall not lie, for catching cold.
                                        [*She gathers up the letter.*]
Jul. I see you have a month's mind to them.
Luc. Ay, madam, you may say what sights you see;
I see things too, although you judge I wink.
Jul. Come, come, will 't please you go?   *Exeunt.*   140

---

130. S.D.] *F2.*   134. you] *F;* thou *Pope.*   them,] *F4;* them; *F.*   137. see] *F;*
see that *Keightley.*   to them] *F;* unto them *Collier ii;* to them, minion *Hanmer.*
138. say...see] *F;* see...think *Collier ii.*

131. *your father*] See Introduction, pp. xviii–xix.

134. *respect*] value.

135. *taken up*] reprimanded; cf. *Cym.,* II. i. 4–5: 'a whoreson jackanapes must take me up for swearing'.

136. *for catching cold*] lest they should catch cold.

137. *month's mind*] inclination. Originally a 'month's mind' was a religious commemoration of a deceased person on a day one month after his death: *Martin's Month's Minde* (1589), describing Martin Marprelate's death and funeral, shows an application of this sense. The phrase seems, however, to have acquired, in the late sixteenth century, the sense of a 'longing' such as that experienced by a pregnant woman in the last month of pregnancy. Staunton argues that the celebration for the dead implies a 'strong affection' and thus traces the transition of meaning (though he does not mention pregnancy). Cf. Tilley, M1109. *month's,* if the line is to be taken as verse, is disyllabic ('monthes' or 'moneths').

139. *wink*] close my eyes; cf. II. iv. 93, v. ii. 14, Tilley, W500, and Sonnet 43: 'When most I wink, then do mine eyes best see'.

SCENE III

Enter ANTONIO *and* PANTHINO.

Ant. Tell me, Panthino, what sad talk was that
    Wherewith my brother held you in the cloister?
Pan. 'Twas of his nephew Proteus, your son.
Ant. Why, what of him?
Pan.   He wonder'd that your lordship
    Would suffer him to spend his youth at home,   5
    While other men, of slender reputation,
    Put forth their sons, to seek preferment out:
    Some to the wars, to try their fortune there;
    Some, to discover islands far away;
    Some, to the studious universities.   10
    For any, or for all these exercises,
    He said that Proteus, your son, was meet,
    And did request me to importune you
    To let him spend his time no more at home;
    Which would be great impeachment to his age,   15
    In having known no travel in his youth.
Ant. Nor need'st thou much importune me to that
    Whereon this month I have been hammering.
    I have consider'd well his loss of time,
    And how he cannot be a perfect man,   20
    Not being tried and tutor'd in the world:
    Experience is by industry achiev'd,
    And perfected by the swift course of time.

Scene III

SCENE III] *Rowe; Scœna Tertia* F.   S.D. *Enter . . . Panthino*] Enter Antonio and
Panthino. Protheus. F.   1. Panthino] *F;* Panthion *F3.*

1. *sad*] serious.

14.] Cf. *Diana*: 'should spende his
youth idly at home' (Kennedy, p. 87).
Cf. I. i. 7–8.

15–16.] In *Romeus* Friar Laurence
attributes his contentment in old age
to his having travelled much in his
youth (ll. 2097–119).

18. *hammering*] deliberating; cf.

Wint., II. ii. 48–9: 'the queen . . .
Who but to-day hammer'd of this
design'; *Tit.*, II. iii. 39; *2H6*, I. ii. 47.
The use of the term in this sense is a
cliché in late sixteenth-century writing.

23. *perfected*] almost invariably
stressed on the first syllable in Shakespeare; cf. Kökeritz, p. 335.

Then tell me, whither were I best to send him?
Pan. I think your lordship is not ignorant   25
How his companion, youthful Valentine,
Attends the Emperor in his royal court.
Ant. I know it well.
Pan. 'Twere good, I think, your lordship sent him
     thither:
There shall he practise tilts and tournaments,   30
Hear sweet discourse, converse with noblemen,
And be in eye of every exercise .
Worthy his youth and nobleness of birth.
Ant. I like thy counsel: well hast thou advis'd.
And that thou mayst perceive how well I like it,   35
The execution of it shall make known.
Even with the speediest expedition,
I will dispatch him to the Emperor's court.
Pan. To-morrow, may it please you, Don Alphonso
With other gentlemen of good esteem   40
Are journeying to salute the Emperor,
And to commend their service to his will.
Ant. Good company: with them shall Proteus go.

[*Enter* PROTEUS.]

And in good time, now will we break with him.

---

24. whither] *F2;* whether *F.*   32. eye] *F;* the eye *Keightley.*   43. S.D.] *F2*
(*after l. 44*).   44. And ... time,] *F2;* And ... time: *F;* And, ... time, *Theobald;*
And,— ... time:— *Dyce;* And, ... time! *Camb.*

26. *companion*] often but not necessarily (or here) a term of contempt.

27. *Emperor ... court*] See Introduction, pp. xv–xvi.

30. *tilts and tournaments*] In *Diana,*
Don Felix 'by Tylt and Tourneyes ...
made it manifest that he was in love
with' Felismena. She later reminds
him that he used to woo her 'in the
citie with Tilt and Tourneyes' (Kennedy, pp. 83, 238).

32. *be in eye of*] witness.

35–6.] a conflation of two construc-
tions: (1) how well I like it the execution of it shall make known; (2) in

order that thou mayst perceive how
well I like it, the execution of it shall
make it known.

39. *Don Alphonso*] The 'Don' may
derive from the Spanish source: cf. II.
iv. 49.

44. *in good time*] *à propos,* at the right
moment; Bond quotes *R3,* III. i. 95:
'Now, in good time, here comes the
Duke of York'.

break with him] reveal to him what
we have in mind; cf. III. i. 59, and
Caes., II. i. 150–2: 'let us not break with
him; / For he will never follow any
thing / That other men begin.'

Pro. [*Aside*] Sweet love, sweet lines, sweet life!   45
          Here is her hand, the agent of her heart;
          Here is her oath for love, her honour's pawn.
          O that our fathers would applaud our loves
          To seal our happiness with their consents!
          O heavenly Julia!   50
Ant. How now? What letter are you reading there?
Pro. May 't please your lordship, 'tis a word or two
          Of commendations sent from Valentine,
          Deliver'd by a friend that came from him.
Ant. Lend me the letter: let me see what news.   55
Pro. There is no news, my lord, but that he writes
          How happily he lives, how well-belov'd,
          And daily graced by the Emperor;
          Wishing me with him, partner of his fortune.
Ant. And how stand you affected to his wish?   60
Pro. As one relying on your lordship's will,
          And not depending on his friendly wish.
Ant. My will is something sorted with his wish.
          Muse not that I thus suddenly proceed,
          For what I will, I will, and there an end.   65
          I am resolv'd that thou shalt spend some time
          With Valentinus, in the Emperor's court:
          What maintenance he from his friends receives,
          Like exhibition thou shalt have from me.
          To-morrow be in readiness to go.   70
          Excuse it not, for I am peremptory.
Pro. My lord, I cannot be so soon provided:
          Please you deliberate a day or two.

---

45. life!] *F* (*subst.*); life! sweet Julia! *Capell.*   50. O] *F2; Pro.* Oh *F.*   67.
Valentinus] *F;* Valentino *F2;* Valentine *Warburton.*

45.] Capell's conjectural addition to
this line seems unnecessary: it should
end with a pause.

48.] the first indication of parental
opposition: cf. ll. 80–1, and Introduction, p. xviii.

55.] Bond noted the parallel with
the Duke's seizure of Valentine's letter
to Silvia, III. i. 137.

60. *affected*] disposed.

63. *sorted with*] in agreement with.

65. *there an end*] Cf. II. i. 152; also *R2,*
v. i. 69, and *Mac.,* III. iv. 80.

69. *exhibition*] allowance of money
and/or other provisions (the term still
used at universities); cf. *Lr.,* I. ii. 25:
'Confined to exhibition'.

71. *peremptory*] resolved.

Ant. Look what thou want'st shall be sent after thee.
No more of stay; to-morrow thou must go.   75
Come on, Panthino; you shall be employ'd
To hasten on his expedition.

                [*Exeunt* ANTONIO *and* PANTHINO.]

Pro. Thus have I shunn'd the fire, for fear of burning,
And drench'd me in the sea, where I am drown'd.
I fear'd to show my father Julia's letter,   80
Lest he should take exceptions to my love,
And with the vantage of mine own excuse
Hath he excepted most against my love.
O, how this spring of love resembleth
The uncertain glory of an April day,   85
Which now shows all the beauty of the sun,
And by and by a cloud takes all away.

           [*Enter* PANTHINO.]

74. Look] *F;* Look, *Theobald.*   76. Panthino] *F (Panthmo);* Panthion *F3.*
77. S.D.] *Rowe.*   84. this . . . resembleth] *F;* love's spring resembleth in its sun
conj. Becket; this . . . resembleth well *Pope;* this . . . resembleth right *conj. Johnson.*
86. sun] *F;* light *conj. Johnson.*   87. S.D.] *F2.*

74. *Look what*] For the idiom, cf. M.
Eccles, 'Shakespeare's Use of "Look
How" and Similar Idioms', *J.E.G.P.*,
xlii (1943), 386–400, and P. Ure (ed.),
new Arden *R2*, I. i. 87n.

78–9.] 'drenched' in juxtaposition with fire is found in *Romeus*, l.
214: 'In Lethies floud his wonted
flames were quenchd and drenched
deepe'; it is associated with the sea
in l. 2102: 'on the seas to drenching
waves'.

81. *take exceptions*] make objections;
cf. v. ii. 3.

83. *excepted . . . love*] raised the greatest obstacles to my love; the normal
sense of 'except' is 'object', as in II. iv.
150, a line very close in phrasing to
this one.

84. *resembleth*] tetrasyllabic (Theobald); the emendations of Pope and
Johnson disregard this, and Johnson
further wishes to tighten the quatrain

by securing a rhyme for this line and
l. 86.

84–7.] Cf. Tilley, L92a, who quotes
Tourneur, *Revenger's Tragedy*, v. i. 161:
'Alas I shine in teares like the Sunne in
Aprill'; also Sonnets 1, 3, 18, 33, and
34. Harold Brooks suggests Shakespeare may have recalled here two
fine lines from Greene's *Friar Bacon
and Friar Bungay* (publ. 1594), III. i.
93–4: 'Why, thinks King Henry's son
that Margaret's love / Hangs in the
uncertain balance of proud time?',
where a reference to 'the morning sun'
follows.

85. *The uncertain glory*] echoing 'the
vncertayne glory' of the 1587 edition
of *A Mirror for Magistrates* (a corruption of 'the vncertaintye of glory' previously in the text). Harold Brooks has
indicated to me that this comes in a
passage echoed by Shakespeare in
1H6, I. iv. 66–75.

Pan.   Sir Proteus, your father calls for you,
  He is in haste, therefore I pray you go.
Pro.   Why, this it is: my heart accords thereto,   90
  And yet a thousand times it answers 'no'. *Exeunt.*

88. father calls] *F2* (Father call's)*;* Fathers call's *F.* 91. it answers] *F4;* it
answer's *F.* 91. S.D.] *F* (*Exeunt. Finis.*).

88. *father calls*] Tannenbaum, p. 8,
defends the F reading, taking it as
'father's call's', and suggests adding a
S.D. '*Father calls*'.

90–1.] In this scene Shakespeare has
shown Proteus' uncertainty of character, first in his failure to make his
love for Julia known to his father, and
secondly in this final indication of a
divided mind: Julia and 'the Emperor's court' are rivals for his affection, as later Julia and Silvia will
be.

91. *it answers*] Tannenbaum, p. 8,
defends the F reading, taking 'it' as
genitive.

ACT II

SCENE I

Enter VALENTINE *and* SPEED.

Spe. Sir, your glove.
Val. Not mine: my gloves are on.
Spe. Why, then this may be yours; for this is but one.
Val. Ha! Let me see; ay, give it me, it's mine.
    Sweet ornament, that decks a thing divine!   5
    Ah, Silvia, Silvia!
Spe. Madam Silvia! Madam Silvia!
Val. How now, sirrah?
Spe. She is not within hearing, sir.
Val. Why, sir, who bade you call her?   10
Spe. Your worship, sir, or else I mistook.
Val. Well, you'll still be too forward.
Spe. And yet I was last chidden for being too slow.
Val. Go to, sir, tell me: do you know Madam Silvia?
Spe. She that your worship loves?   15
Val. Why, how know you that I am in love?
Spe. Marry, by these special marks: first, you have
    learned (like Sir Proteus) to wreathe your arms like a

ACT II

Scene 1

ACT II SCENE 1] *Rowe; Actus secundus: Scæna Prima F;* Act II. Scene 1. Scene *changes to* Milan *Pope.*   S.D. *Enter . . . Speed*] *Enter Valentine, Speed, Siluia F.*

1.] *NCS* assumes that Valentine drops the glove and Speed picks it up and offers it to him. But it seems more likely (cf. l. 2) that Valentine has not had the glove in his possession before; Parrott (*Shakespearean Comedy,* 1949, p. 117) assumes it was Silvia who dropped it as a love-token.

3. *one*] This is one of the 'at least

three times' when Shakespeare makes an *on/one* pun (Kökeritz, p. 232).

17. *these special marks*] such as Rosalind notes that Orlando has not: *AYL.,* III. ii. 388 ff. The difference is characteristic of the two plays.

18. *wreathe your arms*] Cf. *LLL.,* III. i. 182–3: 'Dan Cupid . . . lord of folded arms'; *Tit.,* III. ii. 5–7: 'Thy niece and

23

malcontent; to relish a love-song, like a robin-
redbreast; to walk alone, like one that had the pesti-   20
lence; to sigh, like a schoolboy that had lost his
ABC; to weep, like a young wench that had buried
her grandam; to fast, like one that takes diet; to
watch, like one that fears robbing; to speak puling,
like a beggar at Hallowmas. You were wont, when   25
you laughed, to crow like a cock; when you walked,
to walk like one of the lions; when you fasted, it was
presently after dinner; when you looked sadly, it was
for want of money. And now you are metamorphosed with a mistress, that when I look on you, I   30
can hardly think you my master.

Val. Are all these things perceived in me?

Spe. They are all perceived without ye.

Val. Without me? They cannot.

Spe. Without you? Nay, that's certain. For without you   35
were so simple, none else would. But you are so
without these follies that these follies are within you,
and shine through you like the water in an urinal;
that not an eye that sees you but is a physician to
comment on your malady.   40

---

20. had the] *F;* hath the *Collier ii.*   29. are] *F;* are so *Collier ii.*   33. ye] *F;*
you *Capell.*

I . . . want our hands, / And cannot
passionate our tenfold grief / With
folded arms.'

19. *relish*] sing (Onions), with the
sense of taking pleasure in it; cf. *Lucr.*,
1126: 'Relish your nimble notes to
pleasing ears'.

23. *takes diet*] follows a prescribed
dietary; cf. *Meas.*, II. i. 114–16: 'such a
one and such a one were past cure of
the thing you wot of, unless they kept
very good diet.'

24–5. *puling . . . Hallowmas*] Tollet
refers to a Staffordshire custom of
'begging and puling' for 'soul-cakes'
on All Saints' Day (Bond).

27. *walk . . . lions*] probably a reference to the lions in the Tower of London; they are referred to, with equal
oddity, in Webster's *White Devil*

(Revels edn), v. vi. 266–7: 'to be like
the lions i' th' Tower on Candlemas
day, to mourn if the sun shine'.

27–8. *when . . . dinner*] Cf. Tilley,
B289.

28. *presently*] immediately.

29–30. *metamorphosed*] Cf. I. i. 66.

34. *Without me?*] Valentine assumes
Speed (l. 33) means 'apart from ye'.

35. *Without . . . without*] playing on
the senses 'outside' and 'unless'.

36. *none else would*] i.e., 'none else
would be so simple' (Johnson), or
'none else would perceive them'
(Bond).

38. *urinal*] glass vessel for testing
urine; cf. *Wiv.*, III. i. 14, 91.

40. *malady*] Speed is in tune with
contemporary thought in regarding
love as a malady, and Proteus takes the

Val. But tell me: dost thou know my lady Silvia?

Spe. She that you gaze on so, as she sits at supper?

Val. Hast thou observed that? Even she I mean.

Spe. Why, sir, I know her not.

Val. Dost thou know her by my gazing on her, and yet   45
know'st her not?

Spe. Is she not hard-favoured, sir?

Val. Not so fair, boy, as well-favoured.

Spe. Sir, I know that well enough.

Val. What dost thou know?   50

Spe. That she is not so fair as, of you, well-favoured.

Val. I mean that her beauty is exquisite, but her favour
infinite.

Spe. That's because the one is painted, and the other out
of all count.   55

Val. How painted? And how out of count?

Spe. Marry, sir, so painted to make her fair that no man
counts of her beauty.

Val. How esteem'st thou me? I account of her beauty.

Spe. You never saw her since she was deformed.   60

Val. How long hath she been deformed?

Spe. Ever since you loved her.

Val. I have loved her ever since I saw her, and still I see
her beautiful.

---

43. observed] *Collier;* obseru'd *F.*   52–3.] *so Capell;* I . . . exquisite, / But . . .
infinite *F.*   63–4.] *so Capell;* I . . . her, / And . . . beautifull *F.*

---

same view in II. iv. 144, referring to the
time when he was 'sick'. See Lawrence A. Babb, *The Elizabethan Malady*,
1951, ch. VI, VII, for an account of the
contrasting Elizabethan attitudes to
love—as a sickness and as an ideal.

42–77.] an extended fantasia on the
love-sight theme.

43. *observed*] It seems likely that this
line is verse, Valentine fittingly using
it as he recalls his gazing on Silvia: the
elision in the F 'obseru'd' may therefore be an error, and we should take
'euen' as 'eu'n'. Harold Brooks has
noted that l. 41 is also an acceptable
verse-line, and that the explanation
just given hardly applies there. Never-

theless, it is in the present line that
verse-utterance becomes for a moment
fully perceptible.

47. *hard-favoured*] ugly.

48, 51. *well-favoured*] (1) gracious;
(2) beloved.

52. *favour*] good-will, kindness.

54–5. *out of all count*] (1) incalcul-
able; (2) inconsiderable.

57–8. *so . . . beauty*] By an odd shift
'painted' now refers to 'favour' (l. 52,
but now with the meaning 'face',
'appearance') and it is Silvia's
'beauty' that is not countable (contrast ll. 54–5).

58. *counts of*] makes account of,
appreciates; so 'account of', l. 59.

Spe. If you love her, you cannot see her.   65
Val. Why?
Spe. Because Love is blind. O that you had mine eyes, or
your own eyes had the lights they were wont to have,
when you chid at Sir Proteus, for going ungartered.
Val. What should I see then?   70
Spe. Your own present folly, and her passing deformity:
for he, being in love, could not see to garter his hose;
and you, being in love, cannot see to put on your
hose.
Val. Belike, boy, then you are in love, for last morning   75
you could not see to wipe my shoes.
Spe. True, sir: I was in love with my bed. I thank you, you
swinged me for my love, which makes me the bolder
to chide you for yours.
Val. In conclusion, I stand affected to her.   80
Spe. I would you were set, so your affection would cease.

73–4. put on your hose] *F*; beyond your nose *or* put spectacles on your nose *or* put
on your shoes *conj. Camb*; put on your clothes *conj. Keightley*; button your shoes
conj. Daniel.   75–6.] *so Rowe*; Belike...morning / You...shooes *F*.   81. set,]
F; set; *Malone*.

65.] Cf. Elyot, *The Gouernour*, ed.
Foster-Watson, p. 189: 'For as Plu-
tarche saieth what so euer he be that
loueth, he doteth and is blynde in that
thinge whiche he dothe loue.'
    67–8. *Because . . . wont to have*] Cf.
Sonnet 137: 'Thou blind fool, Love,
what dost thou to mine eyes, / That
they behold, and see not what they
see', and Sonnet 148: 'O me, what
eyes hath Love put in my head, /
Which have no correspondence with
true sight!'
    67. *Love is blind*] Cf. Tilley, L506;
the proverb appears again at II. iv.
91.
    69. *going ungartered*] Cf. *AYL.*, III. ii.
397–8: 'your hose should be ungar-
tered' (in a list of signs belonging to a
lover).
    72–4. *for he . . . hose*] In Sonnet 113,
love leaves the poet no eyes for his
ordinary affairs: 'Since I left you,

mine eye is in my mind; / And that
which governs me to go about / Doth
part his function and is partly blind, /
Seems seeing, but effectually is out.'
    73–4. *put . . . hose*] The F reading
seems more acceptable than any conjecture: as Bond points out, Speed
does not imply the absence of Valentine's hose but merely their being in
some disarray.
    78. *swinged*] beat.
    80. *affected to*] in love with; cf. *Ven.*,
157: 'Is thine own heart to thine own
face affected?'
    81. *set*] Valentine has said he 'stands
affected': Speed deduces that his
affection would cease if he were seated
(Mason). The same pun appears at
IV. i. 3–4. Other meanings suggested
for 'set' here are 'set (as of the sun)', by
Malone, and 'put down', by Halliwell;
but Mason's interpretation seems
wholly sufficient.

Val. Last night she enjoined me to write some lines to one
    she loves.
Spe. And have you?
Val. I have.   85
Spe. Are they not lamely writ?
Val. No, boy, but as well as I can do them.

               [*Enter* SILVIA.]

    Peace, here she comes.
Spe. [*Aside*] O excellent motion! O exceeding puppet!
    Now will he interpret to her.   90
Val. Madam and mistress, a thousand good-morrows.
Spe. [*Aside*] O, 'give-ye-good-ev'n! Here's a million of
    manners.
Sil. Sir Valentine, and servant, to you two thousand.
Spe. [*Aside*] He should give her interest; and she gives it   95
    him.
Val. As you enjoin'd me, I have writ your letter
    Unto the secret, nameless friend of yours.
    Which I was much unwilling to proceed in,
    But for my duty to your ladyship. [*Gives her a letter.*]   100
Sil. I thank you, gentle servant. 'Tis very clerkly done.

82–3.] *so Pope;* Last . . . me, / To . . . loues *F.*   87. S.D.] *Rowe (after l. 90).*   89,
92, 95. *Aside*] *Capell.*   89–90.] *so Theobald;* Oh . . . Puppet: / Now . . . her *F.*

89–90. *motion . . . to her*] A 'motion'
was a puppet-show. Speed means that
Silvia is a puppet because she has not
been able to speak of her love for
Valentine but has had to employ him
as an 'interpreter': 'to her' means here
'for her', 'on her behalf'. Some commentators (e.g., Hawkins, Staunton)
take 'motion' here to mean 'puppet':
though it can have that meaning, the
speech will run better if we have suc-
cessive references to the puppet-show,
the puppet, and the interpreter. And
it is quite unnecessary to explain the
use of 'puppet' by reference to Silvia's
low stature (Staunton) or her 'fine
dress' (Bond). On the passage as a
whole, cf. *Ham.*, III. ii. 256–7: 'I could

interpret between you and your love,
if I could see the puppets dallying.'
Cf. also Nashe, *Pierce Penilesse* (1592):
'like . . . one's voyce that interprets to
the puppets' (Bond).
    91–4.] For this lavishing of good-
morrows, which Speed mocks, cf. IV.
iii. 6–7 (in which Silvia is again concerned) and *Rom.*, II. ii. 155.
    94. *servant*] 'payer of authorized
attentions, not pledging the lady'
(Bond). Cf. II. iv. 1.
    95. *He . . . interest*] perhaps because
Silvia is about to reveal her love for
Valentine.
    101. *clerkly*] like a scholar. E. I.
Fripp, *Shakespeare Man and Artist*, 1938,
i. 286, notes that the phrase 'clerkly

Val. Now trust me, madam, it came hardly off.
For being ignorant to whom it goes,
I writ at random, very doubtfully.

Sil. Perchance you think too much of so much pains?   105

Val. No, madam; so it stead you, I will write
(Please you command) a thousand times as much.
And yet—

Sil. A pretty period. Well, I guess the sequel;
And yet I will not name it; and yet I care not.   110
And yet take this again; and yet I thank you,
Meaning henceforth to trouble you no more.

Spe. [*Aside*] And yet you will; and yet another 'yet'.

Val. What means your ladyship? Do you not like it?

Sil. Yes, yes; the lines are very quaintly writ,   115
But (since unwillingly) take them again.
Nay, take them.

Val. Madam, they are for you.

Sil. Ay, ay. You writ them, sir, at my request,
But I will none of them: they are for you.   120
I would have had them writ more movingly.

Val. [*taking the letter*] Please you, I'll write your ladyship
another.

Sil. And when it's writ, for my sake read it over,
And if it please you, so; if not, why, so.

Val. If it please me, madam? What then?   125

Sil. Why, if it please you, take it for your labour;
And so good-morrow, servant.   *Exit.*

---

106. stead] *Capell;* steed *F.*   110. and yet] *F;* yet *Pope.*   113. *Aside*] *Rowe.*
yet another 'yet'] *Capell;* yet, another yet *F;* yet—another yet *Staunton.*   114.]
so Pope; What . . . Ladiship? / Doe . . . it *F.*   117. them] *F;* them again
Keightley.   118. for] *F;* writ for *conj. anon (ap. Camb).*   124. not, why, so.]
Capell; not: why so: *F;* not, why so. *F2.*   127. S.D.] *F (Exit. Sil.).*

---

done' appears in Puttenham's *Arte of
English Poesie* (1589), ch. VI (ed. G. D.
Willcock and A. Walker, p. 11).

102. *came hardly off*] was written with
difficulty; cf. *Tim.*, I. i. 29 (of a paint-
ing): 'this comes off well and excellent'
(Steevens).

106. *stead*] be of use to

109. *period*] pause as at the end of a

sentence: Silvia pretends to think that
Valentine does after all repine at the
labour.

sequel] what Valentine was going to
say after 'And yet—'.

113. *and . . . 'yet'*] Speed means that
Silvia will add a further item in her
series of antitheses.

115. *quaintly*] skilfully; cf. III. i. 117.

Spe. O jest unseen, inscrutable, invisible,
　　As a nose on a man's face, or a weathercock on a steeple!
　　My master sues to her; and she hath taught her suitor,
　　He being her pupil, to become her tutor.　　131
　　O excellent device, was there ever heard a better?
　　That my master being scribe, to himself should write
　　　　the letter?
Val. How now, sir? What are you reasoning with your-
　　self?　　135
Spe. Nay, I was rhyming; 'tis you that have the reason.
Val. To do what?
Spe. To be a spokesman from Madam Silvia.
Val. To whom?
Spe. To yourself. Why, she woos you by a figure.　　140
Val. What figure?
Spe. By a letter, I should say.
Val. Why, she hath not writ to me.
Spe. What need she, when she hath made you write to
　　yourself? Why, do you not perceive the jest?　　145
Val. No, believe me.
Spe. No believing you indeed, sir. But did you perceive
　　her earnest?
Val. She gave me none, except an angry word.
Spe. Why, she hath given you a letter.　　150
Val. That's the letter I writ to her friend.
Spe. And that letter hath she delivered, and there an end.
Val. I would it were no worse.
Spe. I'll warrant you, 'tis as well.
　　For often have you writ to her, and she in modesty,　　155

128–9.] *so F; as prose Pope.*　　133.] *so Pope;* That . . . scribe, / To . . . Letter *F.*
scribe] *F;* the scribe *Pope.*　　134–5.] *so Pope;* How . . . Sir? / What . . . selfe *F.*
143. me.] *Capell;* me? *F.*　　144–5.] *so Capell;* What . . . she, / When . . . selfe? /
Why . . . iest *F.*　　147–8.] *so Pope;* No . . . sir: / But . . . earnest *F.*

128–9. *invisible . . . face*] Cf. Tilley,
N215.
　　128–33.] For Speed's doggerel, or
'tumbling', verse, see I. i. 130–3n.
Bond points out that this kind of writing appears also in *LLL.*, *Err.*, and *Shr.*
　　134. *reasoning*] talking. In his reply
Speed characteristically shifts the
meaning to the commoner one: for the

rhyme–reason opposition, cf. Tilley,
R99.
　　140. *figure*] device (normally a rhetorical one). In l. 142 Speed shifts the
meaning to 'number'.
　　148. *her earnest*] (1) her to be serious;
(2) her initial payment to validate a
contract.
　　155–9.] Cf. ll. 128–33. Bond points

Or else for want of idle time, could not again reply,
Or fearing else some messenger, that might her mind
    discover,
Herself hath taught her love himself to write unto
    her lover.
All this I speak in print, for in print I found it.
Why muse you, sir? 'Tis dinner time.   160

Val. I have dined.

Spe. Ay, but hearken, sir: though the chameleon Love
    can feed on the air, I am one that am nourished by
    my victuals; and would fain have meat. O, be not
    like your mistress, be moved, be moved.   *Exeunt.*   165

SCENE II

Enter PROTEUS *and* JULIA.

Pro. Have patience, gentle Julia.
Jul. I must where is no remedy.
Pro. When possibly I can, I will return.
Jul. If you turn not, you will return the sooner;

159–60.] *so F; as prose Camb.*

SCENE II] *Rowe; Scœna secunda F;* Scene II. *Changes to* Verona *Pope.*   S.D. *Enter
. . . Julia*] *Enter Protheus, Iulia, Panthion F.*

out, however, that on this occasion Speed is using regular fourteeners.

156. *want*] lack.

157. *discover*] reveal.

159. *in print*] (1) with exactness (cf. Tilley, M239); (2) in a printed book, etc. The second meaning could suggest that the preceding lines were a quotation.

161. *I have dined*] Bond quotes *Euphues* (ed. Bond, i. 201): 'they all sate downe, but *Euphues* fed of one dish which euer stoode before him, the beautie of *Lucilla*.' In *Damon and Pithias* (M.S.R., 435–62), Stephano, the servant of the two friends, complains like Speed that his masters'

higher preoccupations do not take away his own hunger. See Introduction, p. xxxviii.

162–3. *chameleon . . . air*] The chameleon's nourishing itself on air is frequently referred to (e.g., in *Ham.*, III. ii. 98–9); that love shares this property is mentioned in Lyly's *Endimion*, III. iv. 129: 'Love is a Camelion which draweth nothing into the mouth but air' (Bond). Cf. Tilley, M226, and in this play II. iv. 24–6.

Scene II

1–2.] Cf. Tilley, C922, P111.

4. *turn*] change, prove unfaithful (Rann). Julia, too, can quibble.

Keep this remembrance for thy Julia's sake.   5

[She gives Proteus a ring.]

Pro. Why then we'll make exchange; here, take you this.

[He gives Julia a ring.]

Jul. And seal the bargain with a holy kiss.

Pro. Here is my hand, for my true constancy.
And when that hour o'erslips me in the day
Wherein I sigh not, Julia, for thy sake,   10
The next ensuing hour some foul mischance
Torment me for my love's forgetfulness.
My father stays my coming. Answer not.
The tide is now; nay, not thy tide of tears,
That tide will stay me longer than I should.   15
Julia, farewell.   *[Exit JULIA.]*
          What, gone without a word?
Ay, so true love should do: it cannot speak,
For truth hath better deeds than words to grace it.

[Enter PANTHINO.]

Pan. Sir Proteus, you are stay'd for.

Pro.   Go; I come, I come.
Alas, this parting strikes poor lovers dumb.   *Exeunt.*   20

---

5. S.D.] *Rowe (subst.).*   6.] *so Pope;* Why . . . exchange; / Here . . . this *F.*
6. S.D.] *Sargent (subst.).*   16. S.D.] *Rowe (at l. 15).*   18. S.D.] *Rowe.*
19. I come, I come] *F;* I come *Pope.*

7.] Cf. *Rom.*, v. iii. 114–15: 'seal with a righteous kiss / A dateless bargain' (Fleay); *Tw.N.*, v. i. 159–62: 'A contract of eternal bond of love, / Confirm'd by mutual joinder of your hands, / Attested by the holy close of lips, / Strengthen'd by interchangement of your rings'. Shakespeare gives a deliberately vague impression of a formal betrothal between Julia and Proteus, the legally necessary witness being absent.

14. *tide . . . tide of tears*] Cf. Launce's punning on 'tide' and 'tied' in the next scene, II. iii. 37 ff. The echo can hardly be accidental. See Introduction, p. lxi.

16–18.] Cf. Tilley, L165; also

Romeus, ll. 1535–6: 'Thus muet stoode they both, the eight part of an howre, / And both would speake, but neither had of speaking any powre.'

18.] The dramatic irony here may echo a passage in *Diana* where Don Felix's infidelity is made plain. He reads to his supposed page the letter from Celia which refers to his former love for Felismena. He asks ' "What thinkest thou *Valerius* of these words?" ' and receives the answer 'That your deedes are shewed by them' (Kennedy, p. 96). Cf. Sonnet 69: 'By seeing farther than the eye hath shown. / They look into the beauty of thy mind, / And that, in guess, they measure by thy deeds.'

SCENE III

Enter LAUNCE [*with his dog Crab*].

Lau. Nay, 'twill be this hour ere I have done weeping. All
the kind of the Launces have this very fault. I have
received my proportion, like the prodigious son, and
am going with Sir Proteus to the Imperial's court. I
think Crab my dog be the sourest-natured dog that   5
lives: my mother weeping; my father wailing; my
sister crying; our maid howling; our cat wringing
her hands, and all our house in a great perplexity;
yet did not this cruel-hearted cur shed one tear. He is
a stone, a very pebble stone, and has no more pity in   10
him than a dog. A Jew would have wept to have seen
our parting. Why, my grandam, having no eyes, look
you, wept herself blind at my parting. Nay, I'll show
you the manner of it. This shoe is my father. No, this
left shoe is my father; no, no, this left shoe is my   15
mother; nay, that cannot be so neither. Yes, it is so, it
is so: it hath the worser sole. This shoe with the hole
in it is my mother; and this my father. A vengeance
on't, there 'tis. Now, sir, this staff is my sister; for, look
you, she is as white as a lily, and as small as a wand.   20

Scene III

SCENE III] *Rowe; Scœna Tertia* F.   S.D. *Enter . . . Crab] Pope; Enter Launce
Panthion* F; *Enter Launce leading a dog   Theobald.*

S.D.] Crab (from crab-apple)
means a sour person; cf. *Shr.*, II. i. 229–
30: '*Pet.* . . . you must not look so sour.
Kath. It is my fashion, when I see a
crab.'

2. *kind*] family; cf. *Per.*, v. i. 67–8:
'She . . . Came of a gentle kind and
noble stock'.

3. *proportion, prodigious*] Launce-
language for 'portion', 'prodigal'.

4. *Imperial's court*] See Introduction,
p. xvi. In Beaumont and Fletcher,
Knight of the Burning Pestle, II. ii, the
Citizen's Wife uses the form 'Emperall'.

11–12. *A Jew . . . parting*] This seems
to strengthen the link with *Mer.V.* and

Launcelot Gobbo. See Introduction,
p. lxxi.

14 ff.] Steevens pointed out a resemblance between this passage and one
in Daborne's *A Christian turn'd Turke*
(publ. 1612): 'you shall stand for the
Lady, you for her dogge, and I the
Page: you and that dogge looking one
vpon another, the Page presents himselfe' (sig. G3). The resemblance, however, is probably fortuitous.

17–18. *worser . . . mother*] Launce's
obscenity here is noted by Eric Partridge, *Shakespeare's Bawdy*, 1955,
p. 129.

20. *as white . . . wand*] Cf. Tilley,

This hat is Nan our maid. I am the dog. No, the dog
is himself, and I am the dog. O, the dog is me, and I
am myself. Ay; so, so. Now come I to my father:
'Father, your blessing.' Now should not the shoe
speak a word for weeping; now should I kiss my   25
father; well, he weeps on; now come I to my mother.
O that she could speak now, like a wood woman!
Well, I kiss her. Why, there 'tis: here's my mother's
breath up and down. Now come I to my sister: mark
the moan she makes. Now the dog all this while sheds   30
not a tear; nor speaks a word; but see how I lay the
dust with my tears.

[*Enter* PANTHINO.]

Pan. Launce, away, away; aboard; thy master is
shipped, and thou art to post after with oars. What's
the matter? Why weep'st thou, man? Away, ass,   35
you'll lose the tide, if you tarry any longer.

27. O . . . now,] *F*; Oh . . . now! *conj. Steevens;* O that the shoe could speak now,
Hanmer, conj. Blackstone; (O . . . now!) *Malone, conj. Blackstone;* O . . . more
Sisson.   a wood woman] *Theobald;* a would-woman *F;* an old (ould) woman
Pope; a wold woman *conj. Capell;* a wild woman *Collier (MS.).*   32. S.D.]
Rowe.

L296 and W23; *small* = slender.
Launce here uses language appropriate to the description of a romance
heroine.

21-3. *I am . . . myself*] On the
clown who 'sometimes confuses himself in an impersonated dialogue', see
L. Borinski, 'Shakespeare's Comic
Prose', *Shakespeare Survey* 8, p. 63:
he quotes III. i. 264-71 below after
citing the present episode to exemplify
the 'impersonation of a dramatic
scene'.

27. *a wood woman*] Theobald's 'wood'
(= mad, wild) has been objected to on
the ground that the -l- of 'would' was
pronounced in Shakespeare's day and
therefore a printer's confusion of the
two words was unlikely; but Jonson
rhymes 'would' and 'good', and there
is other evidence that the -l- was not

always pronounced (Kökeritz, p. 311
and n.). Capell's 'wold' indicates a
woman wild as the wold itself, a
countrywoman.

28-9. *my mother's . . . down*] Launce is
holding the shoe close to his face, and
thus perceives the 'breath'. This passage is more vulgar than is suggested
by Sisson, i. 54-5, who finds the
'breath' in the squeaking sound of the
shoe. *up and down* = exactly.

29-30. *mark . . . makes*] *NCS* suggests
Launce swishes the staff through the
air.

31-2. *see . . . tears*] Cf. *Lr.*, IV. vi.199-
201: 'this would make a man a man of
salt, / To use his eyes for . . . laying
autumn's dust.'

36. *you'll . . . tarry*] Cf. Tilley, T323.
tide] Cf. 'river', l. 51. But the river at
Verona is not tidal (*NCS*).

Lau. It is no matter if the tied were lost, for it is the unkindest tied that ever any man tied.

Pan. What's the unkindest tide?

Lau. Why, he that's tied here, Crab my dog.   40

Pan. Tut, man. I mean thou'lt lose the flood, and in losing
the flood, lose thy voyage, and in losing thy voyage,
lose thy master, and in losing thy master, lose thy service, and in losing thy service—why dost thou stop
my mouth?   45

Lau. For fear thou shouldst lose thy tongue.

Pan. Where should I lose my tongue?

Lau. In thy tale.

Pan. In my tail?

Lau. Lose the tide, and the voyage, and the master, and   50
the service, and the tied? Why, man, if the river
were dry, I am able to fill it with my tears; if the
wind were down, I could drive the boat with my
sighs.

Pan. Come; come away, man, I was sent to call thee.   55

Lau. Sir, call me what thou dar'st.

Pan. Wilt thou go?

Lau. Well, I will go.   *Exeunt.*

37–8. tied ... tied that] *Theobald;* tide ... Tide, that *F.*   49. my tail?] *Hanmer;*
thy Taile. *F;* thy tail?— *Theobald;* thy Tail! *Camb;* thy tail! [*kicking him*] *conj.*
anon (*ap. Camb*).   50. tide] *F;* flood *Pope;* tied *Collier.*   51. and the tied?]
Singer; and the tide: *F;* om. *Capell;* The Tide! *conj. Steevens* (*ap. Malone ii*);
indeed! *conj. S. Verges* (*ap. Camb*).

37. *the tied*] Steevens pointed out that
the pun on 'tide' and 'tied' was found
in Lyly's *Endimion,* iv. ii. 9–11; Bond
noted it also in Munday's *Two Italian
Gentlemen,* iv. vi.

47–9. *my tongue ... my tail?*] Bond
compares *Shr.,* ii. i. 214–19: '*Pet.* Who
knows not where a wasp does wear his

sting? In his tail. *Kath.* In his tongue.
Pet. Whose tongue? *Kath.* Yours, if you
talk of tails: and so farewell. *Pet.* What,
with my tongue in your tail?' This
comes shortly before the passage in
which Katharina talks of seeing a
'crab' (see note on opening S.D.,
above).

SCENE IV

Enter VALENTINE, SILVIA, THURIO *and* SPEED.

Sil. Servant,—
Val. Mistress?
Spe. Master, Sir Thurio frowns on you.
Val. Ay, boy, it's for love.
Spe. Not of you.   5
Val. Of my mistress, then.
Spe. 'Twere good you knocked him.
Sil. Servant, you are sad.
Val. Indeed, madam, I seem so.
Thu. Seem you that you are not?   10
Val. Haply I do.
Thu. So do counterfeits.
Val. So do you.
Thu. What seem I that I am not?
Val. Wise.   15
Thu. What instance of the contrary?
Val. Your folly.
Thu. And how quote you my folly?
Val. I quote it in your jerkin.
Thu. My jerkin is a doublet.   20
Val. Well, then, I'll double your folly.
Thu. How!
Sil. What, angry, Sir Thurio? Do you change colour?

Scene IV

SCENE IV] *Rowe; Scena Quarta F; Scene* IV. *Changes to* Milan *Pope.*   S.D. *Enter
. . . Speed] Enter Valentine, Siluia, Thurio, Speed, Duke, Protheus F.*   1. Servant,—]
Theobald; Seruant. F.   2. Mistress?] *Theobald;* Mistris. *F.*   7. him.] *F;*
him. [*Exit. Camb.*   21. I'll] *F;* 'twill *Collier (MS.).*   22. How!] How? *F.*

7. *knocked*] struck.
7.] Camb. editors send Speed off the
stage here, as he does not speak again
in the scene and 'the clown' would not
be kept as 'a mute bystander'. But
Speed is a page, not a clown.
18, 19. *quote*] a homophone of 'coat'
(Kökeritz, p. 99); the sense is 'observe'.
20. *jerkin . . . doublet*] The jerkin was

a long jacket worn over, or instead of,
the doublet.
21. *double*] Bond finds the pun also in
Jonson's *Cynthia's Revels,* III. v. 96–7.
22. *How!*] F's question-mark may
represent an exclamation, which seems
more appropriate here. Thurio is not
making an inquiry.
23–6. *Do . . . air*] Cf. Tilley, C222,
M226; and above, II. i. 162–3. One of

Val. Give him leave, madam, he is a kind of chameleon.

Thu. That hath more mind to feed on your blood than   25
live in your air.

Val. You have said, sir.

Thu. Ay, sir, and done too for this time.

Val. I know it well, sir, you always end ere you begin.

Sil. A fine volley of words, gentlemen, and quickly shot   30
off.

Val. 'Tis indeed, madam: we thank the giver.

Sil. Who is that, servant?

Val. Yourself, sweet lady, for you gave the fire. Sir Thurio
borrows his wit from your ladyship's looks, and   35
spends what he borrows kindly in your company.

Thu. Sir, if you spend word for word with me, I shall
make your wit bankrupt.

Val. I know it well, sir. You have an exchequer of words,
and I think no other treasure to give your followers;   40
for it appears by their bare liveries that they live by
your bare words.

Sil. No more, gentlemen, no more. Here comes my father.

[*Enter* Duke.]

Duke. Now, daughter Silvia, you are hard beset.
Sir Valentine, your father is in good health.   45
What say you to a letter from your friends
Of much good news?

Val.   My lord, I will be thankful

34–6.] *so Pope;* Your . . . fire, / Sir . . . lookes, / And . . . company *F.*   39–42.] *so
Pope;* I . . . words, / And . . . followers: / For . . . Liueries / That . . . words *F.*
43.] *so Pope;* No . . . more: / Here . . . father *F.*   S.D.] *Rowe; Enter Duke,
attended Capell.*

Tilley's examples is from *3H6,* III. ii.
191: 'I can add colours to the chameleon.'

27–8.] Cf. Tilley, S117.

32. *giver*] *NCS* equates this with
'direction-giver' (III. ii. 89), one who
directs an archer's aim; but it is
simpler here to take it as giver of 'the
fire' (l. 34): Valentine is being ingenious, and Silvia has to ask (l. 33) for an

explanation, which laboriously follows,

34–42.] Thurio is first charged with
abuse of his lady's largesse and then
with niggardliness. The two charges
are combined in Sonnet 4: 'niggard,
why dost thou abuse / The bounteous
largess given thee to give?'

36. *kindly*] naturally.

40–2.] See Introduction, p. xviii.

44. *hard beset*] hotly besieged.

To any happy messenger from thence.

Duke. Know ye Don Antonio, your countryman?

Val. Ay, my good lord, I know the gentleman   50
    To be of worth, and worthy estimation,
    And not without desert so well reputed.

Duke. Hath he not a son?

Val. Ay, my good lord, a son that well deserves
    The honour and regard of such a father.   55

Duke. You know him well?

Val. I knew him as myself; for from our infancy
    We have convers'd, and spent our hours together,
    And though myself have been an idle truant,
    Omitting the sweet benefit of time   60
    To clothe mine age with angel-like perfection,
    Yet hath Sir Proteus (for that's his name)
    Made use and fair advantage of his days:
    His years but young, but his experience old;
    His head unmellow'd, but his judgment ripe;   65
    And in a word (for far behind his worth
    Comes all the praises that I now bestow)
    He is complete in feature and in mind,

---

49. ye] *F;* you *F2.*   51. worth] *F;* wealth *Collier ii, conj. W. S. Walker.*   57. knew] *F;* know *Hanmer.*   67. Comes] *F;* Come *Rowe.*

48. *happy messenger*] 'bearer of good news' (Bond); but perhaps Valentine implies that anyone from 'home' is 'happy' from having recently been there.

49. *Don Antonio*] Cf. I. iii. 39n.

51. *worth*] 'wealth', Collier's emendation (by his 'corrector'), may perhaps be justified, but the half-pun, half-redundancy, of 'worth' and 'worthy' is characteristic of this play.

57. *knew*] Hanmer's emendation 'know' is unnecessary and blunting: Valentine at the moment feels that he is now living a new life.

58. *convers'd*] associated with one another.

60. *Omitting*] letting slip (Bond).

61. *mine age*] i.e., when that time comes.

62-9.] Education, discussed in I. i, is appropriately dwelt on here in preparing for the entry of Proteus, who has yet to learn much about love and friendship. Harold Jenkins in *The Rice Institute Pamphlet*, January 1959, p. 21, urges that the play 'sets out to teach him the value of constancy'. There is dramatic irony in Valentine's belief that Proteus is already the complete gentleman, a belief that leads to his imprudent confidences at ll. 175 ff. below.

63. *Made use*] employed to good effect, with a suggestion of drawing interest.

67. *Comes*] the singular form of the verb preceding a plural subject, as found occasionally (cf. Franz, p. 566).

68. *feature*] general personal appearance.

With all good grace to grace a gentleman.
Duke. Beshrew me, sir, but if he make this good   70
 He is as worthy for an empress' love
 As meet to be an emperor's counsellor.
 Well, sir; this gentleman is come to me
 With commendation from great potentates,
 And here he means to spend his time awhile: 75
 I think 'tis no unwelcome news to you.
Val. Should I have wish'd a thing, it had been he.
Duke. Welcome him then according to his worth.
 Silvia, I speak to you, and you, Sir Thurio;
 For Valentine, I need not cite him to it.   80
 I will send him hither to you presently.   *[Exit.]*
Val. This is the gentleman I told your ladyship
 Had come along with me, but that his mistress
 Did hold his eyes lock'd in her crystal looks.
Sil. Belike that now she hath enfranchis'd them   85
 Upon some other pawn for fealty.
Val. Nay, sure, I think she holds them prisoners still.
Sil. Nay, then he should be blind, and being blind
 How could he see his way to seek out you?
Val. Why, lady, Love hath twenty pair of eyes.   90
Thu. They say that Love hath not an eye at all.
Val. To see such lovers, Thurio, as yourself:
 Upon a homely object, Love can wink.

[Enter PROTEUS.]

Sil. Have done, have done: here comes the gentleman.

80. cite] *F*; 'cite *Malone.*   81. S.D.] *Rowe.*   91. all.] *F*; all— *Staunton.*
93. S.D.] *F2; Enter Proteus. Exit Thurio Collier (the 'Exit' at l. 94).*

71–2. *empress' love . . . emperor's coun-*
sellor] Cf. Introduction, p. xvi.
 74. *commendation . . . potentates*] As we
have hitherto had the impression that
Proteus was following Valentine
directly to 'the Emperor's court', it is
obscure that 'great potentates' had
been laid under contribution by 'Don'
Antonio. See Introduction, p. xviii.
 80. *cite*] The F reading can make
good sense ('summon'); Malone's

"cite' ('incite') is a possibility.
 83. *Had come*] would have come.
 85. *enfranchis'd*] set free.
 88–93.] once more the love–sight
theme.
 93. *homely*] plain, unlovely.
 wink] Cf. i. ii. 139.
 93. S.D.] Collier and Camb insert
an exit for Thurio, as F makes him
speak the message from the Duke at
l. 111.

Val. Welcome, dear Proteus. Mistress, I beseech you   95
    Confirm his welcome, with some special favour.
Sil. His worth is warrant for his welcome hither,
    If this be he you oft have wish'd to hear from.
Val. Mistress, it is; sweet lady, entertain him
    To be my fellow-servant to your ladyship.   100
Sil. Too low a mistress for so high a servant.
Pro. Not so, sweet lady, but too mean a servant
    To have a look of such a worthy mistress.
Val. Leave off discourse of disability.
    Sweet lady, entertain him for your servant.   105
Pro. My duty will I boast of, nothing else.
Sil. And duty never yet did want his meed.
    Servant, you are welcome to a worthless mistress.
Pro. I'll die on him that says so but yourself.
Sil. That you are welcome?
Pro.   That you are worthless.   110

[*Enter a* Servant.]

Ser. Madam, my lord your father would speak with you.
Sil. I wait upon his pleasure. Come, Sir Thurio,
    Go with me. Once more, new servant, welcome;
    I'll leave you to confer of home affairs.
    When you have done, we look to hear from you.   115

---

110. welcome] *F;* welcome, sir *Capell.*   That . . . worthless] *F;* No, that . . .
worthless *Johnson.*   S.D.] *Theobald; Re-enter Thurio Collier.*   111. *Ser.*]
Theobald; Thur. F.   112. pleasure.] *F;* pleasure. *Exit Servant. Theobald.*
113. Go] *F;* Go you *Capell;* Come, go *Keightley.*   new servant] *F;* my new
servant *Pope.*

99. *entertain*] take into your service.
103. *of*] from.
109. *die on*] die in fight with; Bond,
following Marshall, quotes *Look About
You*: 'I'll die upon the slanderer'.
110. *welcome? . . . worthless*] Capell
and Johnson suggest additions in
order to make the line metrically complete. Malone, however, suggested
that 'worthless' was trisyllabic. Kökeritz, p. 292, warns us that the pheno-
menon of anaptyxis is rare in Shakespeare. In any event, a line shared

between two speakers is frequently
Irregular.
S.D.] It seems most convenient to
accept Theobald's S.D. Thurio could
speak l. 111, as F indicates, but that
necessitates a very poor exit for him
shortly before (see l. 93n.). Collier's
objection, that Shakespeare would not
use a Servant here because his company could not afford to have an actor
for so small a part, is of course absurd:
the Servant could be the Host or an
outlaw in addition.

Pro. We'll both attend upon your ladyship.

          [*Exeunt* SILVIA, THURIO, SPEED *and* Servant.]

Val. Now tell me: how do all from whence you came?

Pro. Your friends are well, and have them much commended.

Val. And how do yours?

Pro.   I left them all in health.

Val. How does your lady? And how thrives your love?   120

Pro. My tales of love were wont to weary you:

      I know you joy not in a love-discourse.

Val. Ay, Proteus, but that life is alter'd now:

      I have done penance for contemning Love,

      Whose high imperious thoughts have punish'd me   125

      With bitter fasts, with penitential groans,

      With nightly tears, and daily heart-sore sighs,

      For in revenge of my contempt of Love,

      Love hath chas'd sleep from my enthralled eyes,

      And made them watchers of mine own heart's sorrow.

      O gentle Proteus, Love's a mighty lord,   131

      And hath so humbled me, as I confess

      There is no woe to his correction,

---

116. S.D.] *Capell (subst.); Exit Silvia and Thurio Rowe; Exeunt Silvia, Thurio, and Speed Malone.*   125. Whose] *F; Those conj. Johnson.*

116. S.D.] It seems best to give Speed an exit here (following Capell and Malone). See note on l. 7. Though it is not satisfactory to have him go off with Silvia and Thurio—it is possible, but slightly desperate, to assume an eloquent look from Valentine telling him to do so—it yet seems unthinkable to follow Dyce in keeping him on the stage, and silent, throughout the following dialogue between Proteus and Valentine.

118. *have . . . commended*] have sent their warm remembrances; a similar reflexive use is in *Mer.V.*, III. ii. 234–5: 'Signor Antonio / Commends him to you.'

125. *Whose . . . thoughts*] Johnson's conjecture 'Those' has been effectively disposed of by the evidence of Malone and Bond that 'imperious' was a frequent epithet for 'love'; Malone also

noted the relation of 'imperious' to 'Love's a mighty lord' (l. 131). Staunton, followed by *NCS*, wondered whether 'thoughts' needed emending, but the *NCS* suggestion 'thonges' does not seem happy.

129. *enthralled*] enslaved. E. I. Fripp, *Shakespeare Man and Artist*, 1938, i. 287, related ll. 129–30 to Sonnets 27, 28, and 43.

131. *Love's a mighty lord*] Cf. *Romeus*, l. 1432: 'Love is thy Lord, thou oughtst obay and not thy prince accuse.'

132. *humbled*] *O.E.D.* gives this as the first use of the word in this sense ('to render humble'). It is found also at I. ii. 59.

as] that.

133, 134. *to*] in comparison with; Malone quotes Sharpham's *Cupid's Whirligig* (1616): 'There is no comfort

Nor, to his service, no such joy on earth.
Now, no discourse, except it be of love;   135
Now can I break my fast, dine, sup, and sleep
Upon the very naked name of Love.

Pro. Enough: I read your fortune in your eye.
Was this the idol that you worship so?

Val. Even she; and is she not a heavenly saint?   140

Pro. No; but she is an earthly paragon.

Val. Call her divine.

Pro.   I will not flatter her.

Val. O flatter me; for love delights in praises.

Pro. When I was sick, you gave me bitter pills,
And I must minister the like to you.   145

Val. Then speak the truth by her: if not divine,
Yet let her be a principality,
Sovereign to all the creatures on the earth.

Pro. Except my mistress.

Val.   Sweet, except not any,

in the world / To women that are kind.'

139. *idol . . . so*] In *Euphues* (ed. Arber, p. 113) the 'cooling Carde for . . . all fond louers' censures 'the idolatrous worshypping of their Ladyes'. Cf. Sonnet 105: 'Let not my love be call'd idolatry, / Nor my beloved as an idol show.'

140–1. *heavenly . . . paragon*] Malone quotes *Cym.*, III. vi. 43–4: 'By Jupiter, an angel! or, if not, / An earthly paragon!' In *The Gouernour*, Titus falls in love with Gisippus' betrothed because he sees in her 'so heavenly a personage', and in *Diana* Silvia's counterpart is called Celia. The tradition of the lady as the 'corseynt' can be traced as far back as the *Lancelot* of Chrétien de Troyes (see C. S. Lewis, *The Allegory of Love*, 1936, p. 29). Sonnet 21 criticizes the conventional hyperbole: 'So is it not with me as with that Muse / . . . Who heaven itself for ornament doth use / . . . O, let me, true in love, but truly write.'

144.] See II. i. 40n. for the attitude to love. Bond suggests a reminiscence here, and in Valentine's preceding speech, of the scene in *Euphues and his England* where, after Euphues has recanted, Philautus rebukes him for his former attacks on love. Harold Brooks points out that the 'cooling Carde' in *Euphues* (ed. Arber, p. 114) may have provided a hint: 'foolish and franticke louers, will deeme my precepts hard, . . . Sowre potions bring sounde health . . . and the medicine the more bitter it is, the more better it is in working.'

147. *principality*] a spiritual being, belonging to one of the nine orders of angels (the eighth according to Reginald Scot, *Discouerie of Witchcraft*, 1584, p. 500; the seventh according to Dante): this particular order is obviously chosen for the sake of the link with 'Sovereign' in l. 148.

149. *Sweet*] The use of 'sweet', absolutely, as a form of address between man and man on equal terms, is rare in Shakespeare; it is, however, used by Patroclus to Achilles, *Troil.*, III. iii. 222.

Except thou wilt except against my love.   150

Pro. Have I not reason to prefer mine own?

Val. And I will help thee to prefer her too:
　　　She shall be dignified with this high honour,
　　　To bear my lady's train, lest the base earth
　　　Should from her vesture chance to steal a kiss,   155
　　　And of so great a favour growing proud,
　　　Disdain to root the summer-swelling flower,
　　　And make rough winter everlastingly.

Pro. Why, Valentine, what braggardism is this?

Val. Pardon me, Proteus, all I can is nothing   160
　　　To her whose worth makes other worthies nothing:
　　　She is alone.

Pro. Then let her alone.

Val. Not for the world. Why, man, she is mine own,
　　　And I as rich in having such a jewel   165
　　　As twenty seas, if all their sand were pearl,
　　　The water nectar, and the rocks pure gold.
　　　Forgive me that I do not dream on thee,
　　　Because thou seest me dote upon my love.
　　　My foolish rival that her father likes   170
　　　(Only for his possessions are so huge)
　　　Is gone with her along, and I must after,

152. too] *F* (to), *F3.*   157. summer-swelling] *F;* summer-smelling *conj. Steevens*
(*withdrawn*), *Collier ii.*   161. makes] *F2;* make *F.*   163. Then] *F;* Why, then
Hanmer.   her alone] *F;* her be alone *Keightley.*

150.] Cf. I. iii. 83 and note. The
sense seems to be 'Unless you will go
so far as to take exception to my love
(which is unthinkable)'. Bond, however, glosses: 'to place any as her equal
is a detraction from her'.

152. *prefer*] advance, with a shift of
meaning from 'prefer' in l. 151, characteristic of this play.

154–6. *lest . . . proud*] Malone quotes
R2, III. iii. 190–1: 'you debase your
princely knee / To make the base
earth proud with kissing it.'

157. *summer-swelling*] Steevens found
this compound also in Sir Arthur
Gorges' translation of Lucan (1614):
there, as Bond points out, it is applied

to the Nile, not to flowers. There is,
however, no need to emend.

159. *braggardism*] unique in Shakespeare.

161. *worthies*] excellences; cf. *LLL.*,
IV. iii. 235–6: 'her fair cheek, / Where
several worthies make one dignity'.

162. *She is alone*] She is unique.
Proteus' reply makes a characteristic
shift of sense.

168. *do . . . thee*] 'seem careless in my
welcome' (Bond).

171. *for*] because; cf. IV. iii. 24.

his . . . huge] This may clash with ll.
40–2 above and perhaps with V. ii. 29
(see note). See also Introduction,
p. xix.

For love, thou know'st, is full of jealousy.
Pro. But she loves you?
Val. Ay, and we are betroth'd; nay more, our marriage hour,
    With all the cunning manner of our flight,   176
    Determin'd of: how I must climb her window,
    The ladder made of cords, and all the means
    Plotted, and 'greed on for my happiness.
    Good Proteus, go with me to my chamber,   180
    In these affairs to aid me with thy counsel.
Pro. Go on before; I shall enquire you forth.
    I must unto the road, to disembark
    Some necessaries that I needs must use,
    And then I'll presently attend you.   185
Val. Will you make haste?
Pro. I will.   *Exit* [VALENTINE].
    Even as one heat another heat expels,
    Or as one nail by strength drives out another,
    So the remembrance of my former love   190
    Is by a newer object quite forgotten.
    Is it mine eye, or Valentinus' praise,

---

173. know'st, . . . jealousy.] *F2* (*subst.*) *;* know'st . . . iealousie.) *F.*   175. nay more,]
F; nay more, my Proteus, Capell.   marriage hour] *F; marriage Pope.*   185. you]
F; upon you Hanmer; on you Capell.   187. S.D.] *Rowe; at l. 186 F; not in F2;
Exeunt Valentine and Speed Dyce.*   192.] *Malone;* It is mine, or *Valentines* praise *F;*
Is it mine then, or Valentineans praise *F2;* Is it mine then, or Valentino's praise
Rowe; Is it mine eye, or Valentino's praise *Theobald;* Is it mine eyne, or Valen-
tino's praise *Hanmer;* Is it mine own, or Valentino's praise *Capell;* Is it her mien, or
Valentinus' praise *Malone ii, conj. Blakeway;* Is it mine, or Valentine's praise *Camb;*
Is it mine unstaid mind, or Valentine's praise *Bond, conj. Camb;* Is it my mind, or
Valentinus' praise *Alexander;* It is mine eye, or Valentinus' praise *Munro.*

173.] Cf. Tilley, L510, including
Ven., 1137: 'It shall be waited on with
jealousy.'
    177–8.] Cf. *Romeus*, ll. 775–6: 'Of
corde I will bespeake, a ladder by that
time / By which, this night, . . . I will
your window clime.'
    180.] He has just said (l. 172) that he
must follow Silvia at once: see Introduction, p. xix.
    183. *road*] Cf. I. i. 53.
    188–91.] The fire-image is frequent
in Shakespeare, and is combined with
the nail-image in *Cor.*, IV. vii. 54. Cf.
Tilley, F277, N17. Shakespeare cer-

tainly had *Romeus*, ll. 203–10, in his
mind: 'And whilest he fixd on her his
partiall perced eye, / His former love
. . . / Is nowe as quite forgotte . . . / The
proverbe saith, unminded oft are they
that are unseene / And as out of a
planke a nayle a nayle doth drive, / So
novell love out of the minde the auncient love doth rive. / This sodain
kindled fyre in time is wox so great, /
That onely death and both theyr
blouds might quench the fiery heate.'
    192.] Sisson, i. 55–6, draws atten-
tion to omissions of 'eies' after 'theis' in
Believe as you List and of 'eye' after

Her true perfection, or my false transgression,
That makes me reasonless, to reason thus?
She is fair; and so is Julia that I love—   195
That I did love, for now my love is thaw'd,
Which like a waxen image 'gainst a fire
Bears no impression of the thing it was.
Methinks my zeal to Valentine is cold,
And that I love him not as I was wont.   200
O, but I love his lady too-too much,
And that's the reason I love him so little.
How shall I dote on her with more advice,
That thus without advice begin to love her?
'Tis but her picture I have yet beheld,   205

194. me] *F;* me, *Theobald.*

'mine' in Sonnet 113. In the line as emended, there is an effective antithesis between 'eye' (Proteus' sight of Silvia) and 'praise' (what he has heard of her). Munro argues for 'eye' on the ground that the speech echoes *Romeus*, ll. 203–8, in which occurs the line 'And whilest he fixd on her his partiall perced eye' (see preceding note), but he preserves 'It is', taking the question-mark as signifying an exclamation. The F '*Valentines*' may be right (possibly as a tetrasyllable), but 'Valentinus' has been used at I. iii. 67. That Proteus should give 'Valentinus' praise' as one reason for his own love links this passage with one in *The Gouernour*, where Titus exclaims: 'Alas, why forgat ye that our myndes and appetites were ever one? And that also what ye lyked was ever to me in lyke degree pleasaunt?' (Bullough, p. 215). Cf. Sonnet 42: 'Thou dost love her, because thou know'st I love her.'

194. *reasonless . . . thus*] A more extended 'rationalization' on the same subject is in *Romeus*, ll. 429–32: 'Oh how we can perswade, our self to what we like, / And how we can diswade our mynd, if ought our mynd mislyke. / Weake arguments are stronge, our fansies streyght to frame / To pleasing things, and eke to shonne, if we mislike the same.'

197.] 'Alluding to the figures made by witches, as representatives of those whom they designed to torment or destroy' (Steevens).

201. *too-too*] excessively, as frequently in Shakespeare: e.g., *Lucr.,* 174; *LLL.,* v. ii. 532; *Wiv.,* II. ii. 260; *Ham.,* I. ii. 129.

203, 204. *advice*] consideration; cf. III. i. 73, IV. iv. 120. Cf. also *Romeus,* ll. 601–2: 'Advise is banishd quite from those that followe love, / Except advise to what they like.'

205. *picture*] appearance. Bond quotes Beaumont and Fletcher's *Scornful Lady,* v. ii. 110: 'what are shapes and colours else but pictures?' Johnson, taking 'picture' in the sense of 'portrait', thought that Shakespeare had slipped here; *NCS,* noting the antithesis provided by 'when I look on her perfections' (l. 207), suggests that originally Proteus spoke these words before he had seen Silvia. It is odd that Silvia's portrait later comes into the play, in IV. ii. See Introduction, p. xxix. An antithesis between external beauty (here 'picture') and 'virtues' or 'perfections' (l. 207) can be found both in *Diana* (Kennedy, p. 98) and in *The Gouernour* (Bullough, p. 215): it is of

And that hath dazzled my reason's light;
But when I look on her perfections,
There is no reason but I shall be blind.
If I can check my erring love, I will;
If not, to compass her I'll use my skill.   *Exit.* 210

SCENE V

Enter SPEED *and* LAUNCE [*with his dog*].

Spe. Launce, by mine honesty, welcome to Padua.

Lau. Forswear not thyself, sweet youth, for I am not welcome. I reckon this always, that a man is never
  undone till he be hanged, nor never welcome to a
  place till some certain shot be paid, and the hostess   5
  say 'welcome'.

Spe. Come on, you madcap: I'll to the ale-house with you
  presently; where, for one shot of five pence, thou
  shalt have five thousand welcomes. But, sirrah, how
  did thy master part with Madam Julia?   10

Lau. Marry, after they closed in earnest, they parted very
  fairly in jest.

Spe. But shall she marry him?

Lau. No.

Spe. How then? Shall he marry her?   15

206. dazzled] *F* (dazel'd); dazel'd so *F2*.   210. S.D.] *F2*; *Exeunt F*.

Scene v

SCENE V] *Rowe; Scena Quinta F*.   1. Padua] *F*; Milan *Pope*.   4. be] *F*; is *Rowe*.

course part of the seeming–being antithesis generally current.

  206. *dazzled*] trisyllabic; cf. I. iii. 84.
  208. *no reason but*] no doubt that. But
'reason' also suggests the lover's in-
ability to be guided by his reasoning
power: the lover in *Euphues* is told 'thou
hast forgot reason' (ed. Arber, p. 106),
and in *Diana* Don Felix admits that
'Valerius', arguing against his infidelity, has 'the greatest reason in the
world' but his new love 'will not let me

understand it so' (Kennedy, pp. 97,
95).

Scene v

  1. *Padua*] See Introduction, p. xvi.
  5. *shot*] i.e., scot, payment; cf. *1H4*,
v. iii. 30–1: 'Though I could 'scape
shot-free at London, I fear the shot
here.'
  11. *closed*] embraced; cf. Webster,
White Devil (Revels edn), I. ii. 214:
'See now they close.'

Lau. No, neither.

Spe. What, are they broken?

Lau. No; they are both as whole as a fish.

Spe. Why then, how stands the matter with them?

Lau. Marry, thus: when it stands well with him, it stands   20
well with her.

Spe. What an ass art thou, I understand thee not.

Lau. What a block art thou, that thou canst not! My staff
understands me.

Spe. What thou say'st?   25

Lau. Ay, and what I do too: look thee, I'll but lean, and
my staff understands me.

Spe. It stands under thee indeed.

Lau. Why, stand under and understand is all one.

Spe. But tell me true, will 't be a match?   30

Lau. Ask my dog: if he say 'ay', it will; if he say 'no', it
will; if he shake his tail, and say nothing, it will.

Spe. The conclusion is, then, that it will.

Lau. Thou shalt never get such a secret from me but by a
parable.   35

Spe. 'Tis well that I get it so. But, Launce, how say'st thou
that my master is become a notable lover?

Lau. I never knew him otherwise.

Spe. Than how?

Lau. A notable lubber; as thou reportest him to be.   40

23-4.] *so Capell;* What . . . not? / My . . . me *F.*   39. Than] *F* (then), *F4.*

17. *broken*] fallen out; cf. *Cor.*, IV. vi.
47–8: 'It cannot be / The Volsces dare
break with us.'

18. *whole . . . fish*] Cf. Tilley, F301.
According to *NCS*, Launce 'probably
intends an indelicate reference as
well'.

20–1. *when . . . her*] a characteristic
Launce obscenity: cf. Partridge,
p. 194, suggesting that the joke continues with 'staff' (ll. 23, 27).

27. *understands*] i.e., props.

34. *never . . . me*] comic comment on
the serious action, as at III. i. 263 ff.
below. The obligation of secrecy was
a heritage from the courtly love code.
In Sonnet 102, the breach of the obligation is rebuked: 'That love is mer-
chandized whose rich esteeming / The
owner's tongue doth publish every
where.'

35. *parable*] unique in Shakespeare;
'A comparison . . . Also vaguely extended . . . to any kind of enigmatical,
mystical, or dark saying . . .' (*O.E.D.*).

36–7. *how . . . that*] what have you to
say to the fact that.

40. *lubber*] lout. E. I. Fripp, *Shakespeare Man and Artist*, 1938, i. 286,
draws attention to Puttenham's reference to a play on 'lover' and 'lubber':
'And we in our Enterlude called the
woer, plaid with these two words,
lubber and *louer*, thus, the countrey

Spe. Why, thou whoreson ass, thou mistak'st me.

Lau. Why, fool, I meant not thee, I meant thy master.

Spe. I tell thee, my master is become a hot lover.

Lau. Why, I tell thee, I care not, though he burn himself
in love. If thou wilt, go with me to the ale-house; if   45
not, thou art an Hebrew, a Jew, and not worth the
name of a Christian.

Spe. Why?

Lau. Because thou hast not so much charity in thee as to
go to the ale with a Christian. Wilt thou go?   50

Spe. At thy service.   *Exeunt.*

SCENE VI

Enter PROTEUS *solus.*

Pro. To leave my Julia, shall I be forsworn;
To love fair Silvia, shall I be forsworn;

45. in . . . go] *Knight;* in Loue. If thou wilt goe *F;* in love, if thou wilt go *Collier,
conj. Malone.*   ale-house] *F;* Alehouse, so *F2.*   50. ale] *F;* ale-house *Rowe.*

Scene VI

SCENE VI] *Rowe; Scœna Sexta* F.   1, 2. forsworn;] *Theobald;* forsworne? *F.*

clowne came & woed a young maide of
the Citie, and being agreeued to come
so oft, and not to haue her answere,
said to the old nurse very impatiently.
*Iche pray you good mother tell our young
dame, / Whence I am come and what is my
name, / I cannot come a woing euery day. /
Quoth the nurse. They be lubbers not
louers that so vse to say.' (Arte of English
Poesie,* ed. G. D. Willcock and A.
Walker, 1936, p. 203.) For a similar
play on the two words in *Damon and
Pithias,* see Introduction, p. xxxviii.

41. *thou . . . me*] Launce in his reply
takes this in the sense 'thou makest a
mistake about me'.

45. *wilt, . . . ale-house*] This reading
disturbs F least, merely inserting a
comma. Malone's conjecture, that 'If
thou wilt go' is in the same sentence as
what precedes, is attractive.

46. *Hebrew, Jew*] One wonders why

Launce's mind runs on Jews: cf. II. iii.
11–12n.

50. *ale*] ale-house: cf. *O.E.D.,* s.v., 2;
the common use of 'ale' for a rustic
festival at which ale was drunk will
hardly fit the present context. Knight,
however, takes 'ale' in that sense, and
links it to Launce's suggestion that
Speed is a Jew if he will not come to the
church festivity; but by no means all
'ales' (e.g., Robin Hood ale) had even
a nominal connection with the church.

Scene VI

S.D.] See Introduction, p. xix. This
soliloquy quickly follows that concluding II. iv: here Proteus dismisses
the hesitation he had expressed there
and determines to tell the Duke of
Valentine's love.

1 ff.] There is a general resemblance
between the soliloquy and that of

To wrong my friend, I shall be much forsworn.
And ev'n that power which gave me first my oath
Provokes me to this threefold perjury.   5
Love bade me swear, and Love bids me forswear.
O sweet-suggesting Love, if thou hast sinn'd,
Teach me (thy tempted subject) to excuse it.
At first I did adore a twinkling star,
But now I worship a celestial sun: 10
Unheedful vows may heedfully be broken,
And he wants wit that wants resolved will
To learn his wit t' exchange the bad for better.
Fie, fie, unreverend tongue, to call her bad
Whose sovereignty so oft thou hast preferr'd,   15
With twenty thousand soul-confirming oaths.
I cannot leave to love; and yet I do;
But there I leave to love, where I should love.
Julia I lose, and Valentine I lose;
If I keep them, I needs must lose myself;   20

---

7. if thou hast] *F;* if I have *Warburton.*   16. soul-confirming] *F;* soul-confirmed
Pope.

Euphues on his treachery to his friend
(ed. Arber, pp. 62–3).

1, 2.] F's question-marks seem an
obvious error, arising from the 'shall I'
inversion.

7. *sweet-suggesting*] 'Sweetly seduc-
tive' (Onions). Cf. III. i. 34.

if thou hast] Johnson rightly defends
F against Warburton: 'O tempting
Love, if thou hast influenced me to sin,
teach me to excuse it.'

9–10.] Cf. *Romeus,* ll. 227–9: 'He in
her sight did seeme to passe the rest as
farre / As Phoebus shining beames do
passe the brightnes of a starre. / In
wayte lay warlike love' (love being
personified as in Shakespeare's two
preceding lines).

11.] Casuistical argument against
vows is common in early Shakespeare:
cf. *2H6,* v. i. 179–91; *3H6,* i. ii. 15–27;
John, III. i. 270–89; *LLL.,* II. i. 105. Cf.
Tilley, O7.

12, 13. *wit*] (1) mental skill; (2)
mind.

12. *resolved*] determined.

will] volition. Asserting that will
should instruct wit, Proteus reverses
the accepted principle, which is
expressed in *Romeus,* l. 2296: 'she
had done right well by wit to order
will.'

13. *learn*] teach, as frequently. Cf.
v. iii. 3.

t' exchange . . . better] Cf. Tilley, B26.

14. *unreverend*] irreverent, as frequently.

15. *preferr'd*] recommended (Onions)
or, perhaps, asserted.

16. *soul-confirming*] Cf. 'blasting', i. i.
48.

17. *leave*] cease. The phrase 'to
leave of to love' occurs in *Diana*
(Kennedy, p. 52).

20. *I needs . . . myself*] Proteus reverses the argument of Sidney in
Astrophel and Stella, Sonnet XVIII: 'My
wit doth strive, those passions to defend / . . . I see my course, to lose my
self doth bend.'

If I lose them, thus find I by their loss:
For Valentine, myself; for Julia, Silvia.
I to myself am dearer than a friend,
For love is still most precious in itself,
And Silvia (witness heaven that made her fair)   25
Shows Julia but a swarthy Ethiope.
I will forget that Julia is alive,
Rememb'ring that my love to her is dead.
And Valentine I'll hold an enemy,
Aiming at Silvia as a sweeter friend.   30
I cannot now prove constant to myself,
Without some treachery us'd to Valentine.
This night he meaneth with a corded ladder
To climb celestial Silvia's chamber-window,
Myself in counsel, his competitor.   35
Now presently I'll give her father notice
Of their disguising and pretended flight;
Who, all enrag'd, will banish Valentine,
For Thurio he intends shall wed his daughter.
But Valentine being gone, I'll quickly cross,   40
By some sly trick, blunt Thurio's dull proceeding.

24. most] *F;* more *Steevens.*   in] *F;* to *Collier (MS.).*   itself] *F* (it selfe); its
self *Theobald.*

20–1.] Cf. *LLL.,* IV. iii. 361–2: 'Let
us once lose our oaths to find ourselves, / Or else we lose ourselves to
keep our oaths.'

23–4.] Cf. Tilley, N57, especially
Erasmus, *Adagia:* 'Heus proximus sum
egomet mihi'. Erasmus has an oppos-
ing adage: 'Nemo sibi nascitur' (see,
further, Tilley, B141). Proteus' declaration is heresy to the Friendship Cult:
Muriel Bradbrook has pointed out
(*Shakespeare and Elizabethan Poetry,*
p. 100) that it is characteristic of
villains, as in *Spanish Tragedy,* III. ii. 118,
and *R3,* v. iii. 183. Cf. Bodenham's
Belvedere or The Garden of the Muses
(1600, edn 1875), p. 96: 'No man
should loue himselfe more than his
friend.'

26. *swarthy Ethiope*] Malone quotes
LLL., IV. iii. 117–18: 'Thou for whom

Jove would swear / Juno but an
Ethiope were.' In view of the general
relationship of *Gent.* to *Rom.,* it is also
worth noting *Rom.,* I. v. 47–8: 'It
seems she hangs upon the cheek of
night / Like a rich jewel in an Ethiope's
ear.' In each instance the beauty of the
girl is contrasted with the blackness of
the Ethiope.

34. *celestial*] Here, and in l. 10
above, there may be a reminiscence of
the Celia who is Silvia's counterpart in
Diana.

35. *Myself in counsel*] with myself in
the secret.

competitor] associate: 'This is the
commoner S. use' (Onions).

37. *pretended*] intended; cf. *Two
Noble Kinsmen,* I. i: 'omit not any
thing / In the pretended Celebration',
Cf. also 'pretence', III. i. 47.

Love, lend me wings to make my purpose swift
As thou hast lent me wit to plot this drift.   *Exit.*

SCENE VII

Enter JULIA *and* LUCETTA.

Jul. Counsel, Lucetta; gentle girl, assist me,
 And ev'n in kind love I do conjure thee,
 Who art the table wherein all my thoughts
 Are visibly character'd and engrav'd,
 To lesson me, and tell me some good mean   5
 How with my honour I may undertake
 A journey to my loving Proteus.
Luc. Alas, the way is wearisome and long.
Jul. A true-devoted pilgrim is not weary
 To measure kingdoms with his feeble steps,   10

42. Love,] *Theobald; Loue F.*

Scene VII

SCENE VII] *Rowe; Scæna septima F;* Scene x. *Verona Pope.*

42. *Love,*] 'thou' in l. 43 makes it highly probable that 'Love' is here a vocative: the comma is therefore inserted.

make . . . swift] bring about quickly the fulfilment of my purpose.

43. *drift*] scheme; cf. the words of the Vice in John Phillip's *Pacient and Meeke Grissill* (M.S.R., 966–7): 'Not a word more my Lorde Marques entreth the place, / Nowe maist thou contriue thy drift within short space.' Cf. also III. i. 18, IV. ii. 80. Johnson suggested that Shakespeare ended Act II at this point, II. vii being properly III. i. But it seems more appropriate to deal with the first stage of the journeying wholly in the first two acts. See Introduction, p. lxxii.

Scene VII

1 ff.] Bond draws attention to the similar scene between Portia and Nerissa in *Mer.V.*, III. iv. 57 ff. Julia's following her love in male disguise is from *Diana*, but in *Romeus* the same idea is suggested: Juliet proposes to accompany Romeus in man's clothes (l. 1620), and though Romeus rejects the plan (ll. 1681–2), the Friar revives it (ll. 2483–4).

1. *Counsel*] It is perhaps worth noting that this takes up the word used by Proteus at II. vi. 35.

3–4.] In *Diana*, Felismena prepares for her journey with 'the helpe of one of my approoued friends, and treasouresse of my secrets' (Kennedy, p. 87).

3. *table*] writing-tablet.

4. *character'd*] written down. The accent is on the second syllable.

5. *lesson*] instruct.

mean] The singular form is similarly used in *2H6*, IV. viii. 71–2: 'we'll devise a mean / To reconcile you all unto the king.'

Much less shall she that hath Love's wings to fly,
And when the flight is made to one so dear,
Of such divine perfection as Sir Proteus.

Luc. Better forbear, till Proteus make return.

Jul. O, know'st thou not his looks are my soul's food?   15
Pity the dearth that I have pined in,
By longing for that food so long a time.
Didst thou but know the inly touch of love,
Thou wouldst as soon go kindle fire with snow
As seek to quench the fire of love with words.   20

Luc. I do not seek to quench your love's hot fire,
But qualify the fire's extreme rage,
Lest it should burn above the bounds of reason.

Jul. The more thou damm'st it up, the more it burns:
The current that with gentle murmur glides,   25
Thou know'st, being stopp'd impatiently doth rage;
But when his fair course is not hindered,
He makes sweet music with th' enamell'd stones,
Giving a gentle kiss to every sedge

11–13.] At II. vi. 42 Proteus had (reprehensibly) asked for wings from Love: hence there is irony in the present passage, which may have been prompted by this from *Diana*: 'They paint [Love] with wings, because . . . the more perfect he is, with more swiftnes and alienation of himselfe, he goeth to seeke the person of the beloved' (Kennedy, p. 157).

15.] In *Romeus*, l. 218, it is the young man who 'onely seeketh by her sight to feede his houngry eyes'.

18. *inly*] Halliwell quotes from *Hoffman* (publ. 1631): 'the inlie grief'.

19–20.] Cf. Tilley, F284. There is a general resemblance here to Antonio's words in *Mer.V.*, IV. i. 71–80, where he mentions various impossible tasks which 'You may as well' undertake as attempt to soften Shylock's heart with words.

21–8.] Cf. I. ii. 30n. The present passage is developed from Ovid, says T. W. Baldwin, *Shakspere's Five-Act Structure*, p. 754, after E. I. Fripp,

Shakespeare Studies, p. 127. Cf. also Tilley, S929, for the image in ll. 25–6.

21–3.] Cf. Lyly's *Love's Metamorphosis* (II. i. 127–8, 131–2), where Ceres says to Cupid: 'warme us with mild affections: lest being too hotte, we seeme immodest', and Cupid replies: 'So shall your flames warme, but not burne'.

22. *fire's*] disyllabic; cf. I. ii. 30.

23. *above . . . reason*] Cf. *Diana*: 'Love, though it hath Reason for his mother, is not therefore limited or governed by it' (Kennedy, p. 156). In the following passage the conclusion is reached that virtuous as well as vicious love is characterized by excess: 'Who can denie, but that in true and honest love excessive and strange effects are sometimes founde' (Kennedy, p. 157).

24.] Cf. I. ii. 30.

25–6.] *Lucr.*, 1118–19, has 'gentle flood' and 'being stopp'd'.

29–32.] Cf. *Diana*: 'But the faire Shepherdesse leaving that place and citie on the right hand, went softly on

He overtaketh in his pilgrimage.   30
And so by many winding nooks he strays
With willing sport to the wild ocean.
Then let me go, and hinder not my course.
I'll be as patient as a gentle stream,
And make a pastime of each weary step,   35
Till the last step have brought me to my love,
And there I'll rest, as after much turmoil
A blessed soul doth in Elysium.

Luc. But in what habit will you go along?

Jul. Not like a woman, for I would prevent   40
The loose encounters of lascivious men:
Gentle Lucetta, fit me with such weeds
As may beseem some well-reputed page.

Luc. Why, then your ladyship must cut your hair.

Jul. No, girl, I'll knit it up in silken strings,   45
With twenty odd-conceited true-love knots:
To be fantastic may become a youth
Of greater time than I shall show to be.

Luc. What fashion, madam, shall I make your breeches?

Jul. That fits as well as 'Tell me, good my lord,   50
What compass will you wear your farthingale?'
Why, ev'n what fashion thou best likes, Lucetta.

---

32. wild] *F;* wide *Collier ii.*

---

by a path hard by the river towards
that part, where the Cristalline waters
with a gentle and pleasant noise runne
smoothly into the Ocean' (Kennedy,
p. 229).

31. *nooks*] corners.

32. *wild*] Collier's emendation
'wide' has been supported by *NCS,*
persuasively arguing that the 'ocean'
is Julia's 'love' where she will 'rest, as
after much turmoil / A blessed soul
doth in Elysium'. Tannenbaum defends 'wild' by referring to *Ven.,* 819:
'the wild waves will have him seen no
more'; there, however, the context is
markedly different. Sisson, i. 56–7,
quotes from a Chancery case of 1610
the use of 'wild Roade' in the sense of
an unenclosed anchorage, and deduces

that 'wild' in the present passage, in
Err., II. i. 21, and in *Troil.,* I. i. 105,
means 'open, unenclosed'. The case is
strengthened by there being a possible
play on 'willing' and 'wild', and by the
'ocean' that Julia goes to proving 'wild'
in the customary sense as well.

41. *encounters*] accostings, addresses;
cf. the verb 'encounter' in I. ii. 5.

44.] Similarly Zelmane in the
Arcadia cut off her hair when she
dressed as a page.

45–6. *knit ... knots*] Cf. Tilley, L571.

45. *knit it up*] tie with a knot.

48. *greater time*] older years.

52. *likes*] On the circumstances in
which the termination '-est' is commonly reduced to '-es', see Franz,
p. 154.

Luc. You must needs have them with a cod-piece, madam.
Jul. Out, out, Lucetta, that will be ill-favour'd.
Luc. A round hose, madam, now 's not worth a pin   55
    Unless you have a cod-piece to stick pins on.
Jul. Lucetta, as thou lov'st me let me have
    What thou think'st meet, and is most mannerly.
    But tell me, wench, how will the world repute me
    For undertaking so unstaid a journey?   60
    I fear me it will make me scandalis'd.
Luc. If you think so, then stay at home, and go not.
Jul. Nay, that I will not.
Luc. Then never dream on infamy, but go.
    If Proteus like your journey, when you come,   65
    No matter who's displeas'd, when you are gone.
    I fear me he will scarce be pleas'd withal.
Jul. That is the least, Lucetta, of my fear:
    A thousand oaths, an ocean of his tears,
    And instances of infinite of love,   70
    Warrant me welcome to my Proteus.
Luc. All these are servants to deceitful men.
Jul. Base men, that use them to so base effect;
    But truer stars did govern Proteus' birth,
    His words are bonds, his oaths are oracles,   75

---

67. withal] *F2;* with all *F.*   70. of infinite] *F;* as infinite *F2;* of the infinite *Malone ii;* of infinity *conj. Bond.*

54. *Out, out*] expression of reproof; Steevens quotes 'Out, out, I hate ye from my heart' from Chapman's *Iliad*, Bk xiii.

55. *round hose*] 'In the round hose, which is contrasted with "Venetians" by Nashe in *Have with you*, 1596, the close-fitting part of the hose or breeches extended farther up the leg, giving a greater bulge and roundness to the remaining portion. See Halliwell's large folio edition of Shakespeare' (Bond).

not . . . pin] Cf. Tilley, P334.

56. *cod-piece . . . on*] Cf. Webster's *White Devil* (Revels edn), v. iii. 100–1: 'Look you his codpiece is stuck full of pins / With pearls o' th' head of them.'

58. *mannerly*] a pun; cf. iii. i. 373 and note.

61. *scandalis'd*] disgraced.

70. *of infinite*] As Malone pointed out, 'infinite' could be used as a noun with the sense of 'infinity': all his examples, however, are preceded by an article. The only example without an article traced by any commentator is that quoted by Halliwell from Chaucer's *Boethius*: 'And although the life of it be stretched with infinite of tyme'. Bond's suggestion that the right reading in the play may be 'infinity' is reasonable enough, but the meaning of the line is plain as it stands.

75. *His . . bonds*] Cf. Tilley, M458.

His love sincere, his thoughts immaculate,
His tears pure messengers sent from his heart,
His heart as far from fraud as heaven from earth.
Luc. Pray heav'n he prove so when you come to him.
Jul. Now, as thou lov'st me, do him not that wrong,   80
To bear a hard opinion of his truth.
Only deserve my love, by loving him,
And presently go with me to my chamber
To take a note of what I stand in need of,
To furnish me upon my longing journey.   85
All that is mine I leave at thy dispose,
My goods, my lands, my reputation,
Only, in lieu thereof, dispatch me hence.
Come; answer not; but to it presently,
I am impatient of my tarriance.   *Exeunt.*   90

83. *go . . . chamber*] These words exactly repeat Valentine's to Proteus at II. iv. 180.

85-7.] Cf. *Diana*: 'being furnished with the helpe of one of my approoved friends . . . who bought me such apparell as I willed her, and a good horse for my journey, I wente not onely out of my countrie, but out of my deere reputation' (Kennedy, p. 87).

85. *longing*] prompted by longing;

Bond quotes *Pilgr.*, 73-4: 'Cytherea . . . / A longing tarriance for Adonis made'.

86. *at thy dispose*] in thy charge. Julia's leaving Lucetta in charge of 'goods' and 'lands' does not fit with the reference to her father in I. ii or with Proteus' references to parental opposition in I. iii. See Introduction, p. xix.

90. *tarriance*] Cf. quotation in note to l. 85.

ACT III

SCENE I

Enter Duke, THURIO *and* PROTEUS.

Duke. Sir Thurio, give us leave, I pray, awhile,
We have some secrets to confer about.   [*Exit* THURIO.]
Now tell me, Proteus, what's your will with me?

Pro. My gracious lord, that which I would discover
The law of friendship bids me to conceal,   5
But when I call to mind your gracious favours
Done to me, undeserving as I am,
My duty pricks me on to utter that
Which else no worldly good should draw from me.
Know, worthy prince, Sir Valentine my friend   10
This night intends to steal away your daughter;
Myself am one made privy to the plot.
I know you have determin'd to bestow her
On Thurio, whom your gentle daughter hates,
And should she thus be stol'n away from you,   15
It would be much vexation to your age.
Thus, for my duty's sake, I rather chose
To cross my friend in his intended drift,
Than, by concealing it, heap on your head
A pack of sorrows, which would press you down,   20
Being unprevented, to your timeless grave.

ACT III

Scene 1

ACT III SCENE I] *Rowe; Actus Tertius, Scena Prima F;* Act III. Scene 1. Scene *changes to* Milan *Pope.*   S.D. Enter . . . *Proteus*] *Enter Duke, Thurio, Protheus, Valentine, Launce, Speed F.*   2. S.D.] *Rowe.*

4. *discover*] reveal.
18. *drift*] scheme; cf. II. vi. 43.
21. *timeless*] untimely, as normally in Shakespeare (e.g., 'timeless end' in

Rom., v. iii. 162); cf. Marlowe's *Edward II*, I. ii. 5–6: 'This ground . . . / Shall be their timeless sepulchre, or mine.'

Duke. Proteus, I thank thee for thine honest care,
     Which to requite command me while I live.
     This love of theirs myself have often seen,
     Haply when they have judg'd me fast asleep,   25
     And oftentimes have purpos'd to forbid
     Sir Valentine her company and my court.
     But fearing lest my jealous aim might err,
     And so (unworthily) disgrace the man
     (A rashness that I ever yet have shunn'd)   30
     I gave him gentle looks, thereby to find
     That which thyself hast now disclos'd to me.
     And that thou mayst perceive my fear of this,
     Knowing that tender youth is soon suggested,
     I nightly lodge her in an upper tower,   35
     The key whereof myself have ever kept,
     And thence she cannot be convey'd away.
Pro. Know, noble lord, they have devis'd a mean
     How he her chamber-window will ascend,
     And with a corded ladder fetch her down;   40
     For which the youthful lover now is gone,
     And this way comes he with it presently,
     Where, if it please you, you may intercept him.
     But, good my lord, do it so cunningly
     That my discovery be not aimed at;   45
     For love of you, not hate unto my friend,
     Hath made me publisher of this pretence.
Duke. Upon mine honour, he shall never know
     That I had any light from thee of this.
Pro. Adieu, my lord, Sir Valentine is coming.   [*Exit.*]   50

[*Enter* VALENTINE.]

Duke. Sir Valentine, whither away so fast?

50. S.D. *Exit*] *Rowe.*   *Enter Valentine*] *F2 (Enter.).*   51. whither] *F2; whether*
F.

28. *aim*] guess; cf. *Caes.*, I. ii. 163:
'What you would work me to, I have
some aim'.
    33–4.] 'I tell thee that' is to be
understood before l. 35.
    34. *suggested*] tempted; cf. II. vi. 7.
    38. *mean*] Cf. II. vii. 5.

45. *aimed at*] guessed at; cf. l. 28.
    47. *publisher*] one who makes public;
cf. *Lucr.*, 33–4: 'why is Collatine the
publisher / Of that rich jewel'. The
modern restricted sense is dated by
O.E.D. from 1654.
    pretence] purpose; cf. II. vi. 37.

Val. Please it your grace, there is a messenger
    That stays to bear my letters to my friends,
    And I am going to deliver them.
Duke. Be they of much import?   55
Val. The tenor of them doth but signify
    My health, and happy being at your court.
Duke. Nay then, no matter. Stay with me awhile;
    I am to break with thee of some affairs
    That touch me near; wherein thou must be secret.   60
    'Tis not unknown to thee that I have sought
    To match my friend Sir Thurio to my daughter.
Val. I know it well, my lord, and sure the match
    Were rich and honourable. Besides, the gentleman
    Is full of virtue, bounty, worth, and qualities   65
    Beseeming such a wife as your fair daughter.
    Cannot your grace win her to fancy him?
Duke. No, trust me, she is peevish, sullen, froward,
    Proud, disobedient, stubborn, lacking duty,
    Neither regarding that she is my child,   70
    Nor fearing me as if I were her father.
    And may I say to thee, this pride of hers
    (Upon advice) hath drawn my love from her,

---

56. tenor] *Theobald; tenure F.*

59. *break with*] Cf. I. iii. 44.
63–5.] This seems prompted by *Romeus*, ll. 1964–7, where Juliet's father says of Paris: 'for his many vertues sake, a man of great renowne. / Of whom, both thou and I, unworthy are too much, / So riche ere long he shalbe left, his father's welth is such. / Such is the noblenes, and honor of the race'.
63–7.] This somewhat craven pretence makes Valentine resemble Proteus, who in I. iii was fearful of revealing his love for Julia.
64. *rich*] This conflicts with II. iv. 40–2: see Introduction, pp. xviii–xix.
68. *peevish*] In Lyly's *Love's Metamorphosis*, IV. i. 112, this is the epithet for the girls who have refused their suitors.
69–71.] Cf. *Romeus*, ll. 1948–9,

1951–2, 1957, 1969–70, 1988: 'Listen (quoth he) unthankfull and thou disobedient childe; / Hast thou so soone let slip out of thy mynde . . . / How much the Romayne youth of parentes stood in awe / And eke what powre upon theyr seede the fathers had by lawe? / . . . In how straight bondes would they thy stubberne body bynde . . . / The dainty foole, and stubberne gyrle; for want of skill, / Thou dost refuse thy offred weale, and disobay my will. / . . . thou shouldst once for all be taught, thy duetie how to knowe.'
70. *regarding*] taking into account; cf. l. 256.
71. *as . . . father*] apparently elliptical for 'as she should do if I were her father (and I am)'.
73. *advice*] consideration; cf. II. iv. 203; IV. iv. 120.

And where I thought the remnant of mine age
Should have been cherish'd by her child-like duty,   75
I now am full resolv'd to take a wife,
And turn her out to who will take her in.
Then let her beauty be her wedding-dower;
For me and my possessions she esteems not.
Val. What would your grace have me to do in this?   80
Duke. There is a lady in Verona here
Whom I affect; but she is nice, and coy,
And nought esteems my aged eloquence.
Now therefore would I have thee to my tutor
(For long agone I have forgot to court,   85
Besides the fashion of the time is chang'd)
How and which way I may bestow myself
To be regarded in her sun-bright eye.
Val. Win her with gifts, if she respect not words:
Dumb jewels often in their silent kind,   90

---

81. in Verona] *F;* sir, in Milan *Pope;* in Milano *Theobald;* of Verona *Halliwell.*
83. nought] *F2;* naught *F.*

74. *where*] whereas.

74–5.] Cf. *Lr.,* I. i. 125–6: 'I loved her most, and thought to set my rest / On her kind nursery'.

78.] Cf. *Lr.,* I. i. 130–1: 'With my two daughters' dowers digest this third: / Let pride, which she calls plainness, marry her.' Bond has noted the general reminder of *Lr.,* I. i, in the Duke's words. In *Romeus,* ll. 1977–8, Juliet's father threatens to 'geve all that I have away / From thee'.

81. *Verona*] See Introduction, p. xvii.

82. *nice*] shy (Onions) or unwilling (*NCS:* 'particular').

85. *agone*] frequently used as variant of 'ago'.

87. *bestow myself*] conduct myself; cf. *John,* III. i. 224–5: 'make my person yours, / And tell me how you would bestow yourself.'

88. *sun-bright*] *O.E.D.* records this in *The Shepherd's Calendar,* October, 72: 'Sonnebright honour pend in shamefull coupe'; Bond notes it in *1 Tamburlaine,* II. iii. 22.

89–91.] Malone quoted *Hero and Leander:* ''Tis wisdom to give much: a gift prevails / When deep persuasive oratory fails.' Bond points out that ll. 119–20 lend some support to the view that Marlowe is behind this passage, but he also draws attention to the appearance of the sentiment in Lyly's *Sapho and Phao,* II. iv. 105 ('he hath wit ynough, that can give ynough. Dumbe men are eloquent, if they be liberall'), and, perhaps more important, in Ovid's *Art of Love,* ii. 275–8: 'Carmina laudantur: sed munera magna petuntur. / Dummodo sit dives, barbarus ipse placet. / Aurea nunc vere sunt saecula: plurimus auro / Venit honos: auro conciliatur amor.' Cf. also Tilley, W704. These and the following lines are difficult to reconcile with the romantic love that Valentine has been professing and representing in II. i and II. iv.

90–105.] Rhyme here is used, as normally, for sententious utterances. Bond suggests that Shakespeare found

More than quick words, do move a woman's mind.
Duke. But she did scorn a present that I sent her.
Val. A woman sometime scorns what best contents her.
　　Send her another; never give her o'er,
　　For scorn at first makes after-love the more.　　95
　　If she do frown, 'tis not in hate of you,
　　But rather to beget more love in you.
　　If she do chide, 'tis not to have you gone,
　　For why, the fools are mad, if left alone.
　　Take no repulse, whatever she doth say,　　100
　　For 'get you gone' she doth not mean 'away!'.
　　Flatter, and praise, commend, extol their graces;
　　Though ne'er so black, say they have angels' faces;
　　That man that hath a tongue, I say is no man,
　　If with his tongue he cannot win a woman.　　105
Duke. But she I mean is promis'd by her friends

---

92. sent her.] *F4;* sent her, *F;* sent, sir. *conj. Steevens (ap. Malone ii).*　　93. sometime scorns] *F;* sometimes scorns *F3;* scorns sometimes *Steevens.*　　contents] *F;* content *conj. Mason (ap. Malone ii).*　　101. For] *F;* By *conj. Keightley.*

---

it appropriate for Petrarchan love-matter, but his examples from other early plays have not the gnomic character of these lines.

93.] Bond quotes Lyly's *Sapho and Phao,* II. iv. 92 ff.: 'If she seeme at the first cruell, be not discouraged. I tell thee a straung thing, womenne striue, because they would be ouercome.' This and the parallel noted at ll. 89–91 are only a dozen lines apart. On the conjectural emendations of Mason here and of Steevens in l. 92, Malone and Walker are strongly sceptical, but Walker's parallel example of rough rhyming from *Lr.,* III. vi. 119–20, is dubious, being from the quarto only.

95.] Cf. Tilley, S150. For 'after-love', cf. Beaumont and Fletcher, *Knight of the Burning Pestle,* III. i.

99. *For why*] because.

99–101. *the fools . . . 'away!'*] Bond quotes Lyly, *Sapho and Phao,* I. iv. 43–7: 'Wee are madde wenches, if men marke our wordes; for when I say, I

would none cared for loue more then I, what meane I, but I woulde none loued but I? Where we cry "away", doe we not presently say "go too": and when men striue for kisses, we exclaime, "let vs alone", as though we would fall to that our selues.'

101. *For*] by; this usage seems related to *O.E.D.,* 6 (= 'in exchange for').

102–5.] Bond again quotes Lyly, *Sapho and Phao,* II. iv. 60 ff.: 'Flatter, I meane lie . . . Imagine with thy selfe all are to bee won . . . It is vnpossible for the brittle mettal of women to withstand the flattering attemptes of men . . . Be prodigall in prayses . . . There is none so foule, that thinketh not herselfe faire. In commending thou canst loose no labor; for of euery one thou shalt be beleeued.' Cf. also Tilley, W681.

103. *black*] swarthy, but with a strong suggestion of simple ugliness; cf. *Oth.,* II. i. 132: 'How if she be black and witty?'

Unto a youthful gentleman of worth,
And kept severely from resort of men,
That no man hath access by day to her.

Val. Why, then I would resort to her by night.   110

Duke. Ay, but the doors be lock'd, and keys kept safe,
That no man hath recourse to her by night.

Val. What lets but one may enter at her window?

Duke. Her chamber is aloft, far from the ground,
And built so shelving that one cannot climb it   115
Without apparent hazard of his life.

Val. Why, then a ladder quaintly made of cords
To cast up, with a pair of anchoring hooks,
Would serve to scale another Hero's tower,
So bold Leander would adventure it.   120

Duke. Now, as thou art a gentleman of blood,
Advise me where I may have such a ladder.

Val. When would you use it? Pray, sir, tell me that.

Duke. This very night; for Love is like a child
That longs for every thing that he can come by.   125

Val. By seven o'clock I'll get you such a ladder.

Duke. But hark thee: I will go to her alone;
How shall I best convey the ladder thither?

Val. It will be light, my lord, that you may bear it
Under a cloak that is of any length.   130

Duke. A cloak as long as thine will serve the turn?

Val. Ay, my good lord.

Duke.   Then let me see thy cloak,
I'll get me one of such another length.

Val. Why, any cloak will serve the turn, my lord.

---

109. *That*] so that. So in ll. 112, 129.
113. *lets*] hinders.
115. *shelving*] projecting.
116. *apparent*] manifest.
117–18.] *Romeus*, ll. 813–14, has the servant make fast to the 'corden ladder' 'two strong and crooked yron hookes'.
117. *quaintly*] skilfully; cf. II. i. 115.
119, 120. *Hero's tower, bold Leander*] Cf. the reference to Hero and Leander at I. i. 22–6, and the possible echo of

Marlowe's poem in ll. 89–91 of this scene.
120. *So*] provided that.
121. *of blood*] of good parentage; Bond suggests the Duke is here ironic, and notes his very different references to Valentine at ll. 157–8 and at v. ii. 34.
122. *Advise*] inform.
130. *of any length*] of any considerable length.
133. *one . . . length*] another of the same length.

Duke. How shall I fashion me to wear a cloak?   135
    I pray thee let me feel thy cloak upon me.
                          [*He takes Valentine's cloak, and finds*
                                 with it a letter and a corded ladder.]
    What letter is this same? What's here? 'To Silvia'!
    And here an engine fit for my proceeding.
    I'll be so bold to break the seal for once.   [*Reads.*]
        My thoughts do harbour with my Silvia nightly,   140
        And slaves they are to me that send them flying.
        O, could their master come and go as lightly,
        Himself would lodge where (senseless) they are lying.
        My herald thoughts in thy pure bosom rest them,
        While I, their king, that thither them importune,   · 145
        Do curse the grace that with such grace hath blest them,
        Because myself do want my servants' fortune.
        I curse myself for they are sent by me,
        That they should harbour where their lord should be.

136. S.D.] *Hanmer (subst.).*   139. S.D.] *Rowe.*   149. *should be*] *F; would be F2.*

135. *fashion me*] adapt myself.
138. *engine*] device, implement.
140–51.] Bond engages in some unnecessary speculation about whether this poem was written earlier and never sent or whether it was to be drawn up with the ladder before Valentine arrived. He then more significantly notes that ll. 140–9 form a Shakespearian sonnet without the first quatrain (cf. *Ado*, III. i. 107–16, *AYL.*, III. ii. 1–10), and that the sentiment resembles that in Sonnet 27: 'For then [at night] my thoughts, from far where I abide, / Intend a zealous pilgrimage to thee.' There is also some resemblance to a sonnet in *Diana*: 'Goe now my thoughts, where one day you were going, / When neither fortune, nor my love did lower: / Now shall you see that changed day and hower, / Your joies decaied, and uncouth sorrowes growing? / And in the glasse, where I was oft bestowing / Mine eies, and in that sweete and pleasant flower, / A sluggish drone unwoorthely devower / That honie, which for me

sometimes was flowing. / And you shall see to whom I did surrender / My subject life, that causelesse did despise it: / And though this ill no remedy can borrow, / Yet tell her, that my minde did once ingender / A feare of that, wich after to mine eyes yet / She makes more plaine, to end my life in sorrow' (Kennedy, p. 57).
140. My thoughts] Bond suggests there is some confusion in the poem between unwritten thoughts (ll. 141–2) and thoughts on paper (ll. 143–4).
142. lightly] easily.
144. herald] i.e., they declare Valentine's mind, and they go in advance of him.
145. importune] impel; cf. *Meas.*, I. i. 57: 'As time and our concernings shall importune'.
146. grace] (1) fortune; (2) favour.
147. want] lack.
148. for] because.
149. should be] *NCS* observes that F's reading is 'more forcible' than F2's 'would', which most editors have followed.

What's here?   150
   Silvia, this night I will enfranchise thee.
'Tis so; and here's the ladder for the purpose.
Why, Phaëton, for thou art Merops' son
Wilt thou aspire to guide the heavenly car?
And with thy daring folly burn the world?   155
Wilt thou reach stars, because they shine on thee?
Go, base intruder, overweening slave,
Bestow thy fawning smiles on equal mates,
And think my patience (more than thy desert)
Is privilege for thy departure hence.   160
Thank me for this, more than for all the favours
Which (all too much) I have bestowed on thee.
But if thou linger in my territories
Longer than swiftest expedition
Will give thee time to leave our royal court,   165
By heaven, my wrath shall far exceed the love
I ever bore my daughter, or thyself.
Be gone, I will not hear thy vain excuse,
Butt as hou lov'st thy life, make speed from hence. [*Exit.*]

150–1.] *so Malone; one line in F.*   153. Phaëton, for . . . son] *this ed.; Phaeton (for
. . . sonne) F.*   169. S.D.] *F2.*

151. enfranchise] liberate.

153. *Phaëton . . . son*] Phaëton was the son of Phoebus and Clymene (whose husband was Merops): persuading his father to let him drive the chariot of the sun, he was incapable of keeping the horses to the normal course and was destroyed by a thunderbolt from Zeus. What the Duke here appears to express is that Valentine is Phaëton in ambition, but is no god's son: 'for' seems to signify 'for all that'. I owe to J. C. Maxwell the suggestion that the brackets of F are simply a Crane mannerism here and disguise the linking of 'for thou art Merops' son' to 'Wilt thou aspire . . .'. Steevens suggested the wording was prompted by an allusion in *The Troublesome Reign of King John*, Pt II, ll. 234–5: 'as sometime Phaeton / Mistrusting silly Merop for his Sire'. *NCS* thinks that 'Merops' may also contain a pun on 'ropes' (the corded

ladder). Cf. also Lyly's *Midas*, I. i. 15–16: 'least [=lest] desiring things above my reach, I bee fiered with *Phaeton*', where, as in *Gent.*, there is a linking of the Phaëton-image with the idea of reaching without grasping.

156.] Collier quoted Lyly's *Campaspe*, III. v. 37: 'starres are to be looked at, not reched at', and Greene's *Pandosto*: 'Starres are to be looked at with the eye, not reacht at with the hande'. Cf. Tilley, S825.

160. *Is . . . for*] 'grants the privilege of' (Bond).

163–9.] Malone, following a suggestion of Boaden, quoted the banishment of Kent in *Lr.*, I. i. 176–82. Bond, referring to other sentences of banishment in Shakespeare, notably Rosalind's, wisely comments: 'The formula must necessarily be more or less the same.'

Val. And why not death, rather than living torment?   170
　　To die is to be banish'd from myself,
　　And Silvia is myself: banish'd from her
　　Is self from self. A deadly banishment.
　　What light is light, if Silvia be not seen?
　　What joy is joy, if Silvia be not by?   175
　　Unless it be to think that she is by
　　And feed upon the shadow of perfection.
　　Except I be by Silvia in the night,
　　There is no music in the nightingale.
　　Unless I look on Silvia in the day,   180
　　There is no day for me to look upon.
　　She is my essence, and I leave to be,

173. A deadly] *F;* Ah! deadly *NCS.*

170–87.] The strong resemblance between this passage and *Rom.*, III. iii. 12–70, has been pointed out by Marshall: there is the same emphasis on the idea that exile is not more merciful than death but, through the absence of the beloved, is death itself. Cf. also the parting between the Queen and Suffolk in *2H6*, III. ii: see notes below on ll. 170, 174–81, 175, 182–7.

170.] Cf. *2H6*, III. ii. 401: 'From thee to die were torture more than death'; *Romeus*, l. 1430: 'Why dost thou so crye after death, thy life why dost thou hate?'

171–3.] This contrasts with Proteus' 'I needs must lose myself' at II. vi. 20: Valentine is the conventional lover here as Proteus the conventional villain there.

172–3. *Silvia…from self*] Cf. Sonnet 109: 'As easy might I from myself depart', and Sonnet 133: 'Me from myself thy cruel eye hath taken.'

174–81.] Cf. *2H6*, III. ii. 362–4: 'For where thou art, there is the world itself, / With every several pleasure in the world, / And where thou art not, desolation.'

175.] Cf. *2H6*, III. ii. 365–6: '…live thou to joy thy life; / Myself no joy in nought but that thou livest.'

177. *shadow*] image; cf. Lyly's *Love's*

Metamorphosis, III. ii. 20: 'men honour shadowes for substance, because they are men'. For a related use of 'shadow', see IV. ii. 118–28. The opposition of 'shadow' and 'substance' in Shakespeare, illustrated here, has been discussed by Maria Wickert in 'Das Schattenmotiv bei Shakespeare', *Anglia*, lxxi (1953), 274–309: this article relates the matter to the Platonic tradition, and refers specifically to the passage in IV. ii. E. I. Fripp, *Shakespeare Man and Artist*, 1938, i. 287, links the shadow-substance passages in the play with Sonnets 37, 43, 44, 53.

178–81.] Cf. Sonnet 98: 'Yet nor the lays of birds … / Could make me any summer's story tell, / . . . and, you away, / As with your shadow I with these did play.' Cf. also Ovid, *Tristia*, III. iii. 18, and Sidney, *Astrophel and Stella*, Sonnet LXXXIX: 'Stella's eyes that wont give me my daie.'

182–7.] Cf. *Romeus*, l. 1617: 'Thy absence is my death, thy sight shall geve me life', and *2H6*, III. ii. 388–9, 400: 'If I depart from thee, I cannot live; / And in thy sight to die, what were it …? / To die by thee were but to die in jest.'

182. *essence*] very being.
leave] cease; cf. II. vi. 17.

If I be not by her fair influence
Foster'd, illumin'd, cherish'd, kept alive.
I fly not death, to fly his deadly doom: 185
Tarry I here, I but attend on death,
But fly I hence, I fly away from life.

[*Enter* PROTEUS *and* LAUNCE.]

Pro. Run, boy, run, run, and seek him out.
Lau. So-ho, so-ho—
Pro. What seest thou?   190
Lau. Him we go to find. There's not a hair on 's head but
       'tis a Valentine.
Pro. Valentine?
Val. No.
Pro. Who then? His spirit?   195
Val. Neither.
Pro. What then?
Val. Nothing.
Lau. Can nothing speak? Master, shall I strike?
Pro. Who wouldst thou strike?   200

---

185. death, to fly his] *F;* death to fly his *F4;* death; to fly is *Singer;* death, to fly
this *Dyce.*   187. S.D.] *F2.*   189. So-ho, so-ho—] *F* (So-hough, Soa hough—),
Theobald.   191-2.] *so Capell;* Him . . . finde, / There's . . . *Valentine F.*   200.
Who] *F;* Whom *F2.*

---

183. *influence*] 'exercise of personal
power regarded as something akin to
astral influence' (Onions). Bond
quotes *L'Allegro*, 121–2: 'ladies, whose
bright eyes / Rain influence'.

185. *his*] presumably the Duke's,
though *NCS* takes it as 'death's'.

186–7.] i.e., in reverse, death comes
immediately if I go; if I stay, I merely
wait for it.

186. *attend on*] wait for, with perhaps
a suggestion of being Death's servitor.

189. *So-ho, so-ho*] a cry in hare-
hunting and hawking; Bond refers to
an engraving of a fourteenth-century
seal, in Halliwell's possession, showing
a hare with the legend 'So-hov. So
hov'. In the 1647 translation of
Guarini's *Il Pastor Fido*, Silvio cries
'Sogh, hogh, hogh' in searching for his

dog (II. ii). In Middleton's *A Trick to
Catch the Old One*, IV. iv, 'Sa ho, sa ho,
sa ho!' appears as a falconer's cry, and
in Dekker and Middleton's *The Roaring
Girl*, II. ii, the cry 'so ho, ho, so ho!'
gets the response, 'dost thou go a-
hawking after me?'

191. *hair*] Malone suggests a quibble
on 'hare': cf. note to l. 189.

192. *a Valentine*] apparently = a
lover (*O.E.D.*, s.v., 2). Bond suggests
that Launce means each of his hairs is
true to him: rather, perhaps, the idea
is that Valentine is in every particu-
larity a true lover.

200. *Who*] On the change to 'Whom'
in F2, see Franz, p. 296: 'Im 17. Jahr-
hundert, als man grösseren Wert auf
sprachliche Korrecktheit legte, war
man bestrebt, den Obliquus wieder in

Lau. Nothing.
Pro. Villain, forbear.
Lau. Why, sir, I'll strike nothing. I pray you—
Pro. Sirrah, I say forbear. Friend Valentine, a word.
Val. My ears are stopp'd, and cannot hear good news,   205
    So much of bad already hath possess'd them.
Pro. Then in dumb silence will I bury mine,
    For they are harsh, untunable, and bad.
Val. Is Silvia dead?
Pro. No, Valentine.   210
Val. No Valentine indeed for sacred Silvia.
    Hath she forsworn me?
Pro. No, Valentine.
Val. No Valentine if Silvia have forsworn me.
    What is your news?   215
Lau. Sir, there is a proclamation that you are vanished.
Pro. That thou art banish'd—O, that's the news—
    From hence, from Silvia, and from me thy friend.
Val. O, I have fed upon this woe already,
    And now excess of it will make me surfeit.   220

203. you—] *Theobald;* you. *F.*   204. Sirrah, I say] *F;* I say *Pope.*   216. that
you] *F;* you *Pope.*   217–18.] *F (subst.) ;* That . . . banished— / *Val.* Oh, that's
the news! / *Pro.* From . . . friend *conj. Camb.*   217. banish'd] *F;* banished
Singer.

seine alten Rechte einzusetzen, und
daher erscheint häufig in der zweiten
Folio-Ausgabe und in den darauf-
folgenden Ausgaben *whom* an Stelle
eines *who* der älteren Quartos und der
ersten Folio-Ausgabe.' Malone drew
attention to several Shakespearian examples of interrogative 'who' as
object.
    206. *hath*] 'News' could be either
singular or plural in Shakespeare: see
Franz, p. 190.
    211. *No Valentine*] Bond suggests
'no true-love' and relates this to ll.
191–2. That meaning may be in the
term, but it could also indicate simply
that he no longer exists for Silvia (cf.
l. 214).
    sacred] This may seem a strong word
in the context, but Bond quotes

'sacred beauty' in Sonnet 115. Cf. also
Wint., I. ii. 76: 'O my most sacred
lady!'
    216. *vanished*] Bond interestingly
suggests that Launce's mistake may
have been the origin of Shakespeare's
use of 'vanish'd from his lips' (referring
to Romeo's sentence of banishment) in
Rom., III. iii. 10.
    217. *banish'd*] Singer's emendation
would make the line more regular, but
a pause is effective before 'O' and a
trisyllabic 'banished' would seem
oddly affected as a correction of
Launce's 'vanished'. On the other
hand, it seems right that Valentine
should drag out a full line at 221.
    220. *excess . . . surfeit*] Malone
quoted *Tw.N.*, I. i. 2–3: 'Give me
excess of it, that, surfeiting, / The

Doth Silvia know that I am banished?
Pro. Ay, ay; and she hath offered to the doom
(Which unrevers'd stands in effectual force)
A sea of melting pearl, which some call tears;
Those at her father's churlish feet she tender'd,   225
With them, upon her knees, her humble self,
Wringing her hands, whose whiteness so became them
As if but now they waxed pale for woe.
But neither bended knees, pure hands held up,
Sad sighs, deep groans, nor silver-shedding tears   230
Could penetrate her uncompassionate sire;
But Valentine, if he be ta'en, must die.
Besides, her intercession chaf'd him so,
When she for thy repeal was suppliant,
That to close prison he commanded her,   235
With many bitter threats of biding there.
Val. No more; unless the next word that thou speak'st
Have some malignant power upon my life.
If so, I pray thee breathe it in mine ear,

221. banished] *Pope;* banish'd *F.*

appetite may sicken, and so die'; Bond added *Mer.V.*, III. ii. 113–15: 'scant this excess . . . For fear I surfeit.' In *2H6*, III. ii. 348, the Queen parting from Suffolk compares 'grief' with a 'surfeit' (cf. notes above drawing attention to several parallels there with the present scene).

222–36.] As Bond points out, this is an extreme example of the Elizabethan dramatist's readiness to separate real from dramatic time. All that Proteus describes here would have to take place during the time when Valentine was speaking ll. 170–87, if we were thinking of time in those terms. See Introduction, p. xix.

223.] Proteus seems to be emphasizing that the sentence, not having been reversed, remains operative. But Bond interprets 'if unreversed, . . .'.

224.] Cf. Sonnet 34: 'Ah but those tears are pearl which thy love sheds, / . . . and ransom all ill deeds' (Silvia is trying to 'ransom' Valentine here).

225–6.] In *Romeus*, Juliet, summoned before her father for rebuke, 'all bewept, fell groveling at his feete, / Which she doth washe with teares' (ll. 1940–1); then the 'chidden chylde' is left 'kneeling upon the floore' (l. 1994); soon after she is kneeling before the Friar 'on her tender knees' (l. 2009): cf. 'tender'd' here.

234. *thy repeal*] perhaps = the reversal of your sentence. Bond interprets as 'recall', which Onions calls 'The only S. use': however, 'recall' here would have to be understood in a proleptic sense, as Valentine has not yet departed. The modern sense is found in Shakespeare with the verb, and the use of the noun in this context may be a border-line one. Cf. *2H6*, III. ii. 349 (the Queen-Suffolk scene again): 'I will repeal thee.'

235–6.] Cf. *Romeus*, ll. 1979–80, 2018: 'too so close, and to so harde a gaole, / I shall thee wed, for all thy life'; 'Her fathers threats'.

As ending anthem of my endless dolour.   240
Pro. Cease to lament for that thou canst not help,
And study help for that which thou lament'st.
Time is the nurse and breeder of all good.
Here, if thou stay, thou canst not see thy love;
Besides, thy staying will abridge thy life.   245
Hope is a lover's staff: walk hence with that
And manage it, against despairing thoughts.
Thy letters may be here, though thou art hence,
Which, being writ to me, shall be deliver'd
Even in the milk-white bosom of thy love.   250
The time now serves not to expostulate.
Come, I'll convey thee through the city-gate,
And ere I part with thee, confer at large
Of all that may concern thy love-affairs.
As thou lov'st Silvia (though not for thyself)   255
Regard thy danger, and along with me.
Val. I pray thee, Launce, and if thou seest my boy,
Bid him make haste, and meet me at the North
        Gate.
Pro. Go, sirrah, find him out. Come, Valentine.
Val. O my dear Silvia! Hapless Valentine!   260
        [*Exeunt* PROTEUS *and* VALENTINE.]
Lau. I am but a fool, look you, and yet I have the wit to
think my master is a kind of a knave; but that's all

---

240. anthem] *F;* amen *conj. Singer.*   260. S.D.] *F2* (*Exeunt.*).

240. *anthem*] song of mourning; cf.
Phoen., 21.
241.] Cf. *3H6*, v. iv. 37–8: 'what
cannot be avoided / 'Twere childish
weakness to lament or fear', where
Shakespeare may be indebted to
Romeus, l. 1477: 'Foly it is to feare that
thou canst not avoyde.'
245. *abridge*] shorten; this sense
(with reference to time) is the original
one.
247. *manage*] wield. Originally
the word relates to the training of
horses.
250. *milk-white bosom*] For 'milk-
white', cf. Tilley, M931. On Silvia's
bosom as the place for the delivery of

letters, cf. Valentine's verses, esp.
l. 144. Commentators have laboured
to show that sixteenth-century dress
facilitated the carrying of letters in the
bosom.
251. *expostulate*] discuss.
255–6.] Cf. *Romeus*, ll. 513–14: 'I
wishe for lyfe, not for my propre ease, /
But that in it, you might I love'; and
Sonnet 22: 'O, therefore, love, be of
thyself so wary / As I, not for myself,
but for thee will.'
256. *Regard*] take account of; cf.
l. 70.
257. *and if*] if.
261–3. *I am . . . knave*] See Introduction, p. xix.

one, if he be but one knave. He lives not now that
knows me to be in love, yet I am in love, but a team
of horse shall not pluck that from me; nor who 'tis I   265
love; and yet 'tis a woman; but what woman I will
not tell myself; and yet 'tis a milk-maid; yet 'tis not
a maid, for she hath had gossips; yet 'tis a maid, for
she is her master's maid, and serves for wages. She
hath more qualities than a water-spaniel, which is   270
much in a bare Christian. [*Taking out a paper*] Here
is the cate-log of her conditions. 'Imprimis, she can

263. one knave] *F;* one kind of knave *Hanmer;* one kind *Warburton;* one in love
conj. Staunton.   271. S.D.] *Rowe (subst.) (after* 'cate-log').   272. cate-log] *F;*
cat-log *Pope;* catalogue *NCS.*   conditions] *F4;* condition *F.*

263. *one knave*] The weight of opinion
is in favour of keeping the F reading, in
the sense of single, moderate knavery
as contrasted with double: Johnson
argued for it; Farmer supported by
quoting Edwards' *Damon and Pithias*
(M.S.R., 124): 'You lose Money by
him if you sel him for one knaue, for he
serues for twaine'; and Steevens and
Malone found other relevant passages.
To these may be added *Oth.*, I. iii. 399–
400: 'to plume up my will / In double
knavery'.   Capell suggested that
Launce refers to Proteus' double
treachery, to Valentine and to Julia.
Collier added that Launce might be
thinking of the four knaves of a pack of
cards.

263 ff.] Cf. II. v. 34n.

268. *gossips*] Originally sponsors at
baptism, the word came to be used
sometimes for (talkative) women
attending a confinement; Bond noted
an instance in *Piers Plowman* (ed.
Skeat, A.v.154, B.v.310), where it is
applied to a man. It remains a little
obscure whether Launce is saying she
has had lovers (male gossips), women-
visitors at her confinement, or sponsors for the baptism of her child. The
general sense is, however, plain.

269. *her master's maid*] In *Diana*, as a
comic foil to Felismena's love, Don
Felix's page tells her, in her disguise as

Valerius: 'I know where an old
Cannons maide is . . . whom if thou
canst but finde in thy hart to love and
serve as I do . . .' (Kennedy, p. 94).

270. *qualities*] accomplishments.

water-spaniel] Marshall notes the
abilities of the water-spaniel given in
A. Fleming's translation (1576) of Dr
Caius' treatise on English dogs. However, Marshall thinks that it is the
'Spaniel gentle or Comforter' (the
Maltese lap-dog) that is meant here,
as Caius refers to that dog as relieving
a master or mistress of a 'sickness of the
stomach' by taking it on himself.

271. *bare Christian*] Steevens suggested a quibble—(1) mere; (2) naked—
and a contrast between the naked
Christian and the hairy dog.

272. *cate-log*] Bond suggested a pun
on the girl's name; either 'Kate' or
'cat' could suggest a whore (cf. Partridge, p. 136). *NCS* regards the F
spelling as a misprint, but Launce
rarely misses an opportunity.

conditions] qualities. Bond quotes
Mer.V., I. ii. 142–4: 'the condition of a
saint and the complexion of a devil'.
The plural of F4 seems more acceptable in this instance; cf. Phillip's
Patient and Meek Grissill (M.S.R.,
1231): 'If you had Grissils pacyence
and condiseyons excelent'.

272–5. *she . . . jade*] Cf. *Everie Woman*

fetch and carry': why, a horse can do no more; nay,
a horse cannot fetch, but only carry, therefore is she
better than a jade. 'Item, she can milk': look you, a 275
sweet virtue in a maid with clean hands.

[*Enter* SPEED.]

Spe. How now, Signor Launce! What news with your
mastership?

Lau. With my master's ship? Why, it is at sea.

Spe. Well, your old vice still: mistake the word. What 280
news, then, in your paper?

Lau. The black'st news that ever thou heard'st.

Spe. Why, man, how black?

Lau. Why, as black as ink.

Spe. Let me read them. 285

Lau. Fie on thee, jolt-head, thou canst not read.

Spe. Thou lyest; I can.

Lau. I will try thee. Tell me this: who begot thee?

Spe. Marry, the son of my grandfather.

Lau. O illiterate loiterer! It was the son of thy grand- 290
mother. This proves that thou canst not read.

Spe. Come, fool, come; try me in thy paper.

Lau. [*Giving him the paper*] There; and Saint Nicholas be
thy speed.

Spe. 'Imprimis, she can milk.' 295

275. milk': look you,] *Rowe;* milke, look you, *F;* milk', look you; *Capell.*   276.
S.D.] *F2.*   279. master's ship] *Theobald;* Mastership *F.*   295–6.] *om. conj.
Farmer (ap. Malone ii).*   295. Imprimis] *F;* Item *Halliwell.*

in her Humor, 1609, sig. D4: 'What
kinde is your Dogge of Sir? . . . A kinde
of Mungrill, he will carrie, but not
fetch.'

275. *jade*] (1) ill-conditioned horse;
(2) term of contempt for a woman.

280. *your . . . word*] Bond notes that
Speed has the punning habit too. It is,
moreover, frequent with many of this
play's characters. Bernard Spivack,
Shakespeare and the Allegory of Evil, 1958,
p. 202, suggests that Shakespeare is
here referring to the love of word-play
characteristic of the Vice of the
morality plays.

284. *as . . . ink*] Cf. Tilley, I 73.

286. *'olt-head*] blockhead; cf. *Sir
Clyomon and Clamydes* (M.S.R., 627):
'was euer seene such a iolt-headed
villaine as he'.

288–91. *Tell . . . grandmother*] Cf.
Tilley, M1193.

293–4. *Saint . . . speed*] Warburton
pointed out that St Nicholas was
the patron-saint of scholars. Halliwell drew attention to the pun in
'speed'.

295–360.] On the resemblances between this passage and passages in
Err., III. ii. 71–160, and Lyly, *Midas,*

Lau. Ay, that she can.

Spe. 'Item, she brews good ale.'

Lau. And thereof comes the proverb: 'Blessing of your
    heart, you brew good ale.'

Spe. 'Item, she can sew.'   300

Lau. That's as much as to say, 'Can she so?'

Spe. 'Item, she can knit.'

Lau. What need a man care for a stock with a wench,
    when she can knit him a stock?

Spe. 'Item, she can wash and scour.'   305

Lau. A special virtue; for then she need not be washed
    and scoured.

300. sew] *Steevens;* sowe *F.*

II. ii. 11–87, see Introduction, pp.
xxxii–xxxiv.

   295. *Imprimis*] The commentators
have been disturbed by the fact that
Speed begins at the second item (cf.
l. 272) and yet says 'Imprimis'.
Farmer would solve the problem by
omitting ll. 295–6. The possible explanation is that Shakespeare had
thought of another sense of 'milk' (see
following note) and decided to repeat
this particular in order to use it; and
Speed gets a better start for his reading
by beginning with the word 'Imprimis'.

   295–6. *she can milk . . . can*] *NCS*
interprets 'milk' as 'entice by wiles',
quoting Fletcher's *Rule a Wife,* II. iv:
'All this is but in seeming / To milke
the lover on'. Halliwell thought there
might be a pun on 'milk-can'. But it
seems possible that 'milk' is to be taken
in the sense of 'drain away the contents of', ' "bleed" pecuniarily'
(*O.E.D.,* s.v., 4), as in Lyly, *Endimion,*
III. iii. 23: 'Loue hath as it were milkt
my thoughts, and drained from my
hart the very substance of my accus-
tomed courage'. Alternatively, and
perhaps more probably (in view of
'gossips', l. 268, and in view of
Launce's general delight in sexual
reference), it could mean 'suckle'
(*O.E.D.,* s.v., 3), with perhaps a fur-

ther (and indecent) implication linking this with the preceding sense.

   298–9. *Blessing . . . ale*] Cf. Tilley,
B450. Steevens quoted Jonson's
Masque of Augurs, 181–3: 'Our Ale's o'
the best, / And each good guest / Prays
for their souls that brew it.'

   300–1. *sew . . . so?*] There is little
doubt that F's 'sowe' is for 'sew', but
the point of Launce's comment is
obscure. 'Sew' could mean 'drain,
draw off the water from' (*O.E.D.,* v⁴,
1), or 'ooze out' (*O.E.D.,* v⁴, 2). But it
seems more likely that Launce takes
Speed's 'sew' as 'sow' in the sense of
scattering seed (i.e., propagating) and
therefore expresses incredulity with a
pun.

   302. *knit*] *NCS* suggests a quibble on
'knit' meaning 'conceive' (*O.E.D.,*
5d).

   303, 304. *stock*] (1) dowry; (2)
stocking. But cf. preceding note: 'knit
him a stock' may also suggest 'conceive a family for him'.

   306–7. *washed and scoured*] *NCS* interprets as 'knocked down and beaten'.
This depends on interpreting 'wash' as
'a Shakespearian form of "swash" ', on
the evidence of 'washing blow', *Rom.,*
I. i. 70 (1599 Quarto and Folio). As,
the speaker is Launce, it is doubtful whether the implications stop
there.

Spe. 'Item, she can spin.'
Lau. Then may I set the world on wheels, when she can
    spin for her living.   310
Spe. 'Item, she hath many nameless virtues.'
Lau. That's as much as to say 'bastard virtues'; that in-
    deed know not their fathers; and therefore have no
    names.
Spe. 'Here follow her vices.'   315
Lau. Close at the heels of her virtues.
Spe. 'Item, she is not to be kissed fasting in respect of her
    breath.'
Lau. Well; that fault may be mended with a breakfast.
    Read on.   320
Spe. 'Item, she hath a sweet mouth.'

---

315. follow] *F corr.;* followes *F uncorr.*   317. be kissed fasting] *Rowe;* be fasting
F; be — fasting *NCS.*

309. *set . . . wheels*] make life go easily for me; Craig, Herford, *NCS* interpret as 'let things slide'. Bond supports the sense of self-indulgence by referring to the pamphlet by Taylor the water-poet, *The World runnes on Wheeles.* Cf. Tilley, W893; *Ant.*, II. vii. 98–9; *Misogonus*, I. iv. 13: 'lett all go a wheles'; and Beaumont and Fletcher, *Knight of the Burning Pestle*, v. iii: 'the world it runnes on wheeles'. There may be, as Bond suggests, a 'verbal glance at the world as the spinning-wheel'.

311. *nameless*] more than can be named (Bond), inexpressible (Onions); cf. *R2*, II. ii. 40: 'nameless woe'. But Hilda M. Hulme, *Explorations in Shakespeare's Language*, 1962, pp. 336–7, deduces from Stratford inventories of household goods that the proper significance in Launce's catalogue is 'too small to be worth detailed description', and this seems altogether better. For Launce's interpretation in the following line, cf. *Lucr.*, 522: 'Thy issue blurr'd with nameless bastardy'.

317. *kissed fasting*] Rowe's addition seems right, and Dyce supported it by quoting Webster, *Duchess of Malfi*

(Revels edn), II. i. 38–40: 'I would sooner eat a dead pigeon, taken from the soles of the feet of one sick of the plague, than kiss one of you fasting.' Bond assumes that it is the kisser who should not be fasting, but it seems more likely that 'kissed (when she is) fasting' is what is meant.

321. *sweet mouth*] As Johnson pointed out, the obvious sense here is 'sweet tooth'. Steevens suggested that it meant (1) she sang sweetly (which will not do, for it is her vices that are here being catalogued) or (2) she had a lecherous mouth. Malone quoted Hall's *Satires*, IV. ii. 47–8 (1599): 'Let sweete mouth'd *Mercia* bid what crowns she please, / For halfe-red Cherries, or greene garden-pease'; Bond linked 'sweet tooth' and 'lecherous mouth' by quoting *Euphues* (ed. Bond, ii. 83): 'I am glad that my Adonis hath a sweet tooth in his head, and who knoweth not what followeth?' —the last words being a translation of Ovid's 'Caetera quis nescit?', which in context has a wanton sense. Launce's reply is probably to be taken as indicating a welcome for her wantonness: Speed's statement must therefore be

Lau. That makes amends for her sour breath.

Spe. 'Item, she doth talk in her sleep.'

Lau. It's no matter for that; so she sleep not in her talk.

Spe. 'Item, she is slow in words.'   325

Lau. O villain, that set this down among her vices! To
    be slow in words is a woman's only virtue. I pray
    thee out with 't, and place it for her chief virtue.

Spe. 'Item, she is proud.'

Lau. Out with that too: it was Eve's legacy, and cannot   330
    be ta'en from her.

Spe. 'Item, she hath no teeth.'

Lau. I care not for that neither; because I love crusts.

Spe. 'Item, she is curst.'

Lau. Well; the best is, she hath no teeth to bite.   335

Spe. 'Item, she will often praise her liquor.'

Lau. If her liquor be good, she shall; if she will not, I
    will; for good things should be praised.

Spe. 'Item, she is too liberal.'

Lau. Of her tongue she cannot, for that's writ down she   340

---

323. sleep] *F*; slip *Collier ii.*   326–8.] *so Pope;* Oh . . . vices; / To . . . vertue: /
I . . . vertue *F.*   326. villain, that set this] *F corr.;* villanie, that set this *F uncorr.*
330–1.] *so Pope;* Out . . . too: / It . . . her *F.*

---

taken in a different sense, and the only
available one is 'sweet tooth'. Cf.
Tilley, T420, and these lines from the
passage in Lyly's *Midas* referred to in
the note to ll. 295–360: '*Licio.* . . . Then,
sir, hath she a calues tooth. *Pet.* O monstrous mouth! I would then it had been
a sheepes eye, and a neates tongue.
Licio. It is not for the bignes, but the
sweetnes: all her teeth are as sweet as
the sweet tooth of a calfe. *Pet.* Sweetly
meant.'

324. *sleep . . . talk*] A meaning is clear
enough, and the Collier MS. change is
unnecessary. But a *double entendre* may
be suspected.

326–7. *To . . . virtue*] Bond quotes
Mer.V., I. i. 111–12: 'silence is only
commendable / In a neat's tongue
dried and a maid not vendible', and
Lr., v. iii. 272–3.

327. *only*] unique, peerless; cf.

Ham., III. ii. 131: 'O God, your only
jig-maker', and *1H6*, IV. vii. 77: 'Is
Talbot slain, the Frenchmen's only
scourge'.

329. *proud*] *NCS* interprets as 'lascivious', as *Lucr.*, 712: 'The flesh being
proud'.

334. *curst*] shrewish.

335. *no . . . bite*] Launce takes the
alternative meaning of 'curst'—i.e.,
savage—used of bears in *Wint.*, III. iii.
135, and of the boar in *Ven.*, 887.

336. *praise*] appraise, test (by sip-
ping); Bond quoted (as a doubtful
instance) *Tw.N.*, I. v. 267–8: 'Were
you sent hither to praise me?' Launce
(ll. 337–8) takes 'praise' in the normal modern sense.

339. *liberal*] gross, licentious; Bond
quoted *Ham.*, IV. vii. 171: 'liberal
shepherds'. Launce (ll. 340–3) takes it
in the common sense of 'bountiful'.

is slow of; of her purse she shall not, for that I'll keep
shut. Now, of another thing she may, and that cannot I help. Well, proceed.

Spe. 'Item, she hath more hair than wit, and more faults
than hairs, and more wealth than faults.'   345

Lau. Stop there. I'll have her. She was mine, and not
mine, twice or thrice in that last article. Rehearse
that once more.

Spe. 'Item, she hath more hair than wit.'

Lau. More hair than wit: it may be. I'll prove it: the   350
cover of the salt hides the salt, and therefore it is
more than the salt; the hair that covers the wit is
more than the wit; for the greater hides the less.
What's next?

Spe. 'And more faults than hairs.'   355

Lau. That's monstrous: O that that were out!

Spe. 'And more wealth than faults.'

Lau. Why, that word makes the faults gracious. Well,

---

344. hair] *F corr.;* haires *F uncorr.*   347. that last] *F corr.;* that *F uncorr.*
350. wit: it may be. I'll prove it:] *Theobald (subst.)*; wit: it may be ile proue it: *F;*
wit it may be; I'll prove it: *Craig.*   358. Why . . . Well] *so Pope;* Why . . .
gracious: / Well *F.*

---

344. *more . . . wit*] Cf. *Err.*, II. ii. 83–4:
'there's many a man hath more hair
than wit'; Tilley, B736. Bond quoted
Euphues (ed. Bond, II. xviii. 10): 'Thou
hast caryed to thy graue more graye
haires than yeares: and yet more
yeares, then virtues.'

hair] The singular of the corrected
state of F is better with the singular
'wit'; after 'faults', the plural (l. 345)
is preferable.

346. *I'll have her*] This, repeated at
l. 359, comes in oddly before the rest of
Launce's speech here. It looks as if
ll. 346 ('She was mine . . .') –359 were
an afterthought.

347. *Rehearse*] recite.

350. *More hair . . . prove it*] Cf. the
mock academic disputation in *Err.*, II.
ii. 85 ff., on Time and hair.

it may be. I'll prove it] A full stop or
Theobald's semi-colon seems essential

here. Launce does not mean 'perhaps
I'll prove it', either in the sense of
'establish' or 'test'; rather, he means
'perhaps so; I'll test it'.

351–2. *cover . . . than the salt*] Malone
pointed out that formerly salt-cellars
were large, ceremonial, and covered.
NCS suggests a quibble on 'salt' in the
sense of 'wit', but 'salt' can also mean
'lewd' (e.g., *Ant.*, II. i. 21: 'Salt Cleopatra'). In this speech the idea of pubic
hair seems not far away.

353. *greater . . . less*] Cf. Tilley, G437.

355–6.] Launce seems to interpret
'fault' here in the sense of 'an unsound
or damaged place; a flaw, crack'
(*O.E.D.*, 4).

358. *gracious*] acceptable; cf. *3H6*,
III. iii. 117: 'is he gracious in the
people's eye'. Steevens interpreted as
'graceful', Bond as 'full of grace
(religious)'.

I'll have her. And if it be a match, as nothing is
impossible—   360
Spe. What then?
Lau. Why, then will I tell thee that thy master stays for
thee at the North Gate.
Spe. For me?
Lau. For thee? Ay, who art thou? He hath stayed for a   365
better man than thee.
Spe. And must I go to him?
Lau. Thou must run to him; for thou hast stayed so long
that going will scarce serve the turn.
Spe. Why didst not tell me sooner? 'Pox of your love-   370
letters!   [*Exit.*]
Lau. Now will he be swinged for reading my letter; an
unmannerly slave, that will thrust himself into
secrets. I'll after, to rejoice in the boy's correction. *Exit.*

SCENE II

Enter Duke *and* THURIO.

Duke. Sir Thurio, fear not but that she will love you
        Now Valentine is banish'd from her sight.
Thu. Since his exile she hath despis'd me most,

---

360. impossible—] *Rowe;* impossible. F.   371. S.D.] *Capell.*   374. S.D.]
Capell; Exeunt F.

Scene II

SCENE II] *Rowe; Scena Secunda* F.   S.D. Enter . . . *Thurio]* Enter Duke, Thurio,
Protheus F; Enter Duke, and Thurio; Protheus behind *Capell.*

359-60. *nothing is impossible*] Cf.
Tilley, N299.

365-6. *stayed . . . thee*] 'The humour
lies in Launce's having no legitimate
score here, to stay for a person being a
mark of condescension not of contempt' (Bond).

369. *going*] walking, going on foot at
an ordinary pace; cf. *Tp.*, III. ii. 21-2:
'Ste. We'll not run, Monsieur Monster.
Trin. Nor go neither.'

372. *swinged*] beaten; cf. II. i. 78.

373. *unmannerly*] with a quibble, 'not
an adult man'; cf. 'mannerly' (II. vii.
58) and 'boy's' (l. 374). See also
Introduction, p. xxvi.

373-4. *thrust . . . secrets*] with a sexual
implication as well as the obvious
meaning; see preceding note.

Scene II

1. *but . . . will*] i.e., that she will not.
3-4.] As Proteus in l. 13 reports that
Valentine has just gone, there is not

Forsworn my company, and rail'd at me,
That I am desperate of obtaining her.   5
Duke. This weak impress of love is as a figure
Trenched in ice, which with an hour's heat
Dissolves to water, and doth lose his form.
A little time will melt her frozen thoughts,
And worthless Valentine shall be forgot.   10

[*Enter* PROTEUS.]

How now, Sir Proteus, is your countryman,
According to our proclamation, gone?
Pro. Gone, my good lord.
Duke. My daughter takes his going grievously?
Pro. A little time, my lord, will kill that grief.   15
Duke. So I believe; but Thurio thinks not so.
Proteus, the good conceit I hold of thee
(For thou hast shown some sign of good desert)
Makes me the better to confer with thee.
Pro. Longer than I prove loyal to your grace   20
Let me not live to look upon your grace.
Duke. Thou know'st how willingly I would effect
The match between Sir Thurio and my daughter?

---

10. S.D.] *Rowe.*   14. grievously?] *F corr.;* heavily? *F uncorr.;* heauily. *F4;*
grievously. *Capell.*   19. better] *F;* bolder *conj. Capell.*   23. daughter?] *F;*
daughter. *Rowe.*

time for Silvia's harsh treatment of
Thurio to have taken place. But see
note to III. i. 222–36.

5. *That*] so that.

6. *impress*] impression.

7.] A near-parallel is in *Romeus*, l. 98:
'[the lover] melts awaye, as snow
against the sonne'.

7. *Trenched*] cut.

hour's] disyllabic; cf. 'fire', I. ii. 30.

8. *his*] i.e., its (the figure's).

9. *melt . . . thoughts*] This both repeats
the image (her thoughts, 'frozen' in the
form of the 'impress of love', now growing fluid again) and suggests that she
will be less icy to Thurio.

12. *proclamation*] We need not
understand a proclamation in the legal
sense, but simply the declaration of

III. i. 163–9; cf. *All's W.*, I. iii. 180: 'the
proclamation of thy passion'.

14. *grievously*] with grief or distress;
cf. *O.E.D.*, 5 ('1582 EARL SHREWSBURY
in Ellis *Orig. Lett.* Ser. II. III. 61 My
wyffe taketh my doughter Lennoux
deathe so grevouslie that she neither
dothe nor can thincke of any thinge
but of lamentinge'). This would seem
preferable to 'heavily' in being more
closely related to 'grief' in l. 15.

15.] Cf. Tilley, T322, citing Lyly's
Endimion, I. iv. 46: 'This will weare out
with time, that treadeth all things
down but trueth.'

17. *conceit*] opinion; cf. *H8*, II. iii.
74–5: 'the fair conceit / The king hath
of you'.

19. *better*] more readily.

Pro. I do, my lord.

Duke. And also, I think, thou art not ignorant   25
How she opposes her against my will?

Pro. She did, my lord, when Valentine was here.

Duke. Ay, and perversely she persevers so.
What might we do to make the girl forget
The love of Valentine, and love Sir Thurio?   30

Pro. The best way is to slander Valentine,
With falsehood, cowardice, and poor descent:
Three things that women highly hold in hate.

Duke. Ay, but she'll think that it is spoke in hate.

Pro. Ay, if his enemy deliver it.   35
Therefore it must with circumstance be spoken
By one whom she esteemeth as his friend.

Duke. Then you must undertake to slander him.

Pro. And that, my lord, I shall be loath to do:
'Tis an ill office for a gentleman,   40
Especially against his very friend.

Duke. Where your good word cannot advantage him,
Your slander never can endamage him;
Therefore the office is indifferent,
Being entreated to it by your friend.   45

Pro. You have prevail'd, my lord: if I can do it
By aught that I can speak in his dispraise,
She shall not long continue love to him.
But say this wind her love from Valentine,

---

25. I] *F;* I doe *F2*.   26. will?] *F;* will. *Rowe.*   49. wind] *Keightley, conj.*
Marshall; weede *F;* wean *Rowe;* wend *conj. NCS;* woo *Sisson.*

34. *spoke*] On this as a past participle, see Franz, p. 166.

35. *deliver*] report.

36. *circumstance*] particulars (Onions,
following Johnson); Bond takes it as
'circumlocution and hesitation'. These
two senses overlap, but they are to be
distinguished from the uses of the
word in 1. i. 36, 37.

41. *very*] special. Bond quotes from
Gascoigne's *Works* (1572): 'G. T. to
his very friend H. W.'

43. *endamage*] Bond (following
Schmidt) quotes from *1H6*, II. i. 77:
'lay new platforms to endamage them'.

44. *indifferent*] neither good nor bad;
cf. *Ham.*, II. ii. 231: 'the indifferent
children of the earth'.

49. *wind*] The F 'weede' has been
kept by most editors, but the sense is
unsatisfactory. Sisson, i. 58–9, argues
that we should have to interpret as
'clear the weed of her love from the
garden of Valentine's mind'—which
approaches the absurd; but Harold
Brooks (while endorsing 'wind' as at
least probably correct) puts to me the
idea that 'her love' is here the noxious
love she has for Valentine, while in
l. 51 the meaning has shifted to 'her

It follows not that she will love Sir Thurio.   50
Thu. Therefore, as you unwind her love from him,
Lest it should ravel, and be good to none,
You must provide to bottom it on me;
Which must be done by praising me as much
As you in worth dispraise Sir Valentine.   55
Duke. And, Proteus, we dare trust you in this kind,
Because we know (on Valentine's report)
You are already Love's firm votary,
And cannot soon revolt, and change your mind.
Upon this warrant shall you have access   60
Where you with Silvia may confer at large.
For she is lumpish, heavy, melancholy,
And, for your friend's sake, will be glad of you;
Where you may temper her, by your persuasion,

55. worth] *F;* word *conj. Capell.*

capacity for loving'. Bond's suggestion that we might take 'from' as 'of'— 'weed Valentine from the garden of her mind'—is implausible. Moreover, this garden-image does not seem to fit well with what follows. Sisson argues for 'woo' (spelt 'wooee' in the copy for F, Sisson having met that form in manuscript); *NCS*'s conjecture 'wend' has the sense of 'make to wind', but this, except in a nautical context, seems rare in Elizabethan times. A regular feature of this play is the taking up of a word from one speech to another (cf. 'grievously' and 'grief', ll. 14, 15), and in the present instance this gives weight to Marshall's conjecture 'wind', which is here adopted. Against it we must note Sisson's view that it is not 'graphically probable'. Bond quotes, in support of 'wind,' Tourneur's *Revenger's Tragedy*, III. i. 20–1: 'some trick and wile, / To winde our yonger brother out of prison'.

51–3. *unwind . . . bottom*] Johnson points out that the 'housewife's term for a ball of thread wound upon a central body' is a 'bottom of thread': thus Thurio is asking to be made the 'bottom' on which the love-thread is wound while it is being unwound from

Valentine. Steevens quoted *Grange's Garden* (1577): 'A bottome for your silke it seemes / My letters are become,/ Which oft with winding off and on / Are wasted whole and some'. In *Shr.*, IV. iii. 138, we have 'a bottom of brown thread'. The same image seems to lurk in Hotspur's words about 'the smug and silver Trent': 'It shall not wind with such a deep indent, / To rob me of so rich a bottom here' (*1H4*, III. i. 104–5).

52. *ravel*] become entangled; cf. *Mac.*, II. ii. 37: 'the ravell'd sleave of care'.

61. *at large*] fully.

62. *lumpish*] low-spirited (unique in Shakespeare).

63, 65. *your friend's, my friend*] There may be a deliberate absurdity in the Duke's instructing Proteus to help 'my friend' at the expense of 'your friend'. In l. 45 the Duke himself claimed to be 'your friend'. The friendship theme does, of course, easily become absurd, and an attempt to help it in that direction may be suspected in these lines. See Introduction, pp. lx–lxi.

64. *Where*] whereas: 'Welcomed for Valentine's sake, *yet* you may persuade her against him' (Bond). But the

To hate young Valentine, and love my friend.   65
Pro. As much as I can do, I will effect.
  But you, Sir Thurio, are not sharp enough:
  You must lay lime, to tangle her desires
  By wailful sonnets, whose composed rhymes
  Should be full-fraught with serviceable vows.   70
Duke. Ay, much is the force of heaven-bred poesy.
Pro. Say that upon the altar of her beauty
  You sacrifice your tears, your sighs, your heart.
  Write till your ink be dry; and with your tears
  Moist it again; and frame some feeling line   75
  That may discover such integrity.
  For Orpheus' lute was strung with poets' sinews,
  Whose golden touch could soften steel and stones,
  Make tigers tame, and huge leviathans

71. Ay, much] *F;* Much *Pope;* Ay, / Much *NCS.* 75. line] *F;* lines *conj. S. Verges (ap. Camb).* 76. such integrity] *F;* such integrity / As her obdurate heart may penetrate *conj. Malone;* strict integrity *Collier (MS.);* love's integrity *conj. S. Verges (ap. Camb).*

meaning may be no more than 'in which circumstance'; cf. *Tw.N.*, v. i. 88–9: 'Drew to defend him when he was beset: / Where being apprehended . . .'.

 temper] mould, like wax; Malone quoted *2H4*, IV. iii. 140–2: 'I have him already tempering between my finger and my thumb, and shortly will I seal with him.'

 68. *lime*] birdlime; cf. *Ham.*, III. iii. 68: 'O limed soul'.

 tangle] enmesh. As Bond points out, this changes the image from lime to nets.

 69. *sonnets*] poems written in praise, normally of a mistress; not necessarily in the sonnet form; cf. Gascoigne's *Posies*, 472: 'There are Dyzaynes & Syxaines . . . which some English writers do also terme by the name of Sonnettes' *(O.E.D.).*

 composed rhymes] 'carefully wrought verses' (Bond).

 70. *serviceable vows*] vows of service.

 71.] Odd praise of poetry, which in this instance is to be used to capture Silvia's love for the wretched Thurio:

men can become ridiculous when they praise poetry for the wrong reasons or in the wrong circumstances. See Introduction, p. lxiv.

 74, 78.] Cf. *LLL.*, IV. iii. 342–3, 347.

 75. *Moist*] Cf. the Countess of Pembroke's *Antony*, 600: 'His sworde Alreadie moisted is in his warme bloude' *(O.E.D.).* The verb is also to be found in Golding's Ovid (Bond).

 76. *discover*] reveal.

 such integrity] i.e., such single-heartedness as your weeping shows that you have. Malone's conjecture that a line is missing is an unnecessary one, but the expression here is certainly laboured.

 77.] This is an elaborate way (so elaborate that Warburton deduced a reference to Orpheus as law-giver) of saying that the poets share in Orpheus' power to control the world and its creatures. Orpheus and his music appear again in *Mer.V.*, v. i. 80, and *H8*, III. i. 3; they are also elaborately introduced into Bk IV of the *Diana* (Kennedy, pp. 143–53).

 79. *Make tigers tame*] Cf. Ovid,

Forsake unsounded deeps, to dance on sands.   80
After your dire-lamenting elegies,
Visit by night your lady's chamber-window
With some sweet consort; to their instruments
Tune a deploring dump: the night's dead silence
Will well become such sweet complaining grievance. 85
This, or else nothing, will inherit her.

Duke. This discipline shows thou hast been in love.

Thu. And thy advice, this night, I'll put in practice:
Therefore, sweet Proteus, my direction-giver,
Let us into the city presently   90
To sort some gentlemen, well skill'd in music.
I have a sonnet that will serve the turn
To give the onset to thy good advice.

Duke. About it, gentlemen.

Pro. We'll wait upon your grace till after supper, 95
And afterward determine our proceedings.

Duke. Even now about it. I will pardon you.   *Exeunt.*

85. sweet complaining] *F;* sweet-complaining *Capell.*

Tristia, IV. i. 17, on comparable exploits.

81. *elegies*] 'love-poems, like the *Elegiae* of Tibullus' (Bond); cf. *AYL.,* III. ii. 377–80: 'There is a man . . . hangs odes upon hawthorns and elegies on brambles'.

83. *consort*] either company of musicians (see quotation in next note) or piece of music. The latter sense is supported by 'sweet', the former by 'their', but neither piece of evidence is conclusive: the adjective could loosely refer to what the consort was to play, and Malone has pointed out that Shakespeare's pronouns can take a form appropriate to an implied idea, as in *Oth.,* III. iv. 64–5: 'bid me, when my fate would have me wive, / To give it her'.

84. *dump*] mournful melody; cf. Munday, *Two Italian Gentlemen* (M.S.R., 1095–6): 'The third Act being doone, the Consort sounds a sollemne Dump.'

85. *grievance*] lamenting; Bond, following Rolfe, quotes Sonnet 30, l. 9, where the context demands this meaning. Contrast the sense at I. i. 17 and IV. iii. 37.

86. *inherit*] win; Bond, following Rolfe, quotes *Rom.,* I. ii. 28–30: 'even such delight . . . shall you this night / Inherit at my house'.

87. *discipline*] learning; cf. *Troil.,* II. iii. 32–3: 'heaven bless thee from a tutor, and discipline come not near thee!'

89. *direction-giver*] one who directs an archer's aim; cf. v. iv. 100: 'her that gave aim to all thy oaths'.

90. *presently*] at once.

91. *sort*] choose; cf. Ford, *Lover's Melancholy* (ed. W. Bang), II. i. 860: 'Wee shall sort time to take more notice of him'.

93. *onset*] E. I. Fripp, *Shakespeare Man and Artist,* 1938, i. 287, suggests that Thurio is unconsciously punning on 'sonnet', l. 92.

97. *I . . . you*] i.e., I give you leave to go.

ACT IV

SCENE I

Enter certain Outlaws.

1 Out. Fellows, stand fast: I see a passenger.

2 Out. If there be ten, shrink not, but down with 'em.

[*Enter* VALENTINE *and* SPEED.]

3 Out. Stand, sir, and throw us that you have about ye.
    If not, we'll make you sit, and rifle you.

Spe. Sir, we are undone; these are the villains   5
    That all the travellers do fear so much.

Val. My friends—

1 Out. That's not so, sir: we are your enemies.

2 Out. Peace; we'll hear him.

3 Out. Ay, by my beard will we; for he is a proper man.   10

Val. Then know that I have little wealth to lose;
    A man I am, cross'd with adversity:
    My riches are these poor habiliments,

ACT IV

Scene 1

ACT IV SCENE 1] *Rowe; Actus Quartus. Scœna Prima F;* Act IV. Scene I. Scene *a Forest Rowe.* S.D. *Enter . . .* Outlaws] *Enter Valentine, Speed, and certaine Outlawes F.* 2. S.D.] *Rowe.* 3–4.] *so F; as prose Pope.* 4. you sit] *F;* you sir *F3.* 5–6.] *so F; as prose Pope.* 7. friends—] *Theobald (subst.);* friends. *F.*

1. *passenger*] traveller.

4. *sit*] in facetious antithesis to 'Stand', l. 3: the F3 compositor apparently failed to see the joke. Cf. II. i. 80–1.

rifle] rob (unique in Shakespeare); cf. Rowlands, *Dr. Merrie-man,* 3: 'Vnto a Wood hard by, they hale him in, / And rifle him vnto his very skin' (*O.E.D.*); *Damon and Pithias* (M.S.R., 1579): 'Let vs riffell him so that he

haue not one pennie to blesse him'.

10. *proper man*] 'fine-looking fellow, rather of stature than feature' (Bond).

12. *cross'd with*] thwarted by; cf. *Rom.,* Prol. 6: 'star-cross'd lovers'.

13.] Bond compares *Taming of a Shrew*: 'Euen in these honest meane abiliments, / Our purses shall be rich, our garments plaine'; in *Shr.,* IV. iii. 172–3, 'rich' appears as 'proud', 'plaine' as 'poor'.

Of which if you should here disfurnish me,
You take the sum and substance that I have.   15
2 Out. Whither travel you?
Val. To Verona.
1 Out. Whence came you?
Val. From Milan.
3 Out. Have you long sojourned there?   20
Val. Some sixteen months, and longer might have stay'd,
If crooked fortune had not thwarted me.
1 Out. What, were you banished thence?
Val. I was.
2 Out. For what offence?   25
Val. For that which now torments me to rehearse:
I kill'd a man, whose death I much repent,
But yet I slew him manfully, in fight,
Without false vantage, or base treachery.
1 Out. Why, ne'er repent it, if it were done so;   30
But were you banish'd for so small a fault?
Val. I was, and held me glad of such a doom.
2 Out. Have you the tongues?
Val. My youthful travel therein made me happy,
Or else I often had been miserable.   35
3 Out. By the bare scalp of Robin Hood's fat friar,
This fellow were a king for our wild faction.

---

18. Whence] *F; And whence Capell.*   34. travel] *F* (trauaile). *F3.*   35. often
had been] *F2; often had beene often F; had been often Collier.*

14. *disfurnish*] deprive; cf. *Per.*, IV. vi.
11–12: 'she'll disfurnish us of all our
cavaliers'.

26. *rehearse*] relate; cf. III. i. 347.

27–9.] We are given no indication why Valentine should actually
lie here, although of course it can be
argued that he was under an obligation as a 'courtly lover' to conceal
his real reason for leaving 'Milan'.
His account is substantially that
of Brooke's *Romeus.* See Introduction,
p. xliii.

29. *false vantage*] unfair advantage.

32. *doom*] sentence.

33. *tongues*] i.e., a knowledge of
languages.

34. *travel*] This could be either
'travel' or 'study' (travail). Bond
illustrates both meanings from Ber-
cher's *Nobylytye off Wymen* (1559): 'tra-
velenge in sutche maner of Stodye as
then was there ... approved ... To this
I thought good to add an experyence
of travell and knowledge off more con-
tris then myne owne'.

36. *Robin ... friar*] Friar Tuck, well-
known to English audiences as a mem-
ber of Robin Hood's band: he appears
in Munday and Chettle's *Downfall of
Robert Earl of Huntingdon* and *Death of
Robert Earl of Huntingdon* (1598), which
constituted a two-part Robin Hood
play.

1 Out. We'll have him. Sirs, a word.

Spe. Master, be one of them: it's an honourable kind of
    thievery.   40

Val. Peace, villain.

2 Out. Tell us this: have you anything to take to?

Val. Nothing but my fortune.

3 Out. Know, then, that some of us are gentlemen,
    Such as the fury of ungovern'd youth   45
    Thrust from the company of awful men.
    Myself was from Verona banished,
    For practising to steal away a lady,
    An heir, and near allied unto the Duke.

2 Out. And I from Mantua, for a gentleman,   50
    Who, in my mood, I stabb'd unto the heart.

1 Out. And I, for such like petty crimes as these.
    But to the purpose: for we cite our faults,
    That they may hold excus'd our lawless lives;

39–40.] *so Pope;* Master . . . them: / It's . . . theeuery *F.*   it's . . . thievery] *F;*
It is . . . thievery *Capell;* It is a kind of honourable thievery *Steevens.*   46. awful]
F; lawful *conj. Hawkins* (*ap. Steevens*).   49. An heir, and near] *Theobald;* And
heire and Neece *F;* An heir, and Neice *F3.*   51. Who] *F;* Whom *Pope.*

41. *villain*] rascal, often used good-
humouredly.

42. *take to*] have recourse to; cf. *Per.*,
III. iv. 10: 'A vestal livery will I take
me to'.

46. *awful*] Despite doubts, the editors have kept this F reading, taking
the sense as 'commanding respect'
(*NCS*), 'reverend, worshipful' (Johnson), 'of worth and station' (Staunton). Elsewhere in Shakespeare we
find 'awful' rule, duty, sceptre, but the
nearest to the present usage is in *2H4*,
IV. i. 176: 'We come within our awful
banks again.' *O.E.D.* illustrates the
sense 'profoundly respectful or rever-
ential' (6) from Stock's *On Malachi*
(1641): 'An awful child will hardly be
drawn . . . to do aught that his father
hath . . . forbidden him.' This meaning
may well be the right one for the present context.

47–9.] The Third Outlaw tells, substantially, Valentine's own story, as
Valentine had told that of the Second

Outlaw (ll. 50–1). The dramatist was
doubtless saving the trouble of further
invention, but see Introduction, p. lxv.

48. *practising*] plotting.

49. *heir*] commonly used of both
sexes.

near] Theobald's emendation has
been accepted by most editors. *NCS*
points out that the converse error
('neere' for 'neece') is found in *John*,
II. i. 424; Sisson, i. 59, reports frequent
errata of 'c' for 'r' and vice versa. Bond
defends 'niece allied' as 'a formal ceremonial term, or else as meaning
"niece by marriage" ': there is, however, no evidence for such a use.

Duke] Bond points out that Verona
had no Duke at the conceivable time
of the play's action, having passed
under the dominion of the Venetian
Republic at the beginning of the
fifteenth century.

51. *mood*] anger.

52.] the burlesque touch, perhaps
already evident in l. 31.

And partly seeing you are beautified   55
With goodly shape, and by your own report
A linguist, and a man of such perfection
As we do in our quality much want—
2 Out. Indeed because you are a banish'd man,
Therefore, above the rest, we parley to you: 60
Are you content to be our general?
To make a virtue of necessity,
And live as we do in this wilderness?
3 Out. What say'st thou? Wilt thou be of our consort?
Say 'ay', and be the captain of us all: 65
We'll do thee homage, and be rul'd by thee,
Love thee, as our commander, and our king.
1 Out. But if thou scorn our courtesy, thou diest.
2 Out. Thou shalt not live to brag what we have offer'd.
Val. I take your offer, and will live with you,   70
Provided that you do no outrages
On silly women or poor passengers.
3 Out. No, we detest such vile base practices.

58. want—] *Theobald;* want. *F.*   63. this] *F;* the *F2.*

55. *beautified*] Dover Wilson uses this passage to defend Hamlet against the charge of irony in his use of the word to Ophelia (*What Happens in Hamlet,* 1935, p. 113). But the whole tone of this scene makes such a deduction precarious.

57. *linguist*] This seems a rather desperate expedient to give the outlaws a motive for adopting Valentine as their king. J. S. Smart, *Shakespeare Truth and Tradition,* 1928, p. 164, refers to this passage as illustrating the popular Elizabethan enthusiasm 'for travel, foreign fashions, and polyglot attainments'. See Introduction, p. lxv.

58. *quality*] profession, as commonly of the actor's; cf. 'excelent in the qualitie he professes' (Chettle's reference to Shakespeare in the prefatory address to *Kind-Heart's Dream,* 1592).

want—] The dash inserted by Theobald has been adopted by most editors. Tannenbaum urges the preservation of the F full stop, taking ll. 55–8 as a

continuation of ll. 53–4, with 'seeing' = 'because we see'. That is possible, and the speech is in any event loosely constructed: it does, however, seem more graspable with the dash.

60. *above the rest*] more than for any other reason.

parley to] Bond, following Schmidt, quotes *2H6,* IV. vii. 82: 'This tongue hath parley'd unto foreign kings'.

62.] Cf. Chaucer, *Knight's Tale,* l. A3042: 'To maken vertue of necessitee'; *R2,* I. iii. 278: 'There is no virtue like necessity' (Tilley, V73). The line from *Gent.* seems to be echoed in Richard Brathwaite's poem *The Wooer* (1615): 'No cure he finds to heale this maladie, / But makes a vertue of necessity' (*Shakespeare Allusion Book,* i. 256).

64. *consort*] company; cf. III. ii. 83.
72. *silly*] defenceless; cf. *Ven.,* 1098: 'silly lamb'.

passengers] Cf. l. 1n.
73.] This hardly fits with ll. 1–8

Come, go with us, we'll bring thee to our crews,
And show thee all the treasure we have got;   75
Which, with ourselves, all rest at thy dispose.   *Exeunt.*

SCENE II

Enter PROTEUS.

Pro. Already have I been false to Valentine,
And now I must be as unjust to Thurio:
Under the colour of commending him,
I have access my own love to prefer.
But Silvia is too fair, too true, too holy,   5
To be corrupted with my worthless gifts.
When I protest true loyalty to her,

---

74. crews] *F* (Crewes); cave *Collier ii;* caves *Singer;* crew *NCS, conj. Delius;*
cruives *conj. Bullock (ap. Camb).*   76. all] *F;* shall *Pope.*

Scene ii

SCENE II] *Rowe; Scœna Secunda F;* Scene II. *Changes to* Milan *Pope.*   S.D. *Enter*
Proteus] *Enter Protheus, Thurio, Iulia, Host, Musitian, Siluia F.*   1. have I] *F;*
I've *Pope.*

(unless we take it that Valentine and
Speed, not being 'poor', are fair game
in this Robin Hood world) or with
v. iv. 16–17. Yet, as Valentine is now
the outlaws' king, we can hardly
assume they are mocking him. The
notion of romantic outlawry is surely
being burlesqued. See Introduction,
p. lxv.
    74. *crews*] The plural may be wrong
but is not impossible: it seems therefore best to keep the F reading. The
word 'crew' is several times used of a
band of outlaws in Heywood's *Four
Prentices of London.* On the resemblances between Shakespeare's and
Heywood's outlaws, see Introduction,
pp. xlvi–xlvii.
    76. *dispose*] disposal.

Scene ii

1 ff.] The staging of this scene has
been thoroughly considered by Long,
pp. 52–61. He assumes the three doors

of the stage represent (1) a corner of
Silvia's house and a path leading to the
city, left; (2) the entrance to Silvia's
apartment, centre; (3) a path leading
to another side of the apartment,
right. At l. 1 Proteus enters left, with
lute. Other entries and exits, as deduced by Long, will be noted at relevant points of this scene: a substantial
case can, however, be made against
him, as the ensemble effect of the
scene will be much greater if the singing is done in the physical presence of
Julia and the Host.
    3. *colour*] pretext; cf. *Wint.,* IV. iv.
566–7: 'What colour for my visitation
shall I / Hold up before him?'
    4. *prefer*] advance.
    7 ff.] This assumes a state of affairs
which has continued for some time,
contrary to the time-scheme of the
quick-moving plot. The double effect
is common in Shakespeare, the best-
known examples being in *Oth.* Cf. also

She twits me with my falsehood to my friend;
When to her beauty I commend my vows,
She bids me think how I have been forsworn   10
In breaking faith with Julia, whom I lov'd.
And notwithstanding all her sudden quips,
The least whereof would quell a lover's hope,
Yet, spaniel-like, the more she spurns my love,
The more it grows, and fawneth on her still.   15

[*Enter* THURIO *and* Musicians.]

But here comes Thurio; now must we to her window,
And give some evening music to her ear.
Thu. How now, Sir Proteus, are you crept before us?
Pro. Ay, gentle Thurio, for you know that love
        Will creep in service where it cannot go.   20
Thu. Ay, but I hope, sir, that you love not here.
Pro. Sir, but I do; or else I would be hence.
Thu. Who? Silvia?
Pro.   Ay, Silvia, for your sake.
Thu. I thank you for your own. Now, gentlemen,
        Let's tune; and to it lustily awhile.   25

[*Enter* Host *and* JULIA *in boy's clothes.*]

15. S.D.] *Rowe (after l. 17).*   23. Who] *F;* Whom *F2.*   25. S.D.] *Rowe.*

J. W. Lever (ed.), new Arden *Meas.*, pp. xiv–xvii.

7–11.] Cf. *Euphues:* 'Ah fonde wench, doest thou thincke *Euphues* will deeme thee constant to him, when thou hast ben vnconstant to his friend? Weenest thou that he will haue no mistrust of thy faithfulnes, when he hath had tryall of thy ficklenesse?' (ed. Arber, pp. 57–8).

7–8.] Cf. *Euphues:* 'she that hath beene faithlesse to one, will neuer be faithfull to any' (ed. Arber, p. 58).

9. *commend*] direct.

12. *sudden quips*] sharp retorts; Malone quoted Wilson's *Arte of Rhetorique* (1553): 'And make him at his wit's end through the sudden quip'.

14. *spaniel-like*] Bond quoted *Euphues* (ed. Bond, i. 249): 'Wilt thou resemble the kinde Spaniell, which the more he is beaten the fonder he is?' Cf. Tilley, S705, and *MND.*, II. i. 203.

15. S.D.] The entry is through the left door (Long).

18, 20. *crept, creep*] Thurio uses the word in the sense of to 'move quietly and stealthily so as to elude observation' (*O.E.D.*, 2); Proteus uses it in the sense of 'crawl', proverbially contrasted with 'go' (*O.E.D.*, 1b, quoting *Towneley Mysteries*, 114: 'Kynde wille crepe Where it may not go'). In *Wily Beguilde* (M.S.R., 2445) we find 'A man may see that loue will creepe where it cannot goe'. Cf. Tilley, K49.

25. S.D.] Proteus, Thurio, and the musicians exeunt through the right door; Julia and the Host enter left, crossing the stage as they talk; the

Host. Now, my young guest, methinks you're allycholy. I
    pray you, why is it?

Jul. Marry, mine host, because I cannot be merry.

Host. Come, we'll have you merry: I'll bring you where
    you shall hear music, and see the gentleman that you   30
    asked for.

Jul. But shall I hear him speak?

Host. Ay, that you shall.

Jul. That will be music.   [*Music plays.*]

Host. Hark, hark!   35

Jul. Is he among these?

Host. Ay; but peace, let's hear 'em.

Song

Who is Silvia? What is she
That all our swains commend her?
Holy, fair, and wise is she,   40
The heaven such grace did lend her,
That she might admired be.

34. S.D.] *Capell (at l. 35).*   41. *heaven*] *F;* heav'ns *Johnson.*

tuning of instruments is heard as they
approach the right door (l. 34); they
look through the door (Long). But see
above, ll. 1 ff., n.

26. *allycholy*] This corruption of
'malecholie' (variant of 'melancholy'
found in *LLL.*, IV. iii. 14, 15, and in
Dekker and Middleton's 1 *The Honest
Whore*, III. i) occurs also in *Wiv.*, I. iv.
164.

28. *because . . . merry*] Cf. Tilley, S14.

30. *hear music*] Cf. *Diana*: 'mine host
. . . tolde me if I was desirous to heare
some brave musicke, I should arise
quickly, and open a window towards
the street' (Kennedy, p. 88).

30–1. *gentleman . . . for*] Bond points
out that in Montemayor the girl dares
not ask the Host about her lover, and
he suggests that without departing
from this Shakespeare 'could hardly
have brought the Host and Julia on
the stage'. But there would seem
no difficulty in contriving that,
and the change may rather be due
to Shakespeare's consistently more

forceful presentation of his heroine.

32–4.] Malone quotes *Err.*, II. ii.
116–20: 'never words were music to
thine ear . . . Unless I spake'. Cf. Beaumont and Fletcher's *Philaster*, v. v:
'I did hear you talk, / Far above
singing'.

37. S.D. Song] According to Long,
the song is sung off-stage by Proteus,
accompanied by the consort: cf. ll. 1 ff.
n. R. Noble, *Shakespeare's Use of Song*,
1923, pp. 39 ff., states that this song
'had its origin' in 'caricature of the
conventional sonnet'. With Long, I
find it difficult to see traces of caricature. Noble, unlike Long, assumes the
presence of the musicians on stage
during the song and the following
consort-performance. Without this,
Harold Brooks contends (and I largely
agree with him), the dramatic effect of
the simultaneous action is quite lost—
sacrificed to the idea (which is con-
stantly disproved in the theatre) that
simultaneous action is more than an
audience can keep in focus.

> *Is she kind as she is fair?*
> *For beauty lives with kindness.*
> *Love doth to her eyes repair,*   45
> *To help him of his blindness;*
>   *And, being help'd, inhabits there.*
>
> *Then to Silvia let us sing,*
> *That Silvia is excelling;*
> *She excels each mortal thing*   50
> *Upon the dull earth dwelling.*
>   *To her let us garlands bring.*

Host. How now? Are you sadder than you were before?
   How do you, man? The music likes you not.

Jul. You mistake: the musician likes me not.   55

Host. Why, my pretty youth?

Jul. He plays false, father.

Host. How, out of tune on the strings?

Jul. Not so; but yet so false that he grieves my very
   heart-strings.   60

Host. You have a quick ear.

59–60.] *so Pope;* Not . . . yet / So . . . -strings *F.*

43–7.] Cf. Sonnet 152: 'I have sworn deep oaths of thy deep kindness, . . . / And, to enlighten thee, gave eyes to blindness . . . / For I have sworn thee fair.'

44.] 'Beauty without kindness dies unenjoyed, and undelighting' (Johnson).

45–6. Love . . . blindness] Cf. Sidney, *Astrophel and Stella*, Sonnet LXV, where Astrophel has done Love a similar service: Love, 'being blinded / By nature borne, I gave to thee mine eyes'; and Sonnet XXXII, where Stella provides an education for blind eyes: 'My *Stella* I descry / Teaching blind eyes both how to smile and weepe'.

45. repair] resort.

51. dull earth] Malone notes this phrase in *Ven.*, 340; Bond quotes *Mer.V.*, III. v. 87–8: 'the poor rude world / Hath not her fellow' (of Portia).

53–60.] There is a brief pause in the music while they talk (Long).

53. *Are . . . before*] Cf. *Diana*: the music was of 'such sweetnes' that it 'could not chuse but delight any . . . who were so farre from it as I' (Kennedy, p. 91); and *Romeus*, ll. 1769–70: 'When pleasant songes he heares while others do rejoyce / The melody of Musike doth styrre up his mourning voyce'. Cf. also Sonnet 8: 'Music to hear, why hear'st thou music sadly?'

54, 55. *likes*] (1) pleases; (2) a quibble on 'pleases' (for the Host) and 'loves' (for Julia).

58–9. *out . . . yet*] Cf. Sonnet 8, as in l. 53: 'the true concord of well-tuned sounds / . . . do offend thine ear.'

61–77.] There is a brisk dance-tune as they continue to talk (Long). In *Diana*, Long points out, Felismena first hears a consort and then Felix singing first a 'romance' to the accompaniment of a 'dulcayne' and a harp, and

Jul. Ay, I would I were deaf: it makes me have a slow
    heart.

Host. I perceive you delight not in music.

Jul. Not a whit, when it jars so.   65

Host. Hark, what fine change is in the music!

Jul. Ay; that change is the spite.

Host. You would have them always play but one thing?

Jul. I would always have one play but one thing.
    But, host, doth this Sir Proteus, that we talk on,   70
    Often resort unto this gentlewoman?

Host. I tell you what Launce his man told me, he loved
    her out of all nick.

Jul. Where is Launce?

Host. Gone to seek his dog, which to-morrow, by his   75
    master's command, he must carry for a present to his
    lady.   *[Music ceases.]*

Jul. Peace, stand aside, the company parts.

68. You would] *F;* You would then *Malone ii;* You would not *Collier (MS.).*
always play] *F;* play always *F4.*   thing?] *Pope;* thing. *F.*   72–3.] *so Pope;*
I . . . me, / He . . . nicke *F.*

then a 'soneto' or short song. Shakespeare wishes to use the Host as someone to whom Julia can express her
grief, but ambiguously, so that he cannot understand: this is done by their
talk about the music. To achieve this
effect, Shakespeare reverses the order
in Montemayor, so that Proteus' infidelity can be at once apparent to
Julia and she can comment during the
consort when it follows the song. However, in *Diana* consort music also follows the second of the two songs there
given, so there may be no need to
deduce a reversal on Shakespeare's
part. Long also argues that it was
necessary to have the serenade off-
stage, so that the emphasis during the
consort could be on the conversation:
cf. ll. 1 ff. n. The necessary emphasis
could, however, surely be achieved
without Julia and the Host having the
stage to themselves.

    61, 62. *quick, slow*] perceptive;
heavy.

    66. *change*] variation; cf. Sonnet 76:

'Why is my verse . . . So far from varia-
tion and quick change?' In l. 67 Julia
of course refers to the 'change' in Proteus' love. There is no need to assume
that the music begins again at this
line: the Host is drawing attention
to a special modulation now being
achieved.

    69. *play*] Julia's use of the word
seems to involve a theatre-image: i.e.,
a man should play only one part.

    73. *out . . . nick*] beyond all reckoning
or count: it was a host's practice to
keep a score by means of nicks or
notches on a stick (Warburton).

    74–7.] Julia and Launce have never
met in the play: Proteus' messenger in
i. i, ii, was Speed (and even him Julia
did not actually see), and Launce was
not present when Julia and Proteus
parted in ii. ii. What is more significant
here is that the Host's statement about
the dog is unexplained nonsense until
we reach iv. iv. See Introduction,
p. xx.

    78. *parts*] departs. At this point Julia

Pro. Sir Thurio, fear not you, I will so plead,
    That you shall say my cunning drift excels.   80
Thu. Where meet we?
Pro.   At Saint Gregory's well.
Thu.   Farewell.
                            [*Exeunt* THURIO *and* Musicians.]

                        [*Enter* SILVIA, *above.*]

Pro. Madam; good even to your ladyship.
Sil. I thank you for your music, gentlemen.
    Who is that that spake?
Pro. One, lady, if you knew his pure heart's truth,   85
    You would quickly learn to know him by his voice.
Sil. Sir Proteus, as I take it.
Pro. Sir Proteus, gentle lady, and your servant.
Sil. What's your will?
Pro.   That I may compass yours.
Sil. You have your wish: my will is even this,   90
    That presently you hie you home to bed.

81. S.D.s] *Rowe.*   82. even] *F* (eu'n); evening *Malone ii.*

and the Host move back against the
wall at one side of the right door; the
serenaders re-enter through the left
door (Long). But see above, ll. 1 ff. n.
    80. *drift*] Cf. II. vi. 43, III. i. 18.
    excels] Cf. 'excelling', l. 49.
    81. *Saint Gregory's well*] This was an
actual well near Milan, of which
Halliwell reproduced a print from a
view of Milan in Braun's *Civitates Orbis
Terrarum* (1582). The accuracy of this
detail in the play is indeed surprising,
and may well suggest that a now lost
additional source existed.
    81. S.D.] According to Long, Silvia
appears at the central door. Rowe's
insertion of 'above', however, seems
justified by the reference to 'window'
in l. 16. And it may be dramatically
more effective for Silvia to appear on
the upper stage, in order to emphasize
her remoteness from Proteus.
    83.] Thurio and the musicians
exeunt left, having been thanked by
Silvia (Long). But Silvia may more

effectively speak after the musicians
have left, with only Proteus and Julia
to hear her.
    89. *compass yours*] win your goodwill
(with a play on 'will' in the sense of
sexual desire). Knight suggested 'have
you within my power', which seems
over-bold for Proteus at this point.
    90. *my will*] As Johnson pointed out,
Silvia now plays upon the word, taking
it as 'wish'.
    91, 92. *you, Thou*] The sudden
change to 'Thou' at the beginning of
Silvia's formal denunciation of Proteus
should be remarked; cf. Franz, p. 264:
'Höherstehende bedienen sich im Ge-
spräch mit Personen niederen Standes
oder Ranges gern des familiären *thou.*
Es bedeutet wohlwollende Herab-
lassung, Erkenntlichkeit, Vertrauen
und Sympathie oder es ist der Aus-
druck des Missmuts, des Zorns und der
Wut. In letzterem Falle ist *thou* häufig
von beleidigenden und entehrenden
Beiworten begleitet.'

Thou subtle, perjur'd, false, disloyal man,
Think'st thou I am so shallow, so conceitless,
To be seduced by thy flattery,
That hast deceiv'd so many with thy vows?   95
Return, return, and make thy love amends.
For me, by this pale queen of night I swear,
I am so far from granting thy request,
That I despise thee for thy wrongful suit;
And by and by intend to chide myself,   100
Even for this time I spend in talking to thee.

Pro. I grant, sweet love, that I did love a lady,
But she is dead.

Jul. [*Aside*]   'Twere false, if I should speak it;
For I am sure she is not buried.

Sil. Say that she be; yet Valentine thy friend   105
Survives; to whom (thyself art witness)
I am betroth'd; and art thou not asham'd
To wrong him with thy importunacy?

Pro. I likewise hear that Valentine is dead.

Sil. And so suppose am I; for in his grave,   110
Assure thyself, my love is buried.

Pro. Sweet lady, let me rake it from the earth.

Sil. Go to thy lady's grave and call hers thence,
Or, at the least, in hers sepulchre thine.

Jul. [*Aside*] He heard not that.   115

Pro. Madam: if your heart be so obdurate,
Vouchsafe me yet your picture for my love,

---

103. *Aside*] Pope.   106. thyself] *F*; even thyself *Hanmer*.   110. his] *F2*; her *F*.
115, 123. *Aside*] Pope.   116. if] *F*; if that *Warburton*.   116-17. so obdurate, /
Vouchsafe . . . love] *F* (*subst.*); so / Obdurate, oh! vouchsafe me yet your picture
Hanmer.

92. *subtle*] cunning.

93-5.] Cf. *Diana*: 'there shall not
want another to make thee forget thy
second' (Kennedy, p. 95).

93. *conceitless*] witless (Onions).

96. *make . . . amends*] Cf. in *Diana* the
words of Valerius (Felismena) when
Don Felix invites comment on his reply
to Celia: 'it is needlesse . . . to make the
Gentlewoman amendes, to whom it is
sent, but her, whom you do injurie so
much with it' (Kennedy, p. 97).

103. *if*] even if.

104. *buried*] trisyllabic, as in l. 111.

108. *importunacy*] importunity.

109.] This excuse is so feeble that it
reflects from the incompetence of Proteus to that of the dramatist.

112. *rake*] Proteus continues Silvia's
image but makes it rather more con-
crete and thus violent; cf. *H5*, II. iv.
97-8: 'if you hide the crown / Even in
your hearts, there will he rake for
it'.

The picture that is hanging in your chamber:
To that I'll speak, to that I'll sigh and weep;
For since the substance of your perfect self   120
Is else devoted, I am but a shadow;
And to your shadow will I make true love.

Jul. [*Aside*] If 'twere a substance, you would sure deceive it,
And make it but a shadow, as I am.

Sil. I am very loath to be your idol, sir;   125
But, since your falsehood shall become you well
To worship shadows, and adore false shapes,
Send to me in the morning, and I'll send it.
And so, good rest.

126. your falsehood] *F;* you're false, it *conj. Johnson;* your falsehood, *conj. Tyrwhitt (ap. Malone).*

120–7.] See III. i. 177n. Since Silvia's substance is vowed to someone else, Proteus is reduced to a shadow of himself and therefore fittingly can make love to her 'shadow' (picture). Julia comments that, if the picture were real, Proteus would deceive it and reduce it to such a shadow as she is. Silvia adds that, as Proteus is false, he ought to worship false things, i.e., shadows, i.e., pictures. The false shape, when worshipped, becomes an 'idol' (l. 125). Cf. *Mer.V.*, III. ii. 126–9: 'Yet look, how far / The substance of my praise doth wrong this shadow / In underprizing it, so far this shadow / Doth limp behind the substance'; Day, Rowley, Wilkins, *Travailes of the Three English Brothers*, sc. i: 'Thinke it a picture which may seeme as great / As the substantiall selfe'.

121. *else devoted*] vowed to someone else.

123–4.] For the play on 'shadow' and 'substance', cf., e.g., Sonnet 37: 'this shadow doth such substance give'.

123–8.] Cf. Lyly's *Endimion*, v. iii. 254–5: 'so much of Endimion as his picture commeth to possesse and play withall'. In *Campaspe* there is frequent play on the girl's picture, shadow, and substance, with the use of the picture as a stage-property.

124. *shadow*] applied to portraits in Lyly's *Campaspe*, I. ii. 71: 'to shadow a ladies face' (Bond), and in *Euphues*: 'Appelles shadowes' (ed. Bond, II. 42, l. 20).

126–7. *since . . . shadows*] The construction is elliptical, but Johnson's and Tyrwhitt's conjectures seem unnecessary: 'since it shall become your falsehood well to worship shadows' (Bond), or 'since your falsehood shall adapt, or render you fit, to worship shadows' (Douce).

128.] Bond, taking a suggestion from Victor's adaptation (see Introduction, p. xlviii), excuses this conduct of Silvia by saying that she may have wished to lull suspicion of her intended flight. But Silvia is not a suitable character for psychological probing: the dramatist was to use the picture effectively in IV. iv, and in this play that was doubtless reason enough for Silvia's 'touch of coquetry' (as Bond describes it). Harold Brooks suggests that the gift is a 'stinging rebuke', as Proteus is to be satisfied with a shadow (portrait) of a shadow (outward appearance); but this may make Silvia's behaviour too heavily allegorical, and hardly accords with long-established implications in the giving of a portrait to a lover.

Pro.   As wretches have o'ernight
        That wait for execution in the morn.   130
                        [*Exeunt* PROTEUS *and* SILVIA.]
Jul. Host, will you go?
Host. By my halidom, I was fast asleep.
Jul. Pray you, where lies Sir Proteus?
Host. Marry, at my house. Trust me, I think 'tis almost day.
Jul. Not so; but it hath been the longest night   135
        That e'er I watch'd, and the most heaviest.   [*Exeunt.*]

SCENE III

Enter EGLAMOUR.

Egl. This is the hour that Madam Silvia
        Entreated me to call, and know her mind:
        There's some great matter she'd employ me in.
        Madam, madam!

                [*Enter* SILVIA, *above.*]

Sil.   Who calls?
Egl.   Your servant, and your friend;
        One that attends your ladyship's command.   5
Sil. Sir Eglamour, a thousand times good morrow.

---

130. S.D.] *F2 (Exeunt).*   134.] *so Pope;* Marry ... house: / Trust ... day *F.*
136. S.D.] *F2.*

SCENE III] *Rowe; Scœna Tertia F.*   S.D. *Enter Eglamour*] *Enter Eglamore, Siluia F.*
4. Madam, madam] *F;* Madam *Hanmer.*   4. S.D.] *Rowe.*

---

130. S.D.] Silvia withdraws centre, Proteus left (Long). But see above, l. 81 S.D. n.

132. *halidom*] a weak asseveration, originally the relics on which oaths were made.

133. *lies*] lodges.

136. *watch'd*] stayed awake.

most heaviest] the double superlative, as frequently in Shakespeare; cf. Franz, pp. 210–11.

S.D.] The Host and Julia follow Proteus through the left door (Long).

Scene III

S.D.] On the use of 'Eglamour' here and at I. ii. 9, see Introduction, p. xviii.

2. *mind*] purpose.

4. S.D.] Rowe's '*above*' seems justified by Eglamour's calling and by Silvia's asking his identity. But, of course, as in IV. ii, the staging could be managed on one level.

6–7. *a ... yourself*] We have met this

Egl. As many, worthy lady, to yourself.
　　According to your ladyship's impose,
　　I am thus early come, to know what service
　　It is your pleasure to command me in.　　　　　10
Sil. O Eglamour, thou art a gentleman
　　(Think not I flatter, for I swear I do not)
　　Valiant, wise, remorseful, well accomplish'd.
　　Thou art not ignorant what dear good will
　　I bear unto the banish'd Valentine;　　　　　15
　　Nor how my father would enforce me marry
　　Vain Thurio, whom my very soul abhorr'd.
　　Thyself hast lov'd, and I have heard thee say
　　No grief did ever come so near thy heart
　　As when thy lady and thy true love died,　　　20
　　Upon whose grave thou vow'dst pure chastity.
　　Sir Eglamour: I would to Valentine,
　　To Mantua, where I hear he makes abode;
　　And for the ways are dangerous to pass,
　　I do desire thy worthy company,　　　　　　25
　　Upon whose faith and honour I repose.
　　Urge not my father's anger, Eglamour,
　　But think upon my grief, a lady's grief,
　　And on the justice of my flying hence,
　　To keep me from a most unholy match,　　　30
　　Which heaven and fortune still rewards with plagues.
　　I do desire thee, even from a heart

17. abhorr'd] *F;* abhors *Hanmer;* abhorreth *Keightley.*

language before, at II. i. 91–4, and
again it is difficult to believe that, on
the dramatist's part, it is wholly
serious.

8. *impose*] command.

13. *remorseful*] pitiful.

17. *abhorr'd*] The F past tense can be
kept here: the 'would' in the previous
line may suggest that the Thurio-
project is in the past; since she met
Valentine, and especially since she
decided to follow him into exile,
Thurio has ceased to exist for her; her
abhorrence is therefore a memory.

23. *To Mantua*] The only reason for
the introduction of this place seems to

be that it is the refuge of Romeus in
Brooke's poem after his banishment.

24. *for*] because; cf. II. iv. 171.

26. *repose*] rely.

30. *most unholy match*] In using this
expression Shakespeare may have
been thinking of Juliet's proposed marriage to Paris, which would be more
certainly 'unholy' than Silvia's marriage to Thurio. Cf. Mozelle Scaff
Allen, 'Brooke's *Romeus and Juliet* as a
Source for the Valentine–Silvia Plot in
The Two Gentlemen of Verona' (University of Texas Publication No.
3826: Studies in English 1938, pp.
25–46).

As full of sorrows as the sea of sands,
To bear me company, and go with me;
If not, to hide what I have said to thee,   35
That I may venture to depart alone.

Egl. Madam, I pity much your grievances,
Which, since I know they virtuously are plac'd,
I give consent to go along with you,
Recking as little what betideth me,   40
As much I wish all good befortune you.
When will you go?

Sil.   This evening coming.

Egl. Where shall I meet you?

Sil.   At Friar Patrick's cell,
Where I intend holy confession.

Egl. I will not fail your ladyship. Good morrow, gentle lady.

Sil. Good morrow, kind Sir Eglamour.   *Exeunt.* 46

SCENE IV

Enter LAUNCE [*with his dog*].

Lau. When a man's servant shall play the cur with him,
    look you, it goes hard: one that I brought up of a

37–8. grievances, / Which] *F;* grievances, / And the most true affections that you
bear; / Which *Collier ii;* grievances / And sympathize with your affections, /
Which *conj. Keightley.*   38. plac'd] *F;* caused *conj. Staunton.*   40. Recking] *Pope;*
Wreaking *F.*   42. evening coming] *F;* evening coming on *Capell;* coming evening *conj. anon (ap. Camb).*   43. Where ... you] *F;* Where / Shall ... you *Hanmer.*
45.] *so Camb;* I...Ladiship:/Good...Lady.) *F;* I...fail:/Good...lady *Hanmer.*

Scene IV

SCENE IV] *Rowe; Scena Quarta F.*   S.D. *Enter ... dog*] *Enter Launce, Protheus,
Iulia, Siluia F.*

37. *grievances*] distresses; cf. 1. i. 17.
38.] Collier's MS. 'corrector' effect-
ed a simpler relationship between this
and the preceding line; but the ellipsis
does not seem unusually violent.
    40. *Recking*] heeding.
    40–1.] The degree of his heedless-
ness on his own behalf is equated with
the degree of his wishes for her.
    41. *befortune*] befall. The word has

not been traced elsewhere before the
nineteenth century.
    43–4. *At ... confession*] A rendezvous
at a friar's cell, with the girl announcing that she will go to confession, takes
us again to *Romeus and Juliet.*

Scene IV

    1. *play the cur*] The phrase seems an
analogue of 'play the devil'.

puppy; one that I saved from drowning, when three
or four of his blind brothers and sisters went to it. I
have taught him, even as one would say precisely   5
'Thus I would teach a dog'. I was sent to deliver him
as a present to Mistress Silvia, from my master; and
I came no sooner into the dining-chamber, but he
steps me to her trencher, and steals her capon's leg.
O, 'tis a foul thing, when a cur cannot keep himself in   10
all companies: I would have (as one should say) one
that takes upon him to be a dog indeed, to be, as it
were, a dog at all things. If I had not had more wit
than he, to take a fault upon me that he did, I think
verily he had been hanged for 't; sure as I live he had   15
suffered for 't. You shall judge: he thrusts me himself into the company of three or four gentleman-like
dogs, under the Duke's table; he had not been there
(bless the mark) a pissing while, but all the chamber
smelt him. 'Out with the dog', says one; 'What cur is   20
that?' says another; 'Whip him out', says the third;
'Hang him up', says the Duke. I, having been ac-

5–6. even . . . precisely 'Thus . . . dog'] F (subst.); even . . . say 'precisely . . . dog'
Bond.   6. was sent] F; went Theobald.   12. to be a dog indeed] F; to be a dog,
to be a dog indeed conj. Johnson.

2–3. of a puppy] from the time when
he was a puppy.

4. went to it] died; Bond quotes Ham.,
v. ii. 56: 'So Guildenstern and Rosen-
crantz go to 't.'

5–6. even . . . dog] in exactly ('precisely') the way that corresponds with
one's ideal of canine instruction.
Bond's emendation gives the meaning
'all would say the teaching was just
what it should be' or 'I have taught
him the most precise manners: so I
think dogs should be taught'.

6. was sent] See Introduction, p. xx.

9. trencher] wooden plate.

10. keep himself] restrain himself.

13. a . . . things] adept at all things;
cf. John Kirke, Seven Champions of
Christendome (ed. G. Dawson), 595: 'I
am old dogge at that, yfaith'; Tilley,
D506.

15. sure . . . live] Cf. Tilley, L374.

19. bless the mark] This (or 'save the
mark') seems to have been originally
a formula to avert an evil omen, and
hence used by way of apology when
anything disagreeable or improper has
been mentioned or to express impatient scorn at something said (Onions).
Bond quotes Brewer's Dictionary of
Phrase and Fable as giving the origin in
archery, i.e., as a wish that a well-
placed arrow may not be displaced by
a later; he considers it more likely,
however, to be a reference to the
'mark' of the Cross in coins, etc.
O.E.D., 18, rejects Brewer's explanation and quotes another, that the
phrase was first used by midwives
at the birth of a child bearing a
'mark'.

a pissing while] Cf. Tilley, P355.

quainted with the smell before, knew it was Crab;
and goes me to the fellow that whips the dogs:
'Friend,' quoth I, 'you mean to whip the dog?' 'Ay,   25
marry do I,' quoth he. 'You do him the more
wrong,' quoth I; ''twas I did the thing you wot of.'
He makes me no more ado, but whips me out of the
chamber. How many masters would do this for his
servant? Nay, I'll be sworn I have sat in the stocks,   30
for puddings he hath stolen, otherwise he had been
executed; I have stood on the pillory for geese he
hath killed, otherwise he had suffered for 't. Thou
think'st not of this now. Nay, I remember the trick
you served me, when I took my leave of Madam   35
Silvia: did not I bid thee still mark me, and do as I
do? When didst thou see me heave up my leg, and
make water against a gentlewoman's farthingale?
Didst thou ever see me do such a trick?

[*Enter* PROTEUS *and* JULIA.]

Pro. Sebastian is thy name? I like thee well,   40
And will employ thee in some service presently.
Jul. In what you please; I'll do what I can.
Pro. I hope thou wilt. [*To Launce*] How now, you
whoreson peasant,

25. dog?] *Rowe;* dog: *F.*   36. Silvia] *F;* Julia *Warburton.*   39. S.D.] *Rowe.*
40. name?] *Rowe;* name: *F.*   42. I'll do] *F;* I'll do, sir *F2;* I will do *Malone.*
43.] *so Pope;* I ... wilt. / How ... pezant *F.*   S.D.] *Johnson.*

24. *fellow . . . dogs*] Steevens illustrated this functionary's duties from
Mucedorus: 'I'll prove my office good;
for look you, sir, when . . . a dog chance
to blow his nose backward, then with a
whip I give him good time of the day,
and strew rushes presently'.

29–30. *How . . . servant?*] There is an
evident relationship between this and
l. 90, Launce burlesquing the serious
action, as often. In this instance the
burlesque comes before the thing burlesqued. See Introduction, p. lxvi.

31. *puddings*] A 'pudding' was primarily the 'stomach or one of the
entrails of a pig, sheep, or other ani-

mal, stuffed with a mixture of minced
meat, suet, oatmeal, seasoning, etc.,
boiled and kept till needed' (*O.E.D.*,
1).

36. *Silvia*] Warburton's emendation
is needless: Launce has just visited
Silvia; she is a Duke's daughter, which
makes the joke richer; and Launce, as
far as we have seen, has not met Julia
(cf. iv. ii. 74–7n.).

40. *Sebastian*] another link between
this play and *Tw.N.*: Julia in her disguise, and in the service of the man she
loves, takes the name of the twin-
brother of Viola, herself in disguise and
serving the man she loves.

Where have you been these two days loitering?

Lau. Marry, sir, I carried Mistress Silvia the dog you   45
bade me.

Pro. And what says she to my little jewel?

Lau. Marry, she says your dog was a cur, and tells you
currish thanks is good enough for such a present.

Pro. But she received my dog?   50

Lau. No, indeed did she not: here have I brought him
back again.

Pro. What, didst thou offer her this from me?

Lau. Ay, sir, the other squirrel was stolen from me by the
hangman boys in the market-place, and then I   55
offered her mine own, who is a dog as big as ten of
yours, and therefore the gift the greater.

Pro. Go, get thee hence, and find my dog again,
Or ne'er return again into my sight.
Away, I say: stayest thou to vex me here?   60
A slave, that still an end turns me to shame!

[*Exit* LAUNCE.]

Sebastian, I have entertained thee,

48. was] *F; is conj. Capell.*   51–2.] *so Pope;* No . . . not: / Here . . . againe *F.*
53. this] *F; this cur Collier ii.*   54–7.] *so Pope;* I . . . me / By . . . place, / And . . .
dog / As . . . greater *F.*   54. other squirrel] *F* (Squirrill); other, Squirrel,
Hanmer.   54–5. the hangman boys] *Singer;* the Hangmans boyes *F;* the hangmans boy *F2;* a hangman boy *Collier ii.*   61. still an end] *F;* still an-end *NCS.*
S.D.] *F2* (*Exit*).

47–53. *my . . . me*] Proteus is here
made to look absurd, and this goes
along with other matters indicated, to
prevent us from taking the story too
seriously.

54. *squirrel*] Hanmer makes this the
dog's name. But, as Steevens suggests,
Launce may well use the word con-
temptuously in reference to the dog's
diminutive size—i.e., 'the other, a
mere squirrel'. Bond points out that
squirrels were actually carried about
by ladies, and quotes Lyly, *Endimion,*
II. ii. 137: 'What is that the gentlewoman carrieth in a chaine? *Epi.* Why
it is a Squirrill.'

55. *hangman boys*] 'Hangman' was
commonly used as a general term of
reprobation. Cf. *Common Conditions* (*c.*

1576), l. 1698: 'O God this littell hangman is iustling maides aginst the
wall?'; *Ado,* III. ii. 11–12: 'the little
hangman [Cupid] dare not shoot at
him'.

61. *still an end*] continuously; Staunton quotes Cartwright, *Ordinary:* 'I /
Do feel such aguish qualms, and
dumps, and fits, / And shakings still an
end'. The phrase can mean 'notwithstanding' (Sc. 'still and on'), as in *The
Buggbears* (ed. R. W. Bond), IV. v. 27:
'still an end, it should not be true', but
that seems unlikely here.

62. *entertained*] Cf. *Diana:* 'he entertained me for his Page . . . where, being
but a few daies with him, I sawe the
messages, letters, and gifts, that were
. . . caried on both sides' (Kennedy,

Partly that I have need of such a youth,
That can with some discretion do my business:
For 'tis no trusting to yond foolish lout;   65
But chiefly for thy face, and thy behaviour,
Which (if my augury deceive me not)
Witness good bringing up, fortune, and truth.
Therefore, know thou, for this I entertain thee.
Go presently, and take this ring with thee,   70
Deliver it to Madam Silvia;
She lov'd me well deliver'd it to me.   [*He gives her a ring.*]

Jul. It seems you lov'd not her, to leave her token:
She is dead belike?

Pro.   Not so: I think she lives.

Jul. Alas!   75

Pro. Why dost thou cry 'Alas'?

Jul. I cannot choose but pity her.

Pro. Wherefore shouldst thou pity her?

Jul. Because methinks that she lov'd you as well
As you do love your lady Silvia: 80
She dreams on him that has forgot her love,
You dote on her that cares not for your love.
'Tis pity love should be so contrary;
And thinking on it makes me cry 'Alas'.

Pro. Well; give her that ring, and therewithal   85

---

69. know thou] *F2;* know thee *F.*   73. to leave] *F2;* not leaue *F;* nor love
NCS, conj. Johnson.   74. belike?] *F;* belike. *F2.*   78. Wherefore] *F;* Why
Hanmer.   81. him that has] *F;* you that have *conj. Daniel.*   85. Well] *F;* Well,
well *Dyce, conj. S. Walker.*   her] *F;* to her *Collier (MS.).*   therewithal] *F;*
give therewithal *Pope;* give her therewithal *Capell.*

p. 94); 'entertain' is repeated at ll. 69
and 91 below, and 'give her that ring',
'letter', and 'message' come in ll. 85,
86, 88, and 90.

69. *thou*] Malone defended F's
'thee' in that Shakespeare often wrote
'whom' for 'who' and therefore might
be irregular with other pronouns.

72. *deliver'd*] i.e., who delivered. On
the 'omission' of the relative, cf.
Franz, pp. 313–16.

73. *leave*] part with; Mason quoted
Mer.V., v. i. 172–3: 'I dare be sworn
for him he would not leave it / Nor
pluck it from his finger', and v. i.

196: 'how unwillingly I left the ring'.

81–3.] Bond compares this to the
Helena–Demetrius–Hermia situation
in *MND.,* as well as to that in *Tw.N.*
(see note on ll. 93–107).

83.] Cf. *Diana*: 'cruell love is of so
strange a condition, that he bestoweth
his contents without any good order
and rule, and giveth there greatest
favours, where they are lest esteemed'
(Kennedy, p. 104).

85. *give . . . ring*] another, though
slighter, link with *Tw.N.*: there Olivia
pretended that Orsino had sent a ring
to her by Viola.

This letter. [*He gives her a letter.*] That's her chamber.
    Tell my lady,
I claim the promise for her heavenly picture.
Your message done, hie home unto my chamber,
Where thou shalt find me sad, and solitary.   [*Exit.*]

Jul. How many women would do such a message?   90
Alas, poor Proteus, thou hast entertain'd
A fox, to be the shepherd of thy lambs.
Alas, poor fool, why do I pity him
That with his very heart despiseth me?
Because he loves her, he despiseth me,   95
Because I love him, I must pity him.
This ring I gave him, when he parted from me,
To bind him to remember my good will;
And now am I (unhappy messenger)
To plead for that which I would not obtain;   100
To carry that which I would have refus'd;
To praise his faith which I would have disprais'd.
I am my master's true confirmed love,
But cannot be true servant to my master,
Unless I prove false traitor to myself.   105

89. S.D.] *F2.*

88–9.] In *Diana*, Felismena finds Don Felix sometimes 'sad and pensive' when she is carrying messages between him and Celia (Kennedy, p. 101).

91–2. *thou . . . lambs*] Cf. *2H6*, III. i. 252–3: 'were 't not madness, then, / To make the fox surveyor of the fold'; and Tilley, W602.

93. *Alas, poor fool*] Julia refers to herself; cf. 'poor monster' in the quotation in the note on ll. 93–107.

93–6. *why . . . pity him*] In *Diana*, Felismena even invents messages from Celia to Don Felix, 'because I could not see him (whom I loved so deerly) so sad and pensive', and refers to 'the pittie, that I had on him' (Kennedy, pp. 101, 98).

93–107.] Cf. *Tw.N.*, I. iv. 40–2: 'I'll do my best / To woo your lady: [*Aside*] yet, a barful strife! Whoe'er I woo, myself would be his wife'; and

II. ii. 34–42: 'How will this fadge? my master loves her dearly; / And I, poor monster, fond as much on him; / And she, mistaken, seems to dote on me. / What will become of this? As I am man, / My state is desperate for my master's love; / As I am woman,— now alas the day!— / What thriftless sighs shall poor Olivia breathe! / O time! thou must untangle this, not I; / It is too hard a knot for me to untie!'

94. *despiseth*] perhaps suggested by *Romeus*, l. 1600: 'Disdayneth me, his stedfast frend, and scornes my frendship so'.

100.] Cf. *Diana*: 'to be the intercessour of a thing so contrarie to mine owne content' (Kennedy, p. 97).

101, 102. *would have*] wish to have.

105. *false . . . myself*] Cf. Proteus' soliloquy, II. vi. 31–2; also Sonnet 10: ''gainst thyself thou stick'st not to con-

Yet will I woo for him, but yet so coldly,
As (heaven it knows) I would not have him speed.

[*Enter* SILVIA.]

Gentlewoman, good day. I pray you be my mean
To bring me where to speak with Madam Silvia.
Sil. What would you with her, if that I be she?   110
Jul. If you be she, I do entreat your patience
To hear me speak the message I am sent on.
Sil. From whom?
Jul.   From my master, Sir Proteus, madam.
Sil. O, he sends you for a picture?
Jul.   Ay, madam.
Sil. [*calling*] Ursula, bring my picture there.   115
                              [*The picture is brought.*]
Go, give your master this. Tell him from me,
One Julia, that his changing thoughts forget,
Would better fit his chamber than this shadow.
Jul. Madam, please you peruse this letter.

[*She gives her a letter.*]

Pardon me, madam, I have unadvis'd   120
Deliver'd you a paper that I should not;

---

107. S.D.] *F2; Enter Silvia, attended Malone; Enter Silvia and Ursula Chambers.*
108. Gentlewoman] *F;* Lady *Pope.*   113. From my master, Sir Proteus] *F;* My
master, from Sir Proteus *Capell;* From Sir Proteus, my master *conj. Keightley.*
114. picture?] *F;* picture; does he not? *Capell.*   115. The . . . brought] *Capell*
(*subst.*).   119. please you peruse] *F;* may't please you to peruse *Pope;* wilt
please you to peruse *Capell;* so please you to peruse *Collier ii;* if't please you to
peruse *Marshall.*

---

spire'—a line immediately preceding
an image paralleled at v. iv. 8 ff. See
note on v. iv. 9.
  108. *mean*] Cf. II. vii. 5, III. i. 38.
  110–11. *What . . . she*] Silvia's mo-
mentary withholding of identity and
Julia's doubt present, in little, the situation between Olivia and Viola in
Tw.N., I. v. 177–98.
  115–18.] Cf. IV. ii. 123–8n.
  115. *Ursula*] the name of an atten-
dant on Hero in *Ado*. Here it seems convenient to use Capell's passive S.D.,
as the entry is a curiously silent one.

  118. *shadow*] Cf. IV. ii. 120–7n.
  120. *unadvis'd*] thoughtlessly; cf. II.
iv. 203, III. i. 73.
  121.] This by-play might be difficult
to make significant to an audience.
Presumably Julia carried about with
her a letter from Proteus, and her mistake here is introduced in order to
reveal the fact and display its pathos. But Julia makes another similar
mistake (presumably a deliberate
one on that occasion) with the
rings in v. iv. 90–4. See Introduction,
pp. xx–xxi.

This is the letter to your ladyship.

[*She gives another letter and takes back the first.*]

Sil. I pray thee let me look on that again.

Jul. It may not be: good madam, pardon me.

Sil. There, hold.   125

I will not look upon your master's lines:
I know they are stuff'd with protestations,
And full of new-found oaths, which he will break
As easily as I do tear his paper. [*She tears the second letter.*]

Jul. Madam, he sends your ladyship this ring.   130

[*She offers the ring.*]

Sil. The more shame for him, that he sends it me;

For I have heard him say a thousand times
His Julia gave it him at his departure:
Though his false finger have profan'd the ring,
Mine shall not do his Julia so much wrong.   135

Jul. She thanks you.

Sil. What say'st thou?

Jul. I thank you, madam, that you tender her:

Poor gentlewoman, my master wrongs her much.

Sil. Dost thou know her?   140

Jul. Almost as well as I do know myself.

To think upon her woes, I do protest
That I have wept a hundred several times.

Sil. Belike she thinks that Proteus hath forsook her?

Jul. I think she doth; and that's her cause of sorrow.   145

Sil. Is she not passing fair?

129. S.D.] *Victor (subst.)*.

125.] Capell and Bond assume that Silvia here gives back the first letter. But, in view of 'that' in l. 123, it is difficult to believe that she had it then in her possession. Silvia could conceivably take it from Julia a second time at l. 123 and give it back again at 'There, hold'. But it would be very confusing to an audience to have letters passed over-frequently between the two girls: the words at l. 125 seem to indicate rather that Silvia is about to return the second letter, but then decides to tear it (first?).

132. *heard . . . times*] As Proteus loved Silvia at first sight, it is difficult to believe that he would talk about Julia in Silvia's presence 'a thousand times'. See Introduction, p. xx.

138. *tender*] are concerned for; this is related to the adjectival use at v. iv. 37.

139. *wrongs her much*] Cf. *Diana*: 'you do her . . . the greatest wrong in the world' and 'her whom you do injurie so much' (Kennedy, pp. 95, 97).

146–7.] Cf. *Diana*: '*Celia* began in good earnest to aske me what manner of woman *Felismena* was; whom I an-

Jul. She hath been fairer, madam, than she is:
When she did think my master lov'd her well,
She, in my judgment, was as fair as you.
But since she did neglect her looking-glass,   150
And threw her sun-expelling mask away,
The air hath starv'd the roses in her cheeks,
And pinch'd the lily-tincture of her face,
That now she is become as black as I.
Sil. How tall was she?   155
Jul. About my stature: for at Pentecost,
When all our pageants of delight were play'd,
Our youth got me to play the woman's part,
And I was trimm'd in Madam Julia's gown,

---

153. pinch'd] *F;* pitch'd *Warburton;* pencte, pinc'd *conj. Becket.*

---

swered, that touching her beautie,
Some thought her to be very faire, but
I was never of that opinion, bicause
she hath many daies since wanted the
chiefest thing, that is requisite for it . . .
Content of minde' (Kennedy, p. 99).

146. *passing*] exceedingly.

151. *sun-expelling mask*] Bond, following Rolfe, quotes *Troil.*, I. ii. 286–7:
'my mask, to defend my beauty', and
Cym., v. iii. 21–2: 'faces fit for masks, or
rather fairer / Than those for preservation cased'. Cf. also Heywood's
Woman Killed with Kindness (Revels
edn, vii. 40–3): 'her silver brow, /
That never tasted a rough winter's
blast / Without a mask or fan, doth
with a grace/ Defy cold winter.'

152. *starv'd*] killed with cold.

153–4. *pinch'd . . . I*] Warburton
argued for 'pitch'd', claiming that a
'pinching' cold did not turn the skin
black: rather, he said, it was the heat of
the sun (cf. l. 151) that was referred to,
and 'starv'd' in l. 152 meant 'withered'.
Johnson commented that pinching
turns skin 'black and blue', livid, and
that 'no one ever heard of a face being
pitched by the weather'. Steevens supported Johnson by quoting *Ant.*, I. v.
28: 'with Phoebus' amorous pinches
black'. But 'black' in l. 154 has a suggestion of 'ill-favoured' as well as

'swarthy' (cf. III. i. 103); 'pinch'd' can
refer to 'the painful action of cold,
hunger, exhaustion, or wasting dis-
ease' (*O.E.D.*, *vb*, 6). It appears that,
after referring to the sun in l. 151,
Julia speaks only of the ill-effects of
cold weather: the link, however, is that
without a mask her complexion is exposed to. the elements and their
destructiveness. Knight interpreted
'pinch'd' as 'painted'. Becket's conjectures are intended to carry the
meanings 'painted' and 'pencilled'.

156, 157. *Pentecost, pageants*] Whitsun
was in some places (e.g., Chester) the
time when the miracle cycles were
acted. Bond, following Knight, suggests that secular and classical plays,
taking the place of the earlier religious
drama, would be given at the same
time of year. But there is no evidence
that such a formal substitution occurred. What is referred to might perhaps be a dramatic performance given
on the occasion of a 'Whitsun-ale':
although Chambers said that this was
'a mere beer-swilling' (*Medieval Stage*,
1903, i. 179), there is evidence of a
'lord' and a 'lady' for such occasions
(*ibid.*, *loc. cit.*, n. 6) and this may imply
some dramatic element.

159. *trimm'd*] dressed up; Bond
quotes Sonnet 66: 'needy nothing

Which served me as fit, by all men's judgments,   160
As if the garment had been made for me;
Therefore I know she is about my height.
And at that time I made her weep agood,
For I did play a lamentable part.
Madam, 'twas Ariadne, passioning   165
For Theseus' perjury, and unjust flight;
Which I so lively acted with my tears,
That my poor mistress, moved therewithal,
Wept bitterly; and would I might be dead,
If I in thought felt not her very sorrow.   170

Sil. She is beholding to thee, gentle youth.
Alas, poor lady, desolate, and left;
I weep myself to think upon thy words.
Here, youth: there is my purse; I give thee this
For thy sweet mistress' sake, because thou lov'st her. 175

                                    [*She gives her a purse.*]
Farewell.   [*Exit.*]

Jul. And she shall thank you for 't, if e'er you know her.
A virtuous gentlewoman, mild, and beautiful.

---

160. judgments] *F; judgment Capell.*   170. felt] *F; feel conj. Seward (ap. Camb).*
175–6.] *so F2; one line in F; om. 'Farewell' Pope.*   176. S.D.] *F2; after l. 177 Dyce.*

---

trimm'd in jollity', and points out that the word implies a notion of disguise or dress for a special occasion.

160. *served . . . fit*] fitted me as well; Bond, following Craig, quotes *Cym.*, IV. i. 2–3: 'How fit his garments serve me!'

163. *agood*] in good earnest. Steevens quoted Turberville's translation of Ovid's epistle from Ariadne to Theseus: 'beating of my breast a-good'; Malone added Marlowe, *Jew of Malta*, II. iii. 214: 'I have laugh'd a-good'. Cf. also Nashe, *Choice of Valentines*, 144.

165–6.] Ariadne, who had helped Theseus in his encounter with the Minotaur in Crete, was abandoned by him on the isle of Naxos. One of Ovid's epistles is from Ariadne to Theseus after the desertion (cf. l. 163n.). The story is an appropriate one for Julia to

refer to, and the effect on Silvia is clearly greater because Julia is described (by herself in disguise) as weeping at its presentation before she found herself approximately in Ariadne's position.

165. *passioning*] passionately grieving or lamenting. Bond, following Schmidt, quotes *Tp.*, v. i. 22–4: 'shall not myself . . . Passion as they?' and *Ven.*, 1059: 'Dumbly she passions'.

167. *lively*] For the adverbial use, cf. *Tim.*, v. i. 85: 'Thou counterfeit'st most lively'.

168. *my poor mistress*] 'Sebastian' has not previously indicated that he was in Julia's service. Perhaps 'my . . . mistress' is elliptical for 'the mistress of my master'. But cf. l. 180 and note.

171. *beholding*] beholden (as frequently). Cf. I. i. 48.

I hope my master's suit will be but cold,
Since she respects my mistress' love so much.   180
Alas, how love can trifle with itself!
Here is her picture: let me see; I think
If I had such a tire, this face of mine
Were full as lovely as is this of hers;
And yet the painter flatter'd her a little,   185
Unless I flatter with myself too much.
Her hair is auburn, mine is perfect yellow:
If that be all the difference in his love,
I'll get me such a colour'd periwig.
Her eyes are grey as glass, and so are mine;   190
Ay, but her forehead's low, and mine's as high.

180. my] *F;* his *Hanmer.*

179. *suit . . . cold*] i.e., his wooing will be ineffective; cf. *Mer.V.*, II. vii. 73: 'Fare you well; your suit is cold'.

180. *my mistress' love*] In the previous line she had continued to refer to Proteus as 'my master' even though Silvia had left the stage: still, she is in his service. Now she again calls Julia (i.e., herself) 'my mistress' (cf. l. 168). Hanmer's emendation was intended to avoid this. Collier pointed to l. 181 as indicating that Julia is playing with the story she has invented: this would be made clearer by altering the F punctuation, but as it stands the line seems to fit excellently with the lines that follow. However, as Bond suggests, the words may be used simply 'in playful repetition of the fiction' of l. 168.

183. *tire*] head-dress.

183, 185. *tire, painter*] Cf. Sonnet 53: 'you in Grecian tires are painted new'.

187. *perfect yellow*] 'The natural colour of Queen Elizabeth's, and so the fashionable colour in her time' (Bond). Felismena's hair in *Diana* was golden: cf. quotation in note to l. 189.

189. *such . . . periwig*] a periwig of that colour.

periwig] According to Staunton, periwigs were first introduced into England about 1572. In *Diana* the

account of the attiring of Felismena refers to a periwig and to her forehead (cf. l. 191): 'And tying up her haire with a carnation ribbon of silke and silver, they did put thereon a caule of glittering golde, in euery corner whereof a precious Ruby was set, with a naturall crisped periwigge of her owne haire, matching the brightest golde in colour, which adorned either side of her cristalline forehead' (Kennedy, pp. 138–9).

190–1.] Chaucer's Prioress has 'eyen greye as glas' and a 'fair forheed' (*Canterbury Tales*, General Prologue, ll. 152, 154), implying, it appears, her affinity with heroines of romance. Cf. quotations at l. 191n.

190. *grey as glass*] Theobald quoted Chaucer's *Prologue* (see previous note). Malone argued, from the translation of 'grey' (eye) as 'ceruleus, glaucus' in Coles's Latin Dictionary of 1679, that the Elizabethans meant 'blue' when they said 'grey eye'. Bond was sceptical of this, as apparently is *O.E.D.* Knight, however, stated that Elizabethan glass had a light blue tint.

191.] Johnson pointed out the esteem in which high foreheads were held, and Malone quoted *Tp.*, IV. i. 249–50: 'apes / With foreheads villanous low'. So *Rom.*, II. i. 18: 'By

What should it be that he respects in her,
But I can make respective in myself,
If this fond Love were not a blinded god?
Come, shadow, come, and take this shadow up,   195
For 'tis thy rival. O thou senseless form,
Thou shalt be worshipp'd, kiss'd, lov'd, and ador'd;
And were there sense in his idolatry,
My substance should be statue in thy stead.
I'll use thee kindly, for thy mistress' sake   200
That us'd me so; or else, by Jove I vow,
I should have scratch'd out your unseeing eyes,
To make my master out of love with thee.   *Exit.*

199. statue] *F;* sainted *Hanmer;* statued *Warburton;* a statue *conj.* Steevens; statua *conj.* Reed (*ap. Malone ii*).   202. your] *F;* thy *Hanmer.*   203. S.D.] *F2;* Exeunt *F.*

her high forehead and her scarlet lip', and *Ant.,* III. iii. 36–7: 'her forehead / As low as she would wish it' (from the Messenger's report of Octavia to Cleopatra).

192. *respects*] esteems, values; cf. I. ii. 134.

193.] i.e., which I cannot find the equal of in myself (with a pun on 'respects', l. 192). 'There is nothing ... which he respects or admires in Silvia, but that I can make the same in myself: no excellence which I cannot also claim or bear relation to' (Becket). *O.E.D.,* 6, interprets 'respective' as 'worthy of respect', but that does not seem to fit the construction: it would be odd, too, if no pun were to be found here.

195–9.] Cf. Sonnet 53: 'What is your substance, whereof are you made, / That millions of strange shadows on you tend? / Since every one hath,

every one one shade, / And you, but one, can every shadow lend.'

195. *shadow . . . shadow*] Cf. IV. ii. 120–7n. The first 'shadow' is Julia, the second the picture. Cf. 'substance', l. 199.

take . . . up] Bond points out the play on the 'sense of hostile action or attitude'. Cf. I. ii. 134–5.

198. *his idolatry*] Cf. II. iv. 140–1, IV. ii. 126–7, and notes.

199. *statue*] i.e., as an object of worship. Steevens illustrated the use of the word without an article from Massinger's *Great Duke of Florence*: 'it was your beauty that turn'd me statue'.

202–3. *your, thee*] Hanmer's attempt to regularize spoils the effect. Julia expresses her animus strongly in l. 202, but is quieter and friendlier in the following line: hence the change of pronoun.

ACT V

SCENE I

Enter EGLAMOUR.

Egl. The sun begins to gild the western sky,
      And now it is about the very hour
      That Silvia at Friar Patrick's cell should meet me.
      She will not fail; for lovers break not hours,
      Unless it be to come before their time,   5
      So much they spur their expedition.

[*Enter* SILVIA.]

      See where she comes. Lady, a happy evening.
Sil. Amen, amen; go on, good Eglamour,
      Out at the postern by the abbey wall;
      I fear I am attended by some spies.   10
Egl. Fear not: the forest is not three leagues off;
      If we recover that, we are sure enough.   *Exeunt.*

ACT V

Scene i

ACT V SCENE 1] *Rowe; Actus Quintus. Scœna Prima F;* Act V. Scene 1. Scene *continues in* Milan *Pope.*   S.D. *Enter Eglamour*] *Enter Eglamoure, Siluia F.*   3. That Silvia at Friar Patrick's] *F;* Silvia at Friar Patrick's *Pope;* That Silvia at Patrick's *conj. Steevens (ap. Malone ii).*   6. S.D.] *Rowe (after l. 7).*

1.] Cf. *Romeus,* l. 1527: 'The golden sonne was gonne to lodge him in the west.'

1. *gild*] In this sense ('to cover or tinge with a golden colour or light (said esp. of the sun)') *O.E.D.*'s first recorded usage is from *Tit.,* II. i. 6: 'having gilt the ocean with his beams'. Later examples are frequent in Shakespeare.

4. *lovers . . . hours*] Bond quotes *AYL.,*

IV. i. 44: 'Break an hour's promise in love!' Cf. Tilley, L568.

6.] Cf. Tilley, L481: 'Who so hath love in his breast has spurs at his sides.'

9. *postern*] small back- or side-door.

10. *attended*] watched.

12. *recover*] arrive at; cf. *Tp.,* III. ii. 16–17: 'I swam, ere I could recover the shore, five and thirty leagues'.

sure] safe.

SCENE II

Enter THURIO, PROTEUS *and* JULIA.

Thu. Sir Proteus, what says Silvia to my suit?
Pro. O sir, I find her milder than she was,
    And yet she takes exceptions at your person.
Thu. What? That my leg is too long?
Pro. No, that it is too little.   5
Thu. I'll wear a boot, to make it somewhat rounder.
Jul. [*Aside*] But love will not be spurr'd to what it loathes.
Thu. What says she to my face?
Pro. She says it is a fair one.
Thu. Nay, then the wanton lies: my face is black.   10
Pro. But pearls are fair; and the old saying is,
    Black men are pearls, in beauteous ladies' eyes.
Jul. [*Aside*] 'Tis true, such pearls as put out ladies' eyes,
    For I had rather wink than look on them.

Scene II

SCENE II] *Rowe; Scæna Secunda F.*   S.D. *Enter . . . Julia*] *Enter Thurio, Protheus, Iulia, Duke F.*   7. *Jul.* [*Aside*]] *Collier, conj. Boswell (ap. Malone ii); Pro. F.*
13. *Jul.* [*Aside*]] *Rowe; Thu. F.*

1. *to*] concerning.

3. *takes exceptions*] Cf. I. iii. 83, II. iv. 150.

5. *little*] thin; cf. 'small' at II. iii. 20.

6. *boot*] i.e., riding-boot; cf. 'spurr'd', l. 7 (Bond).

7. *Jul.*] Collier's emendation, following Boswell's conjecture, is evidently right: the line must be spoken aside and thus belongs to Julia's function in this scene.

8–10.] Cf. Sonnet 131: 'Thy black is fairest in my judgement's place.'

9. *fair*] pale-complexioned, which may have a suggestion of 'effeminate'; cf. *Ado*, III. i. 61–2: 'if fair-faced, / She would swear the gentleman should be her sister'. *NCS* interprets 'fair' as 'fair-faced' = 'a specious deceiver'.

10. *wanton*] trifler.

black] swarthy. Here there is no pejorative sense (cf. III. i. 103n.).

11–12. *the . . . eyes*] Cf. Tilley, M79.

Steevens quoted Heywood's *Iron Age*: 'a black complexion / Is always precious in a woman's eye', and Chapman's *Sir Giles Goosecap*: 'to make every black slovenly clown a pearl in her eye'. Cf. also Middleton's *Your Five Gallants*, v. i, where a Latin motto is burlesquely translated as '*A black man a pearl in a fair lady's eye*'; and Burton's *Anatomy of Melancholy* (edn 1849, pp. 517–18): 'a black man is a pearl in a fair woman's eye, and is as acceptable as lame Vulcan was to Venus; for he being a sweaty fuliginous blacksmith, was dearly beloved of her'. Bond, however, following Craig, noted the Elizabethan doctor Vicary using the term 'pearl on the eye' in the sense of 'cataract': this, he suggests, was the original meaning of the saying, and Julia takes this up in ll. 13–14.

14. *wink*] Cf. I. ii. 139, II. iv. 93.

Thu. How likes she my discourse?   15
Pro. Ill, when you talk of war.
Thu. But well, when I discourse of love and peace?
Jul. [*Aside*] But better, indeed, when you hold your peace.
Thu. What says she to my valour?
Pro. O sir, she makes no doubt of that.   20
Jul. [*Aside*] She needs not, when she knows it cowardice.
Thu. What says she to my birth?
Pro. That you are well derived.
Jul. [*Aside*] True: from a gentleman, to a fool.
Thu. Considers she my possessions?   25
Pro. O, ay; and pities them.
Thu. Wherefore?
Jul. [*Aside*] That such an ass should owe them.
Pro. That they are out by lease.
Jul. Here comes the Duke.   30

[*Enter* Duke.]

Duke. How now, Sir Proteus! How now, Thurio!
        Which of you saw Sir Eglamour of late?
Thu. Not I.
Pro.   Nor I.
Duke.   Saw you my daughter?

17. *Thu.*] *F; not in F3.*   peace?] *Pope; peace. F.*   18, 21, 24, 28. *Aside*] *Capell.*
18. hold] *F;* do hold *Capell.*   25. possessions] *F;* large possessions *Collier ii.*
30. S.D.] *Rowe; Enter Duke, angrily Collier ii.*   32. saw Sir] *F4;* saw *F;* say saw
Sir *F2.*

16.] Bond is doubtless right in suggesting that this, like l. 9, gives a hint of effeminacy, but the mockery is laborious indeed.

23. *derived*] descended, with a quibble which Julia makes plain in l. 24. Cf. v. iv. 144.

26. *pities them*] (1) is sorry for them; (2) considers them 'pitiful', of no account.

28. *owe*] own.

29. *out by lease*] The obvious meaning here, as indicated by Mason, is that Thurio's estates are not 'in his own dear hands' and therefore (ironically)

Proteus says that Silvia 'pities them' (l. 26). But Steevens (following, according to Malone, Lord Hailes) suggests that Proteus is using the word 'possessions' in a figurative sense, meaning his 'mental endowments', which are no longer under his control. Bond is understandably sceptical about this gloss, but it has had a curiously wide currency. *NCS* discerns a quibble on 'possession' by a spirit, and on 'leash' ('out by lease' meaning 'out of control'). But the laboured mockery of this scene hardly repays investigation.

Pro.   Neither.

Duke. Why, then, she's fled unto that peasant, Valentine;
       And Eglamour is in her company.   35
       'Tis true: for Friar Laurence met them both
       As he in penance wander'd through the forest.
       Him he knew well; and guess'd that it was she,
       But, being mask'd, he was not sure of it.
       Besides, she did intend confession   40
       At Patrick's cell this even, and there she was not.
       These likelihoods confirm her flight from hence;
       Therefore, I pray you, stand not to discourse,
       But mount you presently, and meet with me
       Upon the rising of the mountain foot   45
       That leads toward Mantua, whither they are fled.
       Dispatch, sweet gentlemen, and follow me.   [*Exit.*]

Thu. Why, this it is to be a peevish girl,
       That flies her fortune when it follows her.
       I'll after; more to be reveng'd on Eglamour   50
       Than for the love of reckless Silvia.   [*Exit.*]

Pro. And I will follow, more for Silvia's love
       Than hate of Eglamour that goes with her.   [*Exit.*]

34.] *so Capell;* Why then / She's . . . *Valentine* F.   47. S.D.] *Rowe; Exit in haste*
Collier (MS.).   51. S.D.] *Capell.*   53. S.D.] *Capell.*

36. *Friar Laurence*] another link with
Rom. F. G. Fleay, *New Shakespere
Society Transactions,* 1874, p. 298, said
this was a mere slip for 'Friar Patrick',
as indeed is probable.

37.] The suggestion for the Friar's
penance seems to come from *Romeus,*
ll. 2996–3004: 'fryer Lawrence . . . /
. . . was discharged quyte' of blame for
the lovers' deaths, 'But of him selfe he
went into an Hermitage, / Two myles
from Veron towne, where he in
prayers past forth his age . . . / Fyve
yeres he lived an Hermite, and an
Hermite dyd he dye.'

39. *being mask'd*] On the Shakespearian use of a present participle without
an obvious (or any) referent, cf.
Franz, pp. 557–8.

41. *even*] evening.

42.] i.e., these pieces of evidence
make her flight seem more probable.

43. *stand*] delay; cf. *Caes.,* v. iii. 43:
'Stand not to answer'.

46. *Mantua . . . fled*] Silvia and Eglamour have gone in the direction of
Mantua (IV. iii. 23), but, unless the
'forest' of l. 37 led nowhere else, the
Duke has no means of knowing it.

48. *peevish*] perverse (Onions), foolish (Steevens): l. 49 gives some support
to 'perverse'. Cf. III. i. 68.

49.] i.e., that disregards Thurio's
wooing. Cf. Tilley, L518: 'Woman,
like a shadow, flies one following.'

51, 53, 55. S.D.s] Capell's insertion
of an '*Exit*' after each speech seems a
decided improvement: both Thurio
and Proteus seem to be uttering exit-
lines, and the parallelism of the
speeches is better pointed if each
speaker departs as he finishes.

Jul. And I will follow, more to cross that love
    Than hate for Silvia, that is gone for love.   *Exit.* 55

SCENE III

[Enter] SILVIA *and* Outlaws.

1 Out. Come, come, be patient; we must bring you to our
    captain.
Sil. A thousand more mischances than this one
    Have learn'd me how to brook this patiently.
2 Out. Come, bring her away.
1 Out. Where is the gentleman that was with her?   5
3 Out. Being nimble-footed, he hath outrun us,
    But Moyses and Valerius follow him.
    Go thou with her to the west end of the wood,
    There is our captain. We'll follow him that's fled;
    The thicket is beset, he cannot 'scape.   10
                [Exeunt 2 and 3 Outlaws.]
1 Out. Come, I must bring you to our captain's cave.

55. S.D.] *Capell; Exeunt F.*

Scene III

SCENE III] *Rowe; Scena Tertia F;* Scene III. *The* Forest *Pope.*   1.] *so Pope;* Come
. . . patient: / We . . . Captaine *F.*   9. We'll follow] *F;* follow *Pope.*   10.
S.D.] *Capell.*

54. *cross*] thwart.

Scene III

3. *learn'd*] taught; cf. II. vi. 13.
6.] Eglamour's quick abandoning of
Silvia has caused a good deal of comment, especially in view of the picture
of him given in IV. iii. 11–26. See
Introduction, p. xx.
7. *Moyses and Valerius*] 'Moyses' is a
form of 'Moses' fairly common in sixteenth-century English. There seems
no need to modernize it here. 'Valerius' is the name used by Felismena as a
page in Montemayor.
9. *There . . . captain*] i.e., where our
captain is.

We'll . . . fled] Why more than
Moyses and Valerius were needed to
pursue Eglamour is obscure. Pope's
emendation (for metre's sake) does not
improve matters, as the Third Outlaw
is clearly going with those he addresses
these words to.
10. *beset*] surrounded.
S.D.] Capell's S.D. has been adopted by Bond and by Victor in his adaptation, and gets the support of Tannenbaum, p. 57. It is surely right: at
l. 11 the First Outlaw makes it evident
that Silvia is in his sole charge, and
this renders plausible her unwelcome
rescue by Proteus, with the accom-
panying charge of attempted rape.

Fear not: he bears an honourable mind,
And will not use a woman lawlessly.
Sil. O Valentine! This I endure for thee.   *Exeunt.*

SCENE IV

Enter VALENTINE.

Val. How use doth breed a habit in a man!
This shadowy desert, unfrequented woods,
I better brook than flourishing peopled towns:
Here can I sit alone, unseen of any,
And to the nightingale's complaining notes   5

Scene IV

SCENE IV] *Rowe; Scœna Quarta F.*   S.D. *Enter Valentine] Enter Valentine, Protheus,*
Siluia, Iulia, Duke, Thurio, Out-lawes F.   2. This shadowy desert] *F;* These
shadowy, desert, *Collier ii.*   woods] *F;* wood *conj. Daniel.*

12–13.] Cf. *3H6*, III. ii. 124: 'Ay,
Edward will use women honourably'
(where the meaning is ironic).

14.] Cf. *Diana*: 'he was the cause of
so much sorrow, as I have passed for
his sake', and 'consider and weigh with
thy selfe the strange effects, which the
force of love hath caused me to passe'
(Kennedy, pp. 86, 238).

Scene IV

1–6.] Bond notes a general resemblance here to the Duke's speech in
AYL., II. i. 1–18, and slight echoes of
l. 2 in *AYL.*, II. vii. 110–12, and of ll.
5–6 in *AYL.*, II. v. 3–4. The setting,
with forest and outlaws, would make
such echoes likely, but there may well
be a common source in Seneca, *Hippolytus*, 483 ff. (the hero's praise of sylvan
and dispraise of city life). See notes on
ll. 2–3, 5, 7–10.

2–3.] Harold Brooks compares
Seneca, *Hippolytus*, 485: 'relictis
moenibus silvas amet'; 494: 'populos
. . . urbes'; 507–9: 'nemoris alti densa
. . . loca, . . . sedesque mutas'; 'flourishing' may have been suggested by 'opes'

(491) and 'dives' (496) applied to city-
dwellers. For 'shadowy desert', cf. the
same speech of Hippolytus (539):
'opaca dederant antra naturas domos'
('antres' are linked with 'deserts' in
Oth., I. iii. 140).

2. *desert*] In Elizabethan times (and
later) 'desert' signified 'any wild, un-
inhabited region, including forest-
land' (*O.E.D.*, 1b); cf. *AYL.*, II. vii.
110: 'this desert inaccessible'. Collier's
emendation, making 'desert' an adjective qualifying 'woods', has won support (and in *Romeus*, l. 2101, 'desert
woodes' has this force), but the line
seems to move better with a central
pause.

4–7.] Cf. *Romeus*, ll. 1761, 1771–5
(on the lover in exile in Mantua): 'Is
he accompanied, is he in place alone?
. . . / But if in secret place he walke
some where alone, / The place it selfe,
and secretnes redoubleth all his mone./
Then speakes he to the beastes to
fethered fowles, and trees, . . . / To
them he shewth his smart, as though
they reason had . . .'.

5.] The 'fethered fowles' of *Romeus*,

Tune my distresses, and record my woes.
O thou that dost inhabit in my breast,
Leave not the mansion so long tenantless,
Lest growing ruinous, the building fall,
And leave no memory of what it was.   10
Repair me, with thy presence, Silvia:
Thou gentle nymph, cherish thy forlorn swain.

                                    [*Shouts within.*]

What halloing, and what stir is this to-day?
These are my mates, that make their wills their law,
Have some unhappy passenger in chase.   15
They love me well; yet I have much to do
To keep them from uncivil outrages.
Withdraw thee, Valentine; who's this comes here?

                                    [*Withdraws.*]

[*Enter* PROTEUS, SILVIA *and* JULIA.]

12. S.D.] *Collier ii (subst.).*   18. S.D. *Enter . . . Julia*] *Rowe.*

l. 1773, combine with the complaining birds of Hippolytus' speech in Seneca, *op. cit.*, 508: 'hinc aves querulae fremunt'. Cf. ll. 1–6n., above.

5–6.] Cf. *Euphues*: 'the byrdes recording theyr sweete notes' (ed. Bond, II. 58, l. 7); *Per.*, IV, Prol. 26–7: 'She sung, and made the night-bird mute, / That still records with moan.'

6. *record*] sing.

7.] Cf. Sonnet 109: 'As easy might I from myself depart / As from my soul which in thy breast does lie'; and Sonnet 22: 'my heart / Which in thy breast doth live'.

7–10.] 'It is hardly possible to point out four lines in any of the plays of Shakespeare, more remarkable for ease and eloquence' (Steevens). Malone compared *Err.*, III. ii. 4: 'Shall love, in building, grow so ruinous?', and Bond added *Rom.*, III. ii. 26–7: 'O, I have bought the mansion of a love, / But not possess'd it.' Ritson also compared Marlowe's *Jew of Malta*, I. ii. 265: 'And leave no memory that e'er I was'. The link be-

tween the topic of woods and birds and that of the mansion now introduced may lie in Hippolytus' reference (though it is unfavourable) to city palaces, 496–7: 'mille . . . tegi / . . . columnis', and 523–4: 'cubili . . . multiplici . . . / domo'. In the Sonnets urging the friend to marry, the ruinated mansion image seems more appropriate, and may have been taken over into the play. Cf. Sonnet 10: ''gainst thyself thou stick'st not to conspire / Seeking that beauteous roof to ruinate / Which to repair should be thy chief desire'; and Sonnet 13: 'Against this coming end you should prepare / . . . Who lets so fair a house fall to decay . . .'. Love as a building, ruined and rebuilt, is in Sonnet 119, and in Sonnet 146 the body is a 'fading mansion'.

12. *forlorn*] accent on first syllable; Bond, following Rolfe, compares Sonnet 33: 'And from the forlorn world his visage hide'.

15. *Have*] For 'omission' of the relative, cf. IV. iv. 72.

passenger] Cf. IV. i. 1.

Pro. Madam, this service I have done for you
    (Though you respect not aught your servant doth)   20
    To hazard life, and rescue you from him
    That would have forc'd your honour and your love.
    Vouchsafe me for my meed but one fair look:
    A smaller boon than this I cannot beg,
    And less than this I am sure you cannot give.   25
Val. [*Aside*] How like a dream is this! I see, and hear:
    Love, lend me patience to forbear awhile.
Sil. O miserable, unhappy that I am!
Pro. Unhappy were you, madam, ere I came;
    But by my coming I have made you happy.   30
Sil. By thy approach thou mak'st me most unhappy.
Jul. [*Aside*] And me, when he approacheth to your presence.
Sil. Had I been seized by a hungry lion,
    I would have been a breakfast to the beast,

---

26. *Aside*] *Theobald.*   this! I see] *F;* this I see *Theobald;* this, I see *Warburton.*
32. *Aside*] *Rowe.*

---

20. *respect*] value; cf. IV. iv. 192.

22.] Tannenbaum argues that the First Outlaw, under Valentine's reformed régime, would not attempt rape: therefore Proteus must be referring to something else. The explanation offered is that ll. 19–54 of this scene, with the exception of ll. 26–7, 32, form a remnant of a now lost scene between Silvia and Proteus in which he tried to convince her that Valentine's intentions were not honourable. However, all we need to deduce is that Proteus here found it useful to assume that the outlaw had rape in mind.

23. *meed*] reward.

26. *this! . . . hear*] Theobald's emendation, though adopted by many editors, seems to weaken the effect. Valentine is amazed to see Proteus and Silvia and to hear Proteus' words.

27.] Collier, taking up a hint from Steevens and anxious to explain the notorious ll. 82–3, suggested that at this point Valentine left the stage, returning at l. 60: he was therefore inclined 'to draw a conclusion against'

Silvia from finding her in the forest with Proteus. In support, Collier pleaded that Valentine would have intervened earlier if he had heard everything and that Proteus could not have got to the point of imminent assault. But this is to raise many difficulties in attempting to solve one: there is no reason for Valentine to withdraw: there is nothing in ll. 19–25 to arouse suspicion of Silvia, though much of Proteus; if there were suspicion of Silvia, Valentine's intervention of ll. 60–1 is barely motivated. We can understand Valentine not immediately breaking silence, for Proteus' words would amaze him; but simple curiosity, allied of course with his love, would keep him within earshot.

31. *approach*] amorous advance. This is an odd instance of a quibble, where the word first used ('coming', l. 30) is changed to a synonym. In 'approacheth' (l. 32) Julia reverts to the original sense.

33.] Cf. *Romeus,* l. 494: 'Lyke Lyons wylde, your tender partes asonder would they teare.'

Rather than have false Proteus rescue me.   35
O heaven be judge how I love Valentine,
Whose life's as tender to me as my soul,
And full as much (for more there cannot be)
I do detest false perjur'd Proteus:
Therefore be gone, solicit me no more.   40

Pro. What dangerous action, stood it next to death,
Would I not undergo, for one calm look?
O 'tis the curse in love, and still approv'd,
When women cannot love where they're belov'd.

Sil. When Proteus cannot love where he's belov'd: 45
Read over Julia's heart, thy first best love,
For whose dear sake thou didst then rend thy faith
Into a thousand oaths; and all those oaths
Descended into perjury, to love me.
Thou hast no faith left now, unless thou'dst two,   50
And that's far worse than none: better have none
Than plural faith, which is too much by one.
Thou counterfeit to thy true friend!

47–9. rend . . . perjury,] *F;* hail . . . Discandied into perjury. *conj. Daniel;* rend . . . re-rented into perjury, *conj. Bond;* candy faith . . . Discandied into perjury. *conj. NCS.*   48. oaths] *F4;* oathes, *F.*   49. love] *F;* deceiue *F2.* me.] *Rowe;* me, *F.*

---

37. *tender*] dear; cf. *Mac.*, I. vii. 55: 'How tender 'tis to love the babe that milks me'. Cf. IV. iv. 138.

43. *still*] continually.

approv'd] confirmed; cf. *Lr.*, II. ii. 167: 'Good king, that must approve the common saw'.

48–9. *all . . . me*] That we have good reason to find this difficult is suggested by F2's change of 'love' (l. 49) to 'deceiue'. But the F reading has been ably defended by Sisson, i. 61: the only necessary alteration, he suggests, is to delete the F comma after 'oaths' (l. 48). First Proteus' 'whole and entire faith' has been broken up (rent) into a thousand small oaths of fidelity; then those oaths have descended to perjury, for the sake of loving Silvia. Bond was doubtful of the passage as a whole, and conjectured 're-rented' (torn again)

for 'descended'. The Daniel and *NCS* conjectures are perhaps a little desperate, but 'discandied' may be supported by *Two Noble Kinsmen*, I. i: 'O my petition was / Set downe in yce, which by hot greefe uncandied / Melts into drops'. One cannot have entire confidence that F here is accurate (particularly with 'rend'), but no satisfactory alteration has been proposed. Harold Brooks draws my attention to the use of a synonym for 'rend' in connection with swearing in Sonnet 152: 'thy . . . new faith torn / In vowing . . .'.

50. *unless thou'dst two*] i.e., unless you can be a faithful lover to Julia and to me at the same time.

53. *counterfeit . . . friend*] elliptical, for 'false friend, whose falseness is made more evident by contrast with your friend's (Valentine's) truth'.

Pro.   In love,
    Who respects friend?
Sil.   All men but Proteus.
Pro. Nay, if the gentle spirit of moving words   55
    Can no way change you to a milder form,
    I'll woo you like a soldier, at arm's end,
    And love you 'gainst the nature of love: force ye.
Sil. O heaven!
Pro.   I'll force thee yield to my desire.
Val. [*coming forward*] Ruffian! Let go that rude uncivil touch,
    Thou friend of an ill fashion.
Pro.   Valentine!   61
Val. Thou common friend, that's without faith or love,
    For such is a friend now. Treacherous man,
    Thou hast beguil'd my hopes; nought but mine eye
    Could have persuaded me: now I dare not say   65
    I have one friend alive; thou wouldst disprove me.
    Who should be trusted now, when one's right hand

---

57. woo] *F*; move *F2*.   63. Treacherous] *F*; Thou treacherous *F2*; Though
treacherous *F3*; Tho', treacherous *Rowe*.   65. now I] *F*; I *Pope*.   67. trusted
now, when one's] *F2*; trusted, when ones *F*; trusted now, when the *Pope*; trusted,
when one's own *Johnson*.

53–4. *In . . . friend?*] Cf. Tilley, L549, citing *Euphues*: 'Where love beareth sway, friendshippe can have no shew.' Cf. also Lyly's *Endimion*, III. iv. 110: 'Love knoweth neither friendshippe nor kindred.'

57. *at arm's end*] 'i.e. at sword's point' (Bond); 'like a soldier' seems to justify this, but it must of course be taken in a vague sense, i.e., 'in a hostile fashion'. However, the phrase is oddly encountered here, for the usual meaning of 'at arm's end' is 'at a distance' (*O.E.D.*, 'arm', *sb.*, 2b); cf. *AYL.*, II. vi. 10: 'hold death awhile at the arm's end'; and *Arcadia*: 'Such a one as can keep him at arms end, need never wish for a better companion' (*O.E.D.*). Schmidt suggests a quibble may be intended: 'i.e., laying hands on thee for my weapons instead of useless words'. Conceivably the quibble is a sexual one, 'arm' being 'weapon' in its common sexual sense (cf. Partridge, p. 219).

62. *common*] 'ordinary, like the rest' (Bond). This is borne out by l. 63, but there may be something here of the sense of the word when used of 'criminals, offenders, and offences', e.g., 'a common homicide' (Grafton's *Chronicle*, 1568), 'common liars' (*Homilies*, 1563) (*O.E.D.*, 8): cf. also 'common woman', etc. (*O.E.D.*, 6b).

that's] Bond, following Malone, interprets as 'i.e.'.

63.] The collation illustrates progressive editorial corruption.

65–7.] *I dare . . . trusted*] Cf. *Euphues*: 'Have I not . . . learned . . . that tryal maketh trust? that there is falshood in felowship?' (Bullough, p. 218).

67. *trusted . . . hand*] The emendations of F2 and of Johnson are both plausible. As Sisson, i. 61, suggests, the repetition of 'now' from l. 65 strength-

Is perjured to the bosom? Proteus,
I am sorry I must never trust thee more,
But count the world a stranger for thy sake.   70
The private wound is deepest: O time most accurst,
'Mongst all foes that a friend should be the worst!

Pro. My shame and guilt confounds me.
Forgive me, Valentine: if hearty sorrow
Be a sufficient ransom for offence,   75
I tender 't here; I do as truly suffer,
As e'er I did commit.

Val.   Then I am paid;
And once again I do receive thee honest.
Who by repentance is not satisfied,
Is nor of heaven, nor earth; for these are pleas'd: 80
By penitence th' Eternal's wrath's appeas'd.
And that my love may appear plain and free,

---

71. time most accurst] *F* (*subst.*); time accurst *Hanmer*; time, most curst *Johnson*; spite accurst *conj. S. Verges* (*ap. Camb*).   82–3.] *F*; transferred to end of Thurio's speech, l. 133, conj. Blackstone (*ap. Malone*); Pro. . . . mine in Julia, I . . . thee *conj. Staunton; Sil.* And . . . thee *conj. Knight* (*withdrawn*).

ens rather than weakens the effect. *one's right hand*] Cf. Tilley, H73.

70. *count*] Cf. ii. i. 58.

71. *private wound*] i.e., the wound received in private life, from a friend or intimate. Cf. Tilley, W930, citing as his sole instance *Euphues*: 'the wound that bleedeth inward is most dangerous.'

73. *confounds*] The singular verb after a double subject (especially with abstract nouns related in meaning) is very common: cf. Franz, pp. 567–8.

74–5, 77.] With Valentine's magnanimity compare the poet's in Sonnets 34, 35, especially in Sonnet 34: '. . . those tears . . . which thy love sheds / . . . are rich, and ransom all ill deeds.'

77. *commit*] sin; cf. *Lr.*, iii. iv. 83–4: 'commit not with man's sworn spouse'.

paid] satisfied. The latest quotation illustrating this sense (1) in *O.E.D.* is dated 1501.

78. *receive thee*] accept you as.

82–3.] Commentators have struggled to explain these lines away. On Collier's notion that Valentine was not sure of Silvia's conduct, see l. 27n. Pope merely thought the matter 'very odd' and assumed Shakespeare was just following his source. Hanmer considered it evidence that 'the main parts of this play' were not by Shakespeare. Capell suggested that Valentine was testing Proteus' penitence, and that the offer was not to be taken seriously by anyone but Proteus: 'something in the action,— a squeeze, a look,—might make such his intention known to Sylvia, and so to an audience'. Blackstone would transfer the lines to the end of Thurio's speech (i.e., after l. 133). This, of course, would leave Julia's swoon to be explained: Blackstone says it is an artifice used merely to discover herself to Proteus. This solution entails (1) a most lame addendum to Thurio's speech; (2) an insufficient motive for the timing of the swoon; (3) a dis-

All that was mine in Silvia I give thee.

Jul. O me unhappy!   [*She swoons.*]

Pro.   Look to the boy.

Val.   Why, boy!
    Why, wag; how now? What's the matter? Look up;   85
    speak.

Jul. O good sir, my master charged me to deliver a ring to
    Madam Silvia; which (out of my neglect) was never
    done.

Pro. Where is that ring, boy?

83. mine] *F; thine conj. Becket.*   84. S.D.] *Pope.*   84-9. Why, boy! . . . done]
F; Why . . . matter? / Look . . . me / To . . . Silvia: / Which . . . done *Capell.*
85. Why, wag; how] *F;* how *Pope.*   87. to deliver] *F;* to give *conj. Steevens (ap.
Malone ii);* deliver *ibid.*

placement of text that would be very
difficult to explain. Knight suggested
transferring the lines to Silvia, with the
'slight alteration' of 'was mine' to 'is
mine': she addresses them to Valentine and means 'I give thee all that is
mine to give'. Baron Field's notion
was to emend 'mine' to 'thine' (i.e.,
Valentine's love would make up for
Proteus' loss of Silvia). Staunton
would give the lines to Proteus and
read 'Julia' for 'Silvia': 'All the love I
once felt for Julia I will henceforth
dedicate to my friendship for you.'
Bond adopted a suggestion of Bateson
that Valentine meant 'I give you my
love as frankly and unreservedly as I
gave it to Silvia: you shall have as
much interest in my heart as she': this
was taken as Valentine meant it, by
everyone except Julia, who 'in her
overwrought mood' took it as the un-
instructed modern reader does, and
therefore swooned. E. I. Fripp,
Shakespeare Man and Artist, 1938, i. 285,
interprets the lines as meaning that
Valentine offered to Proteus only to
release Silvia from her vow to him:
there was no question of withdrawing
his vow to her, unless she herself released him from it. This might explain
Julia's swoon, but the words will not
bear the interpretation and it weakens
the connection of the play with the

renunciation-theme in friendship-
literature. In decidedly different circumstances, Gisippus says to Titus in
The Gouernour: 'Here I renounce to you
clerely all my title and interest that I
nowe have or mought have in that
faire mayden' (Bullough, p. 216).
Shakespeare seems to burlesque his
own lines in *MND.,* III. ii. 164-7: 'And
here, with all good will, with all my
heart, / In Hermia's love I yield you
up my part; / And yours of Helena to
me bequeath, / Whom I do love and
will do till my death.' For further
comment, see Intro., pp. lxvii-lxviii.

84. S.D.] In *Diana* at the dénouement of Felismena's story she is 'in
such a traunce she could scarce
speake' (Kennedy, p. 238).

85. *wag*] mischievous boy (a common form of address).

87-9.] In IV. iv Julia offered the ring
to Silvia: therefore, argues Tannenbaum, p. 68, this matter of the rings
did not come into v. iv in the original
version of the play. But here we have
simply a theatrical means of Julia's
self-revelation, and an audience will
not notice the near-contradiction
with IV. iv: even if it does notice, it
can regard Julia's prevarication as
trifling. The lapse into prose at first
sight looks odd, but see Introduction,
pp. lxvii-lxviii.

Jul.   Here 'tis: this is it.   90
                     [*She gives him a ring.*]
Pro. How! Let me see.
    Why, this is the ring I gave to Julia.
Jul. O, cry you mercy, sir, I have mistook:
    This is the ring you sent to Silvia. [*She shows another ring.*]
Pro. But how cam'st thou by this ring? At my depart   95
    I gave this unto Julia.
Jul. And Julia herself did give it me,
    And Julia herself hath brought it hither.
                      [*She reveals herself.*]
Pro. How! Julia!
Jul. Behold her that gave aim to all thy oaths,   100
    And entertain'd 'em deeply in her heart.
    How oft hast thou with perjury cleft the root!
    O Proteus, let this habit make thee blush.
    Be thou asham'd that I have took upon me
    Such an immodest raiment; if shame live   105
    In a disguise of love!

90. S.D.] *Johnson* (*subst.*).   91–6.] *so F;* How … ring / I … sir, / I … sent /
To … this? (*om.* ring) / At … Julia *conj. Steevens.*   91. see] *F;* see it *conj.*
Steevens.   92. Why, this is] *F;* This is *Pope;* Why, 'tis *conj. S. Verges* (*ap.*
Camb).   94. S.D.] *Johnson.*   95. But how] *F;* How *Pope.*   102. root]
F; root on't *Hanmer.*

93–4.] This repeats the mistake with
the letters at IV. iv. 119 ff. On this
later occasion, however, she doubtless
does it deliberately: Proteus must see
both the ring he gave to Julia and the
ring she gave him (which he sent to
Silvia and which he now asks for), but
the first is the more important. See
Introduction, p. xx. It should be
noted that there is also confusion
about rings in the last acts of *Mer.V.*
and *All's W.*

95. *depart*] departure.

100. *gave aim to*] served as the mark
for. Bond, following Boswell, rightly
points out that ll. 101–2 show that all
of Proteus' oaths, those uttered to
Silvia as well as those to Julia, are
referred to. But he further comments
that the phrase was commonly used of
a 'direction-giver' in archery (cf. III. ii.

89). As Julia aided Proteus in his wooing of Silvia, she could be said to 'give
aim' to him in this sense; cf. Webster's
White Devil (Revels edn), III. ii. 24–5:
'I am at the mark sir, I'll give aim to
you, / And tell you how near you
shoot.' Both meanings make their
presence felt here.

102. *cleft the root*] alluding to 'cleav-
ing the pin' in archery. But here we
should understand 'of her heart'.

103. *habit*] Cf. *Diana*: 'in the habite
of a base page I served thee (a thing
more contrarie to my rest and reputation then I meane now to reherse)'
(Kennedy, p. 239).

105. *Such … raiment*] Cf. Sidney,
Arcadia: '*Zelmane* … whom uncon-
sulting affection … had made bor-
rowe so much of her naturall modestie,
as to leave her more-decent rayments',

It is the lesser blot modesty finds,
Women to change their shapes, than men their minds.

Pro. Than men their minds? 'Tis true: O heaven, were man
But constant, he were perfect. That one error   110
Fills him with faults; makes him run through all th' sins;
Inconstancy falls off, ere it begins.
What is in Silvia's face but I may spy
More fresh in Julia's, with a constant eye?

Val. Come, come; a hand from either;   115
Let me be blest to make this happy close:
'Twere pity two such friends should be long foes.

Pro. Bear witness, heaven, I have my wish for ever.

Jul. And I mine.

[*Enter* Outlaws, Duke *and* THURIO.]

Out.   A prize, a prize, a prize!

Val. Forbear, forbear, I say: it is my lord the Duke.   120
Your grace is welcome to a man disgrac'd,
Banish'd Valentine.

Duke.   Sir Valentine!

---

111. th' sins] *F;* sins *Pope, Halliwell MS.*   119. S.D.] *Rowe.*   120.] *so F;*
Forbear, / Forbear . . . Duke *Dyce.*   122. Banish'd] *Malone;* Banished *F;*
The banish'd *Pope.*

and 'for your sake [I] have put off the
apparel of a woman, & (if you judge
not more mercifully) modestie . . . yet
this breaking of my harte, before I
would discover my paine, will make
you (I hope) think I was not altogether unmodest' (Bullough, pp. 254,
256).

105–6. *if . . . love*] if one needs to be
ashamed of a disguise assumed for
love's sake.

107–8.] i.e., modesty is less blotted
by a change of 'shape' in woman than
by infidelity in men.

108. *shapes*] semblances, appearances; cf. *Wiv.*, IV. ii. 82–3: 'I would
my husband would meet him in this
shape'. The lost play 'too [?two]
shapes' recorded by Henslowe in 1602
may have used the word in this sense.
Also, the Elizabethan theatrical mean-

ings seem relevant (*O.E.D.*, *sb.*, 6, a,
b): 'A part, a character impersonated:
the make-up and costume suited to a
particular part' and 'A stage-dress or
suit of clothes'.

112.] The inconstant man wearies of
a pleasure or pursuit before he has
begun to experience it.

113–14.] i.e., if I am constant, I
shall find all Silvia's beauties present
more vitally in Julia. Schmidt glosses
'fresh' here as 'youthful, florid, in the
prime of life', but Proteus cannot
mean that Julia is the younger (even if
she is). Rather, the constancy of the
lover will give more life to the girl's
beauty.

116. *close*] union, with perhaps
something of 'conclusion'.

121. *grace, disgrac'd*] still a playing
upon the word.

Thu. Yonder is Silvia; and Silvia's mine.

Val. Thurio, give back; or else embrace thy death;
Come not within the measure of my wrath;   125
Do not name Silvia thine. If once again,
Verona shall not hold thee. Here she stands,
Take but possession of her with a touch:
I dare thee but to breathe upon my love.

Thu. Sir Valentine, I care not for her, I: 130
I hold him but a fool that will endanger
His body for a girl that loves him not.
I claim her not, and therefore she is thine.

Duke. The more degenerate and base art thou
To make such means for her, as thou hast done,   135
And leave her on such slight conditions.
Now, by the honour of my ancestry,
I do applaud thy spirit, Valentine,
And think thee worthy of an empress' love:
Know then, I here forget all former griefs,   140
Cancel all grudge, repeal thee home again,
Plead a new state in thy unrivall'd merit,

---

127. Verona ... thee] *F;* Milan shall not behold thee *Theobald;* And Milan shall
not hold thee *Hanmer;* Milano shall not hold thee *Collier ii;* Verona shall not hold
me *conj. Craig (ap. Bond).*   141. again,] *F;* again; *Capell;* again. *Steevens ii, conj.*
Tyrwhitt.   142. Plead a new state] *F;* Plead a new statute *or* Plant a new state
conj. Bond.   unrivall'd] *F;* arrival'd *F2.*

124. *give back*] go back.

125. *measure*] reach, literally 'distance of a fencer from his opponent'
(Onions).

127. *Verona*] See Introduction,
p. xvii.

135. *make such means*] take such
pains; Steevens quoted *R3*, v. iii. 248:
'One that made means to come by
what he hath'; Bond, following Rolfe,
quoted *Cym.*, II. iv. 3: 'What means do
you make to him?' In I. ii Shakespeare
has taken a hint from the passage in
Diana where Felismena exclaims: 'But
see the meanes that *Rosina* made unto
me' (Kennedy, p. 84).

136. *on ... conditions*] when such
slight conditions are proposed, i.e.,
when to keep her you would have to
fight for her (Schmidt, substantially).

139. *empress'*] See Introduction,
p. xvii.

140. *griefs*] causes of complaint,
grievances.

141. *repeal*] recall; cf. III. i. 234.

142. *Plead ... state*] This has produced a crop of interpretations and
some emendations. Bond was dis-
inclined to accept Steevens' full stop at
the end of l. 141, which would make
'Plead' an imperative. Singer, with the
same punctuation, interpreted: 'Put in
a plea for reinstatement'—which is
altogether too grudging. Bond took it
as 'Plead (in excuse for my change)
that your exhibition of such merit
creates a new situation', but was uncertain if this gave a Shakespearian use
of 'state'. He therefore put forward the
conjectures given here in the collation.

To which I thus subscribe: Sir Valentine,
Thou art a gentleman, and well deriv'd,
Take thou thy Silvia, for thou hast deserv'd her.   145
Val. I thank your grace; the gift hath made me happy.
I now beseech you, for your daughter's sake,
To grant one boon that I shall ask of you.
Duke. I grant it, for thine own, whate'er it be.
Val. These banish'd men, that I have kept withal,   150
Are men endu'd with worthy qualities:
Forgive them what they have committed here,
And let them be recall'd from their exile:
They are reformed, civil, full of good,
And fit for great employment, worthy lord.   155
Duke. Thou hast prevail'd, I pardon them and thee:
Dispose of them as thou know'st their deserts.
Come, let us go, we will include all jars,
With triumphs, mirth, and rare solemnity.
Val. And as we walk along, I dare be bold   160

---

158. include] *F;* conclude *Hanmer;* interclude *conj. Becket.*

NCS takes 'state' as a rhetorical term, 'the point in question or debate between contending parties' (*O.E.D.*, 12). It seems indeed best to keep the F punctuation at the end of l. 141, so that 'Plead' is parallel to 'Cancel' and 'repeal', with the meaning 'argue (that there is) a new condition of things in your (now manifest) unrivalled merit'. Schmidt gives 'conditions, situation, circumstances of nature or fortune' for 'state' in this context, and Onions 'condition of things' as one Shakespearian meaning of the word.

unrivall'd] F2's 'arrival'd', which survived until Pope, is probably a simple error (the word is not recorded in *O.E.D.* as a verb), but it would make perhaps plainer sense than F itself offers.

143. *To . . . subscribe*] I bear witness to (or acknowledge) your merit thus (i.e., in saying you are a gentleman and in giving you Silvia).

144. *well deriv'd*] Cf. v. ii. 23.

150. *kept withal*] lived with.

154–5.] This hardly coheres with what Valentine has said at ll. 16–17. See Introduction, p. lxviii.

156. *Thou hast prevail'd*] On this behaviour of the Duke, see Introduction, p. lxviii.

158. *include*] Malone, quoting Cowdrey, *Alphabetical Table of Head English Words* (1604), takes the meaning as 'shut in': the 'jars' were to be confined and to be prevented from getting out by triumphs and the like.

159. *triumphs*] pageants, processions —perhaps including tournaments; Bond, following Rolfe, quotes *Per.,* II. ii. 1, 4–5: 'Are the knights ready to begin the triumph?' and 'our daughter, / In honour of whose birth these triumphs are'.

159, 170–1. *triumphs, mirth . . . marriage . . . feast*] Cf. *Diana:* 'There they were all married with great joy, feasts, and triumphes' (Kennedy, p. 242).

160. *And . . . along*] J. C. Maxwell in *NCS Per.* (1956), p. 195, commenting on v. iii. 83–4 of that play ('Lord

With our discourse to make your grace to smile.
What think you of this page, my lord?
Duke. I think the boy hath grace in him, he blushes.
Val. I warrant you, my lord, more grace than boy.
Duke. What mean you by that saying? 165
Val. Please you, I'll tell you, as we pass along,
That you will wonder what hath fortuned.
Come, Proteus, 'tis your penance but to hear
The story of your loves discovered.
That done, our day of marriage shall be yours, 170
One feast, one house, one mutual happiness. *Exeunt.*

162. page] *F;* stripling page *Collier ii.*
Collier ii.

165. saying?] *F;* saying, Valentine?

Cerimon, we do our longing stay / To hear the rest untold: sir, lead's the way'), remarks that it is 'a typical Shakespeare ending' and compares it with concluding formulas in *Gent., Meas., Mer.V., All's W., Wint.* In the present play the formula awkwardly appears both in this line and in l. 166.

163. *the ... blushes*] Cf. Tilley, B480; Hilda M. Hulme, *Explorations in Shakespeare's Language,* 1962, p. 185.

163, 164. *grace*] virtue.

167. *wonder ... fortuned*] wonder at what has happened.